Praise for *The Mom Inventors Handbook*

"*The Mom Inventors Handbook* helped me to .... dreams can come true! The information in this book and *Your Million Dollar Dream* has provided the information and guidance I needed to launch the **BraTree**. I have sold over 10,000 units so far and it is selling now on QVC.com!"

—Angel Ruelas, creator of BraTree

"I am a grandmother and the *The Mom Inventors Handbook* is the first book that I purchased when I thought about taking my product **Zatswho®** a family-centered Photo Learning Game for children to market. The steps in the book helped to provide the road map I needed, but most importantly, it helped me get past my fear and step out of my comfort zone. I never imagined that my daughter and I would appear live on *Fox and Friends* to share our product with America!"

—Trish Cooper, creator of Zatswho

"I had no background in developing a product, so I didn't know where to start. I had read a few business books, but didn't find them very helpful. My sister-in-law gifted me *The Mom Inventors Handbook* and I didn't start reading it right away because I thought it was just another ra-ra inspirational book for women with not much useable information. When I did pick it up in earnest, I quickly realized how wrong I was. It was just what I needed: no fluff, just chapter after chapter of great, relevant and inspirational information. I went from having no clue where to start, to putting together an action plan for my product **Swagger Tags**."

—Karen Walker, creator of Swagger Tags

"Buy *The Mom Inventors Handbook*! I recommend this book to EVERYONE who asks me about my journey creating the **Dropper Stopper**. Your book is a roadmap on a scary and unknown journey! My copy of the book is hardly recognizable with all the highlights, dog-eared pages and Post-it Notes. I reference your book constantly. I think what I love the most is that it is very honest about the ups and downs and hardships that can come with this industry. I am incredibly grateful for your help and resources along the way. I can honestly say I don't know that I would have taken the first step without you."

—Meredith LaMirande, creator of the Dropper Stopper

"I started **LulyBoo Baby Lounge** after purchasing *The Mom Inventors Handbook*. It taught me everything involved with the business from design, sampling, testing, production, sales, marketing and social media.... Now the LulyBoo is sold at *all* Babies "R" Us stores, *all* BuyBuyBaby stores, Target, Amazon, and many other retailers nationwide. I am grateful for your guidance."

—Pazit Ben-Ezri, creator of LulyBoo Baby Lounge

"*The Mom Inventors Handbook* became my confidant, mentor, cheerleader, and my go-to source to stay on-task, on-message, and on-budget. I crunched numbers, crafted a marketing message and confidently negotiated with suppliers. **CastCoverZ!** is now a million dollar brand and the global leader in orthopedic soft goods with 18 lines. Now, it's your turn! Buy this book, execute, and you, too, could be featured in Tamara's next book!"

—Annette Giacomazzi, creator of CastCoverZ!

"Completely honest answer here: we could NOT have done this without Tamara Monosoff's book *The Mom Inventors Handbook*. Between Karen and me we probably own 50 books on creating a product, running a business, and entrepreneurship yet we ALWAYS ended up going back to Tamara's book—we call it our 'business bible.' It's really the only book we needed all along."

—Sisters Lisa Hoskins-Holmes and Karen Wildman, creators of The Bheestie Bag

"I'm not a mom [or a woman] but I used *The Mom Inventors Handbook* to bring my **Sasquatch! Pet Beds** to market and it won Best New Product Awards at our first two national tradeshows by retailers and consumers alike! The media loves it too; I was just featured on *CBS Early Show* and *Anderson Cooper!*"

—Tony Deitch, creator of Sasquatch! Pet Beds

"I used *The Mom Inventors Handbook* at the beginning of my journey. I still have the pages tabbed and have saved it for memories! My product, **Ava the Elephant**, was selected as one of the winning products on the popular TV Show *Shark Tank* and is now distributed internationally."

—Tiffany Krumins, creator of Ava the Elephant

"Almost every page of my copy of *The Mom Inventors Handbook* is dog-eared and the pages are filled with notes. Not only did I feel armed with useful step-by-step information to enter the world of entrepreneurship but I could hear your voice saying, 'You can do it (just be smart)!' My product the **Doodie Pack** is now being worn by thousands of dogs across the country! Through this process, I have discovered my passion and life's work."

—Kristin Elliott, creator of the Doodie Pack

"When I had the idea for **Carry-Her Doll Carriers** and found *The Mom Inventors Handbook*, I couldn't put it down! The stories in the book about other mom inventors inspired me and I realized that 'I can do this too!' I'm on track to sell 85,000 units this year with my new placements in Toys "R" Us, FAO Schwartz and Walmart for the holiday season! P.S. I was just reminding my husband of the day I read your handbook and told him that night that I'd be in your next edition."

—Roberta Wagner, creator of Carry-Her Doll Carriers

"I have read your book *The Mom Inventors Handbook* cover to cover many times, and it is the basis for which I began my journey to becoming a mommy entrepreneur, following a tragic incident that inspired me to create this product. I just wanted to say thank-you! I feel like you've been a personal mentor to me. It's the way you wrote your book— like you were right there guiding me through the process. I checked out a lot of entrepreneur and inventor books from the local library, and I even ordered a few others online, but I can honestly say that your book was THE BEST. I have scribbled drawings, highlights, and notations all throughout it. I know your new book will help inspire more inventors to follow their dreams of launching or licensing a product. It's the book I refer my friends and family to when they ask how I did it!"

—Molly Lofthouse, creator of Lenz Frenz

THE
mom
Inventors Handbook

Also by Tamara Monosoff

The Mom Inventors Handbook: How to Turn Your Great Idea into the Next Big Thing, (1st edition)

Secrets of Millionaire Moms: Learn How They Turned Great Ideas into Booming Businesses

Your Million Dollar Dream: Regain Control and Be Your Own Boss

The One Page Business Plan for Women in Business (with Jim Horan)

How Hot Is Your Product? Find Out if Your Product Idea will Make or Cost You Money (with Brad Kofoed)

THE
mom
Inventors Handbook

How to Turn Your Great Idea
into the Next Big Thing

REVISED AND EXPANDED SECOND EDITION

Tamara Monosoff

New York   **3 1336 10193 6228**   ɔn   Madrid
Mexico Ci   ʃy   Toronto

1 2 3 4 5 6 7 8 9 0   QFR/QFR   1 0 9 8 7 6 5 4

ISBN 978-0-07-182282-4
MHID 0-07-182282-8

e-ISBN 978-0-07-182288-6
e-MHID 0-07-182288-7

Library of Congress Cataloging-in-Publication Data
Monosoff, Tamara.
   The mom inventors handbook : how to turn your great idea into the next big thing / Tamara Monosoff. — Revised and expanded 2nd ed.
      pages cm
   ISBN 978-0-07-182282-4 (pbk.) — ISBN 0-07-182282-8 (pbk.) 1. New business enterprises—Management. 2. Women-owned business enterprises—Management. 3. Working mothers. 4. Intellectual property. I. Title.
   HD62.5.M655 2014
   658.1′1410852—dc23   2013050209

McGraw-Hill Education books are available at special quantity discounts to use as premiums and sales promotions or for use in corporate training programs. To contact a representative, please visit the Contact Us pages at www.mhprofessional.com.

To my precious daughters,
Sophia and Kiara:
I cherish you. You are my heart

To my sweet husband,
My dearest friend:
I am grateful for you every day

To my lovely parents,
I treasure you:
You are with me always

Contents

Foreword

I have been in retail for 30 years, and my amazing journey began quite by accident. My parents moved my family from Los Angeles to a *very* small town in Arkansas during my junior year in high school. The move was incredibly traumatic and dramatic, not unlike most things in a high school girl's life! Like many young people, I didn't have any specific career in mind; however, I knew several things with absolute certainty: I was *not* staying in this horrible country bumpkin place called Arkansas. I was *not* getting married, and I certainly *never* wanted to have children. And I was *absolutely not* going to work in some office job like my mother did. Well, while I'm far from a "country girl," here I am some 35 years later, still living in the same small town my parents moved me to; married to a country boy, living on a farm with horses, cattle, and a chicken production farm (but I believe it's OK to wear heels to do chores—ha ha ha), with two children and a grandchild (he calls me "G"); and I've been working for Walmart/Sam's Club (yes, in the office!) for 30 years. OK, so I had a couple of things wrong when I was 18, go figure!

Like many of you, I was just trying to pay my bills while I was going to school when I started with Walmart at the Home Office in 1982 as an hourly associate typing dictation. Today, I am the senior director of the Showcase Events team for Sam's Club, the nations' eighth-largest retailer, with more than 47 million members. Sam's

Club is a division of Walmart Stores, Inc. Showcase Events are short-term events that feature unique products outside the normal assortment. Throughout my 30 years in retail, including the last 5 years at Sam's Club, there have been many lessons learned, and I have had the honor of being a part of others' success.

At Sam's Club, our goal is to provide high-quality, differentiated merchandise at a value; this may include highly unique "trend right" items or even aspiration brands. Walmart's goal is clear: "Saving people money so they can live better"—everyday low costs on items the customer wants. Being in tune with key trends is critical to business and plays a critical role in both business models. I am very proud to work for a company that has such a strong commitment to community and ethics; initiatives such as locally produced goods, supporting minority- and women-owned businesses, and Veteran's Welcome Home job commitments, to name just a very few.

Within the Showcase Events program at Sam's Club, we are innovators, and we are continuously looking for new ways to support and promote small businesses and their products inside the club. One thing has remained constant: the critical business role that inventors play through the new products they create—*that's you!* I have personally met and worked with many entrepreneurs all across the country over the past several years. In fact, it was at a Sam's small-business event (sponsored by Sam's Club Giving Program) for women in business, in partnership with Count Me In for Women's Economic Independence (countmein.org), that I first heard Tamara speak and had a chance to meet her. This brings me to the message I would like to convey to you, the readers of the *Mom Inventors Handbook: How to Turn Your Great Idea into the Next Big Thing*, 2nd edition.

Your efforts and success are important to me because Sam's Club and the retail industry are, in many ways, dependent on your creativity, passion, and ultimate success in order to bring newness into the marketplace. A woman came to us with a salsa, My Brother's Salsa, that she had in production and had been selling in a few specialty stores. The whole company had started for her with a salsa recipe she and her brother made that everyone loved and asked for. They were seeing some success, but she had been encouraged by friends and family to take the next step and expand further. This next step she chose was to approach Sam's Club about its interest in the product—a courageous step! While the regular buyer wasn't prepared to take a chance on the product, my team was a perfect fit, and we were intrigued. She had a high-quality product, great packaging, and unique product attributes; she knew her target customer and her target market; and the salsa tasted fantastic as well—a winning combo! She started with just a few Showcase Events that she staffed herself; learned from her successes, feedback, and mistakes; grew her business methodically; and now has products on the shelves at many Sam's Club and now Walmart stores as well! While not every new product may be a fit for our clubs, our buying teams and I are faced with the daily challenge of finding the next great products for our members.

I am asked every day for advice about how to get products onto the shelves of our clubs. The answer to this question is in your hands. Consider the My Brother's Salsa story. Helen came prepared, and that, in large part, set her apart from many others we see from the first meeting. The results demonstrated by others who have followed Tamara's advice is testimony to the value of preparation. As I write this, Kimberly Meckwood, creator of the Click & Carry, is a finalist in Walmart's Get On the Shelf Contest.

> *The Mom Inventors Handbook* was a lifesaver! Not only did it walk me step by step through the product development process, but thanks to you, I have the insurance squared away and my product is safety tested! It also inspired me to stay enthusiastic and to believe in my path. I just sold 20,000 units of my Click & Carry, and I've made it to the final round of Walmart's Get On the Shelf Contest. Thank you a *million*. —Kimberly Meckwood

As Kim will attest, it is essential to start with a deep understanding of your target market and the problem or need that your product addresses. Do not shortchange this step. I ask every new product entrepreneur I meet, "What makes your product unique?" You should be able to answer this question clearly and tell us why we should choose your item over other similar products.

Next, you must follow a proven path to designing and producing your product. And, just as critical, your packaging must convey the key attributes of your product in both its messaging and its appearance. Fundamental to the success of this entire process is the importance of your business plan and the structure that will create a strong foundation for your business to grow—especially in an environment like Sam's. Tamara has outlined this process in a way that few others have or could. Beyond her personal experience and knowledge, what is relevant to anyone wishing to launch a product business is her dedication to helping women in business—a passion that I share.

My final advice to those readers who aspire to see their products on the shelves of the nation's top retailers; *be courageous* and *go for it*! Whether it is through Sam's Showcase Events program, Walmart's Get On the Shelf Contest, other traditional buying channels, or competing retailers; we need your creativity, innovations, and, most important, your tenacity.

Journey on!

Julie Martin-Allen,
Senior Director of Showcase Events, Sam's Club
January 1, 2014

Acknowledgments

First, I wish to thank each of the entrepreneurs who contributed videos, stories, advice, and quotes for this book. Your contributions have brought life and authenticity to the book that would not have been possible any other way.

I also wish to acknowledge the thousands of other entrepreneurs whom I have met or interacted with since the 2005 publication of the first edition of the *Mom Inventor Handbook*. It has been your enthusiasm, drive, and pursuit of success that has inspired me to continue to write and develop educational programs for entrepreneurs.

I am enormously grateful to Julie Martin-Allen, Senior Director of ShowCase Events/Regional Buying for Sam's Club, for contributing such a heartfelt foreword in which she urges readers to "journey on!"

I truly appreciate the special contributions made by experts: Ann Noder, President of Pitch Public Relations; business law and intellectual property attorney John Merchant of J. Merchant Law; video marketing expert Lou Bortone; product development consultant Justin Aiello; and graphic designer, Erika Ruggiero.

A special thank you to Kaywa (http://qrcode.kaywa.com/) for generously donating the QR codes sprinkled throughout this book!

I wish to thank the phenomenal team at McGraw-Hill that has supported me every step of the way: Mary Glenn, Donya Dickerson,

Casie Vogel, and Dannalie Diaz; and also my literary agent, Jessica Faust.

And finally, I am awed by the love and continuous support that I have received from my precious daughters, Sophia and Kiara (ages 12 and 10). Remarkably, I have never heard one complaint while I've been absorbed in this project. In fact, they too feel ownership of this book, as they loved being the first to watch the inspirational videos from the courageous entrepreneurs featured here. And, of course, I am grateful to my husband, Brad Kofoed, who contributed to this book and who edited, read, and reread every word of it.

Introduction

n 2005, McGraw-Hill gave me the opportunity to write and publish the first edition of this book, a privilege for which I will always be grateful.

The book was published shortly after the launch of my first product—the TP Saver, which prevents children and pets from unrolling the toilet paper—and my business, Mom Inventors, Inc., was born. Shortly after the launch, my little gadget was featured on the *Today* show with Katie Couric. I never could have imagined the whirlwind of media activity that would follow and that still continues today—a decade later.

At the time I wrote the first edition, I was writing about experiences and lessons that I was learning at that moment week by week. In other words, the first edition was a documentary of my own process of taking my first products to market. I shared everything I was learning along the way and included my resources, steps, and mistakes in the hope of helping entrepreneurs who were following closely in my footsteps. I distinctly recall the feeling of being barely one step ahead of others who were relying on me for advice.

Nearly 10 years later, it is an honor to be given the opportunity to write the second edition that you now hold in your hands.

Since that time, I have developed, licensed, and launched dozens of new products and have written four additional how-to books for entrepreneurs. Yet, few things inspire me more than the association I have had with the thousands of inventors and entrepreneurs who have benefited from my books, or who have worked with me personally through my Power Mentoring classes or connected with me online via my blog, Facebook, and Twitter. What touches me the most is seeing the perseverance that so many have shown in the face of what many people would consider insurmountable obstacles.

It is this internal drive that entrepreneurs embody that inspires me to forge on with the mission of helping others to build businesses that they love.

When McGraw-Hill asked me to create a second edition of this book, I wondered what more I had to offer. So I sat down with a copy of the first edition and began looking for places where I could insert some new content. Even though I have lived in the midst of the changing entrepreneurial landscape, I was surprised by how dramatically things have actually changed for inventors.

For example, in the first edition, there was nothing unusual about recommending the Yellow Pages as a starting point: "Grab your local Yellow Pages." Today, my daughters don't even know what the Yellow Pages are and, like many others simply say, "Just Google it." Now most inventors consider Google to be their digital

Watch Video Message from Tiffany Krumins

http://www.tamaramonosoff.com/tiffany-krumins/

Tiffany Krumins, founder of the AVA the Elephant brand (www.avatheelephant.com), a talking children's medicine dispenser that takes the fear and anxiety out of administering medicine to children, embodies this kind of stamina. Shortly after launching her product, she was diagnosed with cancer. What became clear to her, as she was battling cancer, was that she was on the right track in creating a product that helps sick children. After her recovery, she forged on and became the first woman to receive funding for her product on ABC's TV show *Shark Tank*.

"best friend" in gaining immediate access to resources. However, there is nothing more helpful than being offered trusted resources firsthand as a starting point. Therefore, it is my goal with this edition to provide you with a detailed road map that is easy to follow, comprehensive, and rich in its content and resources so that you have everything you need in order to succeed.

Interestingly, the top four challenges that have remained the same for entrepreneurs—past and present—are related to funding, manufacturing, publicity, and sales. These topics are much more thoroughly covered in this edition. Also, the resources available to inventors today simply did not exist even a few years ago. Crowdfunding, 3-D printing, social media (it's hard to believe that YouTube was founded the same year the first edition of this book was published and Twitter didn't yet exist!), apps as marketing tools, and thousands of new retail sales opportunities have been born since 2005. In each chapter, I have inserted every vendor and online resource I have found to be valuable.

In addition to the flash of new technology, there are some core business fundamentals that I have also addressed in a whole new way. The importance of market research has never been greater. I have fully leveraged the content and system that Brad Kofoed and I developed in our recent book, *How Hot is Your Product?*, and condensed it so that you have easy-to-follow steps to thoroughly research your market.

There have also been dramatic changes to the U.S. patent laws that have a direct impact on independent inventors, so the legal section has been rewritten with generous expert guidance from my friend, business law and intellectual property attorney John Merchant.

Most important, I have included stories from more than 50 entrepreneurs, mostly moms, but some grandmoms and some "honorary" moms. They have been generous in allowing me to share their challenges, successes, and resources, including their manufacturers, designers, top sales channels, and more. To hear their stories, scan the QR codes sprinkled throughout the book to watch the videos they created for you.

You have a tremendous opportunity before you now. With the resurgent economy, the abundance of new resources provided in this book, and phenomenal new distribution opportunities from hungry new retailers and e-tailers, there has *never* been a better time to launch a product than today.

Chinese philosopher, Lao Tzu wrote, *"The journey of a thousand miles must begin with a single step."*

Let us step forward together.

Onward!

Tamara

Message to Readers

This book is interactive! I am thrilled to show you how to bring it to life. All the QR (Quick Response) codes throughout the book can be scanned with your smartphone or iPad to watch the videos that were created especially for you.

The entrepreneurs featured here have shared a personal message with you about the challenges they have overcome, the rewards of starting a business, the thing that has surprised them the most about being their own boss, and one piece of advice for you. Each of the videos is approximately two minutes long. You will see that these courageous people are just like you. After you hear their messages, I hope you feel inspired and motivated to forge on toward making your dream a reality.

How to Scan the QR Codes in This Book

Step 1: Download a *free* QR code reader onto your smartphone by searching the App Store. I selected the Kaywa Reader because it is free of advertisements. Also, Kaywa has generously donated the QR codes featured in this book.

Step 2: Tap the app once it has downloaded to your phone; this will open up the Kaywa Reader. Tap again, and your camera will appear to be on. Hover over the code you wish to scan, and the camera will automatically take a picture of the QR code; then your phone will be directed to the respective web page on TamaraMonosoff.com that contains each video message.

Enjoy!

Want to generate QR codes for your business? Visit http://qrcode .kaywa.com.

I want to hear from you. Please join me:

Visit my website: TamaraMonosoff.com and sign up to receive free, helpful tips and get up-to-date information about upcoming mentoring classes, new tools, and training.
Twitter: Twitter.com/mominventors
Facebook: Facebook.com/mominvented
YouTube Channel: YouTube.com/TamaraMonosoff

Watch video message from Kaywa

http://www.tamaramonosoff.com/watch-video-message-kaywa/

Note to Non-Moms

I wrote the first edition of this book from the perspective of being a mom and wanting to serve a community that, at the time, was somewhat invisible. Many women have launched products since that time, but many of the challenges have not changed. While the title of this book and most of the stories shared are from moms, this is not intended to exclude others.

Every step, process, and resource in this book is as applicable to non-moms as it is to moms. I get enormous satisfaction when I hear from men who have found my books to be valuable in building their businesses, so I wholeheartedly welcome non-mom readers. So, jump in and turn the page!

Taking Your First Steps

Watch Video Message: Tamara Monosoff Introduces Chapter 1

http://www.tamaramonosoff.com/
tamara-monosoff-introduces-chapter-1/

A Road Map to Get You There

So you have a great idea. And whether it's been percolating in your head for a week or marinating in your mind for years, the key to transforming this idea from concept to profit is *action*. If it is truly a problem-solving idea, you can rest assured that someone else has also thought of it. Acting on that idea is what will differentiate you. But arbitrary action leaves too much to chance. That's why two things need to happen from the beginning: creative thinking and becoming a student *again*.

The Power of Creative Solutions

Part of getting into the inventor mindset is to utilize creative thinking. As a mom, this is a skill that can help you tremendously when you are juggling priorities and dealing with your unique work environment—a workplace that's seldom quiet and doesn't come with a standard eight-hour day.

In fact, you probably already think creatively without even knowing it. As a mom, with so many unexpected curveballs being thrown your way on a daily basis, you are forever devising solutions and strategies to achieve your goals. And whether it's finding an efficient way to feed your family three healthy meals a day or developing a strategy to get the kids to all their activities prepared and on time, there's no doubt that you've created your very own solutions to accomplish these and countless other family-management tasks.

Plan on tapping into these creative-thinking abilities as you go through the entrepreneurial process. What truly sets a successful entrepreneur and inventor apart is how she handles potential obstacles and embraces tough steps during the process. When you are confronted with a challenge, don't change your goals—be creative and change your plan of action. After all, when we think that we have only two options, we often find ourselves in a dilemma. In his book *Profiting from Intellectual Capital: Extracting Value from Innovation*, Patrick H. Sullivan says, "When given the choice between two alternatives, always pick a third!"

 Watch Video Message from Tony Deitch

http://www.tamaramonosoff.com/tony-deitch/

 I love what Tony Deitch, the inventor of Sasquatch! Pet Beds (www. sasquatchpetbeds.com) said about using the first edition of the *Mom Inventors Handbook*, "I'm not a mom. I figured if a busy mother with kids and a family to juggle could learn from Tamara's book, then I could too! It's that simple." Sasquatch! Pet Beds are now sold worldwide.

So even if you're not a mom, you were mom-invented (and dad-inspired), so read on and get started!

So, how can you adopt the proper mindset? Believe in the skills that you already have, and be willing to become a student and *listen* to the information that you find about your product.

And be sure to take time to read—and watch the QR code videos—the stories sprinkled throughout this book to learn from the entrepreneurs who have led the way. They all have different backgrounds and life experiences, and yet they have something in common. They were personally motivated to make it happen.

Give Up the Words "I Can't"

I love what Jack Canfield says in his book *The Success Principles*, "If you are going to be successful, you need to give up the phrase 'I can't' and all of its cousins, such as 'I wish I were able to.' The words I can't actually disempower you and make you weaker when you say them.... Decide that you are capable of doing anything you want and start working toward it now."

Now that we are on the same page, let's start the work needed to figure out whether your first idea is a winner and set the foundation for hitting it big!

Throughout this book, you will find the stories of dozens of inventors to help punctuate points or simply to inspire you. Nearly all of them used the first edition of this book to get their products to market, and in many cases, they achieved satisfaction and wealth they did not imagine.

This is my wish for you, too. And, it is within your reach.

Become a Student: Product Assessment and Market Research

stu·dent *noun* / stü-d(e)nt—*any person who studies, investigates, or examines thoughtfully**

* Source: TheFreeDictionary.com.

Whether or not you enjoyed studying when you were in school, the difference here is that becoming a student when you are bringing a product to market is 100 percent your choice—to fulfill your dream. Becoming a focused student and taking the next important steps will help ensure that you are on the right track.

For the past 10 years, teaching entrepreneurs how to bring products to market successfully has been enormously rewarding for me. It has also made me painfully aware of some of the most common mistakes that inventors make. Many inventors avoid evaluating their products and conducting market research as a first step to see whether there is a big enough market for their product. When I mentor inventors, I always ask, "What market research have you done to make sure that this is a product that people will buy?" The answer is nearly always, "Nothing," or, "My friends and family love it, and that's good enough for me." While nothing is better than

Watch Video Message from Roberta Wagner

http://www.tamaramonosoff.com/roberta-wagner/

Facing her daughter's need to have a way to carry her 18-inch doll, Roberta Wagner created the Carry-Her Doll Carriers (www.carry-her.com). As in most of these stories, her path was full of obstacles that required her to change directions, overcome extreme disappointment, and relish her success. With each disappointment, she pulled herself up by reengaging her network, learning what she could, and forging on. Having gone from using a local manufacturer and hand-packaging her products to getting them placed with some of America's largest retailers, Roberta is now aiming to sell 85,000 units this year.

Tamm Stitt Photography

Emily was the reason that I created Carry-Her, and she's helped me every step of the way. When I started Carry-Her in 2008, it was tough to juggle family and business. Now that Emily's 13, she helps package and print shipping labels. I love proving to her that anything is possible if you believe in yourself and your product.

love from friends and family, this is not enough. For most inventors (including myself), the temptation is to begin with the fun part—building a prototype and bringing your product to life (covered in Chapter 2)—which then often leads to filing a patent and having thousands of units manufactured and shipped to our front doors. However, all too often, reality sets in when people are not rushing to beat down our doors to purchase our product. And the most discouraging part is that at that point, it's often too late to make changes without great expense.

I'm not telling you this to scare you, but instead to share good news. This does not have to happen! In Chapters 1 and 3, you are going to learn the steps that you need to take to honestly evaluate your product before you bring it to market. I think you will be surprised by how much you can learn about the industry in which you plan to sell your product. This newfound knowledge will also help you down the road with consumers, buyers, and investors.

Let's Be Real

While I think that most of the entrepreneurs mentioned in this book would agree with me that taking their own product to market was one of the most interesting and rewarding experiences in their lives, they would also agree that it took work... *hard work*. That said, one of the things I have learned about mom inventors is that "work" is not something that they shy away from. In fact, all of the women—and some men—mentioned in this book have juggled *while* taking their products to market.

Let's get started! Following the steps summarized here and in Chapter 3 will enable you to:

- Determine whether this cool product idea is truly viable as a business.
- Decide among multiple potential product ideas you may be thinking about pursuing.
- Make better decisions and accelerate many of the later steps outlined in this book.

Watch Video Message from Cocreators Stefanie Huber and Janae' Giurlani

http://www.tamaramonosoff.com/Stefanie-Huber/

Stefanie Huber, cocreator of Kuviez Button up! Bedding, bedding that "redefines the way parents keep their children covered at night" (www.kuviez.com), shares her insight on the hard work involved.

Launching products or a business sounds misleading to me. When I think of launching, I think of a rocket taking off.... This is definitely not the case with Kuviez. We are gradually introducing our products to the public.

The First Steps to Inventing

- *Self-assessment.* What are your goals?
- *Market.* What is the realistic targetable market for your product?
- *Competition.* Who is your competition?

Before you embark on these steps, I am going to ask you to place your current belief that your idea is a hit "on the shelf" temporarily and adopt the mindset of a skeptical student who has to sleuth out the answers. Put yourself in the impartial role of someone who is researching someone else's product and needs to make a recommendation to her boss based on her research. You need to determine whether or not this product has proven itself to be a financially viable opportunity. With this in mind, get ready to go through the steps, and be an inquisitive student, assembling the facts like many pieces in a puzzle, and working until a clear picture appears.

Let's get started. First, quickly answer the following questions, as best you can for now. At this point, there are surely gaps in what you know. That is OK; just do your best. Grab a piece of paper or a notebook and answer these questions.

Describe Your Product Idea

Succinctly describe your product. Write down the answers.

What is your idea?

How did you think of it? (What inspired you, and what experiences was it based upon?)

What does it look like? (This should include dimensions, shape, materials, and anything else that is relevant.)

How does it work? (Describe the function of the invention.)

What problem does it solve? (Why is the product needed?)

What are some possible product names?

Draw a picture of your product idea. If you're not artistically inclined, don't worry; this can be a rudimentary sketch. (See Figure 1.1 for the first sketch of TP Saver.) A drawing is important not just to keep a record of how your product began, but also so that you can better communicate with the machinist, engineer, or product developer about what you are trying to achieve when you get to the design or prototype stage (see Chapter 2). An added benefit of an early sketch is that you will be able to revisit it to see how far you have actually come once the product is stocked on retail store shelves.

Write the three to five key features and benefits of the product. (Note the differences between "features" and "benefits" in the following examples.)

Features. (What is it made of? Is it durable? Chemical free? Locally made or grown? What color is it? Is it stylish? Lightweight? Easily cleaned? Inexpensive? Interchangeable?)

Benefits. (What problem does it solve? Does it save money? Save time? Create joy? Reduce pain? Improve health or happiness?)

FIGURE 1.1 **First Sketch of TP Saver in November 2002**

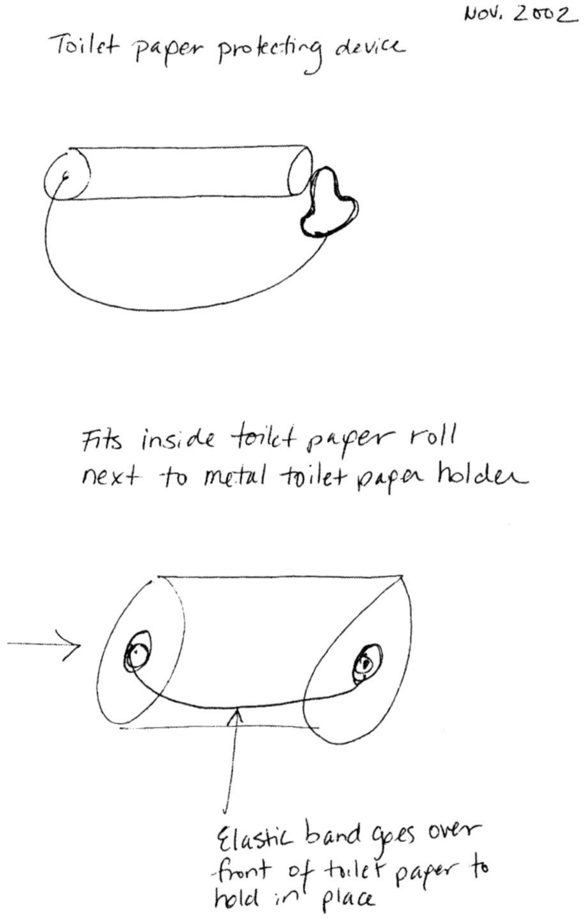

Who specifically will buy it?

_____

_____

_____

_____

_____

How much will this person pay for it?

_____

_____

_____

_____

Why will this customer buy it? How do you know?

_____

_____

_____

_____

I asked you to answer these questions to give you a starting point from which you can measure your progress. By the end of Chapter 3, you will be able to see what you've learned and how your thinking may have shifted or evolved. Now, answer the following questions.

Self-Assessment

Is this a hobby or a serious business endeavor?

_____

_____

Is your goal to build a product manufacturing and distribution business?

_____

_____

Is your goal to license the product to another company?
Licensing means that you sell your idea to another manufacturer, who will make the product and pay you a small percentage (usually 2 to 6 percent), or "royalty," on the net sales, instead of making the product and becoming a manufacturer yourself. *Note:* If licensing is your preferred path, the ability to obtain intellectual property protection—a patent—is important. This is covered in later chapters.

Do you have a different goal?

Do you have specific financial goals or requirements that will determine whether you will pursue this project?

How much money have you set aside to develop the product and invest in your business?

How much outside funding will you need to build your business?

It's also important that you consider other goals beyond financial rewards. What else is important to you?

Risk

How much risk can you tolerate? Some people can tolerate tremendous amounts of risk, while others have no stomach for it. When you start a business, you need to understand where you fall on this "risk tolerance" continuum (see Figure 1.2). For example, you need to know how much you are willing to spend and at what point you are willing to walk away.

First, complete the risk continuum exercise, then describe your own risk comfort level on the following lines.

I met a woman who had spent $80,000 on her prototype, patenting, and marketing for her product business. After many years, she was still not selling her product. To me, this is risky.

Watch Video Message from Kristin Elliott

http://www.tamaramonosoff.com/kristin-elliot/

Kristin Elliott is the creator of the Doodie Pack (www.DoodiePack. com). She is on a mission to "Put Dignity Back in Your Dogwalk." The Doodie Pack is a lightweight pack that allows the dog to carry the empty and full sanitation bags needed for walks. Like the hundreds of mom inventors I have met over the years, she makes it work. As a full-time teacher and mom, her plate is full, but she finds space for her business.

My secret: I take advantage of early morning hours (3:00 a.m. to 6:00 a.m.) when the house is quiet to get work done, and I follow up with spare minutes throughout the day.... Nearly everything that is presented to the public comes through my office, from social media, to PR and advertising, to fulfillment and invoicing. It requires a clear schedule and lots of internal communication. Thankfully, everything is in close proximity to our home, so I can still be that "soccer mom."

FIGURE 1.2   **Reality and Risk Continuum Chart**

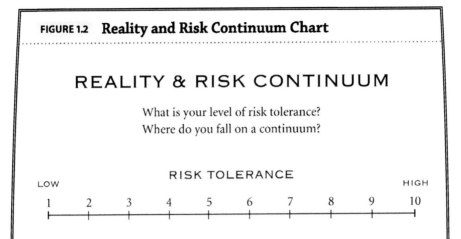

REALITY & RISK CONTINUUM

What is your level of risk tolerance?
Where do you fall on a continuum?

RISK TOLERANCE

LOW   HIGH

1   2   3   4   5   6   7   8   9   10

Instructions:

This exercise is intended to bring clarity by providing you with a visual display of your personal risk profile as it relates to this project. The upside of taking risk can be extraordinary success in many forms: financial, freedom, relationships, leisure, etc.

That said, by nature, "risk" means that there can be negative consequences to a project. It is not our intention to unnecessarily focus on this aspect, or to convince you that you should not accept the risk and proceed, but rather, to help you be fully mindful in the process of accepting risk. Too often, we have witnessed, and experienced ourselves, the tendency to put on blinders to potential risks when there is excitement about a new project. (In our own work, we now see a candid risk assessment as a useful mechanism to help choose between multiple exciting options to pursue.)

Take a different colored pen or marker and place a mark on the continuum based on your answer to each question or statement below. A strong "no" to the statements would place you at or near the "1". Absolute or strong "yes" puts you toward the "10". This is not scientific and you can even add questions that are specifically relevant to you. You decide where each mark goes. Then consider what you see.

Questions:

1) I can afford to lose the money I will be investing in this business.

2) I am comfortable working long hours, for months, with very low pay.

3) I am comfortable with major changes on a regular basis.

4) I have a family and/or solid support system I can rely upon to help tackle the big challenges.

5) I thrive on pressure.

6) I just learned I will appear on national television in three days. I am 1) paralyzed – 10) thrilled.

7) If my business took off and the pace and priorities of my life changed within a few months, I would be 1) displeased – 10) very satisfied.

8) I will be fine if key relationships in my life are impacted by this process.

9) I am comfortable asking people to invest or lend me money.

10) I am comfortable dealing with legal matters and possible disputes.

Effort

How much time and effort are you willing and able to spend on this product business? Please be realistic.

Are you working full-time? Are you a single parent? Are you caring for your aging parents? Look at your schedule and analyze how much time you can realistically block out each day and each week to work on your business. Actually list which hours and days you would use and then test this plan to gauge whether those times are workable for the next two weeks. If the schedule is not working, make adjustments.

Market: What Is the Realistic Targetable Market for Your Product?

One way to determine your potential market is to develop numbers that can help you formulate your likely target customer base. Each market is different. Your data points will be unique as well. We've designed a way to chart this information so that you can create a visual picture (see Figure 1.3). The intention of this tool is to help you move from broad information to specific data. You will want to get as specific as possible about the nature of the customer, placing that information in the center for each market.

In this step, the idea is to quantify the actual size of the potential market, whereas the next section approaches this from the perspective of the benefit to the customer, in as measurable a way as possible.

1. Who is the target customer? Describe the person who will be pulling out her wallet to pay for your product.

2. How many customers of this kind exist? (*Note:* While theoretically the market can be global, we consider the U.S. market to be the best measure of this metric for American inventors.) Later, you can see how you can begin gathering this information at http://www .census.gov.

3. Working from the outside of the target chart (see the complete sample chart in Figure 1.5) and looking in, think through and note the descriptive characteristics of this customer, using the following list to help you think of the key traits.

The number of rings in your target chart can be increased as you identify additional filters to place on your target market. Then, like cutting a pizza, segment the circle based on the different markets in which you intend to sell your product.

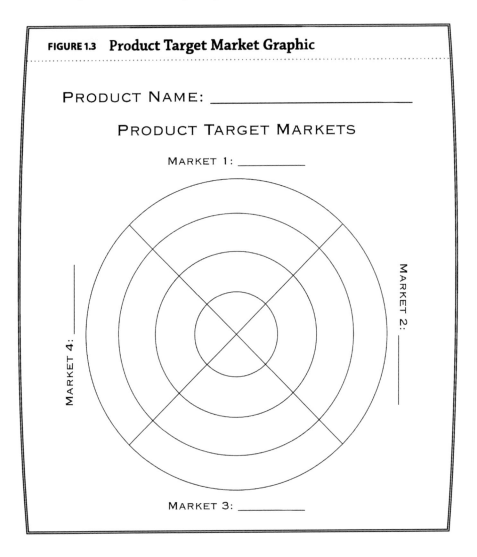

FIGURE 1.3 Product Target Market Graphic

PRODUCT NAME: _____

PRODUCT TARGET MARKETS

MARKET 1: _____

MARKET 2: _____

MARKET 3: _____

MARKET 4: _____

a. Gender.
b. Age/generation.
c. Race.
d. Geographic location and needs (for example, more people buy mittens in Michigan than in Florida).
e. Urban or suburban dweller. Think about the differences. For example, just consider the driving, gardening, shopping— you name it—habits and needs of these types of consumers.
f. Economic class.
g. Professional/blue-collar/student.
h. Parent/nonparent.
i. Educational level.
j. Other characteristics applicable to your product or category.
   i. Active/athletic
   ii. Use of technology
   iii. Hobbies
   iv. Traveler
   v. Pet owners
   vi. Other

The U.S. Census Bureau website (http://www.census.gov) has a wealth of information that will help you identify your market. It takes some time (and patience) to sift through the data to find useful numbers, so be prepared to spend enough time to find precisely what you are seeking. Once you get used to the way the website is organized, the data are quite interesting. These data are especially useful if your product is specifically relevant to particular populations based on demographic specifics such as age, gender, geography, or ethnicity. For example, we know that there are approximately 117 million total U.S. households, of which 71 million are "family" households. Approximately 38 million households have children under 18 years. Also interesting is that more than 30 percent of American households are in just four states: California, Texas, Florida, and New York.

4. How much money is spent annually in this product category? How much money is spent on similar or comparable items?

5. Using a search engine, type, "_____ market statistics" or "sales of _____," and experiment with other search terms. Another often overlooked approach is to simply type your question into a search engine such as Google. For example, "How many _____ are there in America?" Be sure to cross-reference (check facts against multiple sources) to validate your data as much as possible.

6. Look up the industry association that represents the market space your item falls into and read its market statistics. Type your "category + association" into Google to find this association. Search trade publication websites that serve this market and read their statistics. For example, if you are looking for the National Pet Association, but you don't know the exact name, type that phrase into a search engine. When I typed "National Pet Association" into Google, it took me to American Pet Products Association: http://www.americanpet products.org/. You can do this with any industry, and you will often find a plethora of invaluable data to help you understand the market you are trying to reach.

Figure 1.4 shows just a portion of the *amazing* amount of data available at the American Pet Products Association website.

Now, try to answer the question, "How many of these customers in the key market experience the problem or will have their need met by this product?" (See Chapter 3.)

7. As an independent, small entrepreneur, it is important that you leverage other people's efforts as much as possible.

There are specific websites that gather detailed information about companies and their key employees (http://www.zoominfo.com and http://www.hoovers.com). Not only can you learn a lot about the specific company you are researching, but these sites also list the companies that are considered to be its top competitors. Follow this path until you find relevant corporate information.

8. Ask your peers. Identify other people in your business community that you think may have insights into the market. Share what you have learned, and get their thoughts. Ideally, some of these people will be in the retail industry. You will be amazed by what you will learn by first studying this information and then speaking to others who will also have insights to share.

Let's revisit the TP Saver example.

FIGURE 1.4 Industry Statistics and Trends

Industry Statistics & Trends

PET OWNERSHIP

- According to the 2011-2012 APPA National Pet Owners Survey, 62% of U.S. households own a pet, which equates to 72.9 millions homes

- In 1988, the first year the survey was conducted, 56% of U.S. households owned a pet as compared to 62% in 2008

Breakdown of pet ownership in the U.S. according to the 2011-2012 APPA National Pet Owners Survey

Number of U.S. Households that Own a Pet (millions)

Bird	5.7
Cat	38.9
Dog	46.3
Equine	2.4
Freshwater Fish	11.9
Saltwater Fish	0.7
Reptile	4.6
Small Animal	5.0

Total Number of Pets Owned in the U.S. (millions)

Bird	16.2
Cat	86.4
Dog	78.2
Equine	7.9
Freshwater Fish	151.1
Saltwater Fish	8.61
Reptile	13.0
Small Animal	16.0

*Ownership statistics are gathered from APPA's 2011-2012 National Pet Owners Survey

We started with four rings and then sliced the diagram into four markets, although we focused our efforts on only one market (see Figure 1.5). In the outermost ring, start with the total addressable market. In our case, we know that in the United States, there are just over four million babies born each year. Based on our experience and discussions with parents, we know that kids tend to pull the toilet paper when they are one or two years old, which means that there are about eight million kids in this age range. Assuming that some households have two kids in this range, the household number is between four million and eight million; we will estimate six million. So, in the outermost ring, we will write six million. But *don't stop there* the way most new product entrepreneurs do.

Next, we need to figure out, of this number of potential households, how many actually experience this problem?

Large consumer products companies spend a tremendous amount of money on surveys, focus groups, and other research to find out how many people experience the problem that their product addresses. As discussed previously, you can also do this to understand what percentage of people in this demographic experience this problem. Let's say that we learned from our surveys and interviews that one out of four families experienced this problem; we would then write 1.5 million (6 million × 25%) in the second ring. (Remember this rule of thumb: if you don't know what customers think, don't assume or guess. Ask them.)

Next, you need to determine how many of those who experience this problem have enough "pain" or "frustration" associated with it that they will purchase a product to fix it. Again, you will use survey data, target customer interviews, and assumptions to further narrow this down (covered in Chapter 3). From our interviews, we learned that one out of five, or approximately 20 percent of this number, would pay to address this problem, so in the third ring we would write 300,000 (1.5 million × 20%).

Finally, in the center, we need to estimate how many of these potential consumers we could realistically reach.

Because this is a fairly targeted market and there is no other similar product on the market, we think it is plausible that we could

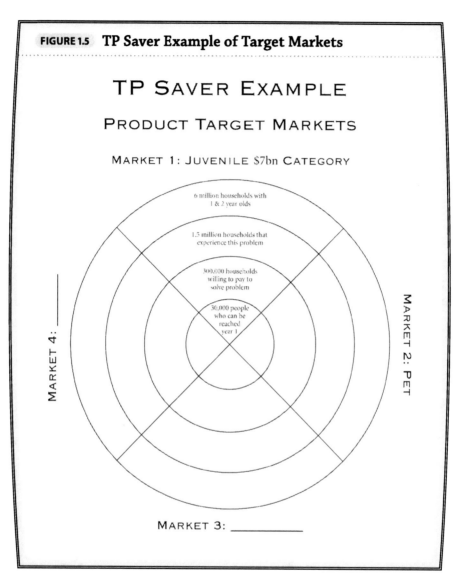

FIGURE 1.5 **TP Saver Example of Target Markets**

TP SAVER EXAMPLE

PRODUCT TARGET MARKETS

MARKET 1: JUVENILE $7bn CATEGORY

6 million households with
1 & 2 year olds

1.5 million households that
experience this problem

300,000 households
willing to pay to
solve problem

30,000 people
who can be
reached
year 1

MARKET 4: _____

MARKET 2: PET

MARKET 3: _____

reach 10 percent of this market each year (which is a very large market share for a small, new company). You can adjust this estimate up or down based on your marketing budget and prowess. But, at this stage, I suggest being conservative.

This represents 30,000 families (300,000 × 10%). As you can see, the center of our target is now 30,000 sales, which you will now multiply by your wholesale price to estimate your sales revenue.

At $1.50 per unit (our initial price estimates were higher than we found would work in the end), that is only $45,000 (30,000 × $1.50 = $45,000) in total annual gross revenue. You will learn about calculating profit margins in Chapter 3, but if our gross profit margin is 50 percent, it appears that our annual gross profit margin would be about $22,500 ($45,000 × 50% = $22,500) per year, at least in the beginning. $22,500 equals less than $2,000 per month in gross profit. After we pay all of our other expenses each month, that leaves very little for salary.

What this means is that making this product is *not* going to meet our own goals unless (1) our sales assumptions are too low, or (2) this item turns out to be a mass-market item and we find other markets to sell into, such as the pet market. Even if we doubled our market share to 20 percent, the total revenue would be just $90,000. On the other hand, if we had a different product that generated, say, $20 in gross margin per sale, the outcome would be very different (30,000 units × $20 = $600,000 gross revenue), or if we had a true mass item and sold a million units (1,000,000 × $1.50 = $1,500,000), this could be a lucrative business.

As you can see, TP Saver was a niche item with a low sale price potential. Not a good combination. While we sold fewer than 200,000 units over the years, it still did work for us because we subsequently launched other items under the same brand.

Note: Visit TamaraMonosoff.com/guides to download a free blank copy of this bulls-eye chart for your use.

Mass or Niche?

In Chapter 7, you will need to closely examine whether your product is best suited for a mass or a niche market. You can see now how important it is to know the answer to this question, as it has a major implication with regard to the financial potential of your product. Most of us dream of a major retailer running with our product. However, that comes with its own challenges. A product

Watch Video Message from Kimberly Duncan

http://www.tamaramonosoff.com/kimberly-duncan/

Kimberly Duncan, creator of the Thumb Glove (www.thumb gloveonline.com), a gadget designed to help children stop thumb sucking, has found that niche sales are her best option.

Probably the biggest success so far has been getting dentists and orthodontists on board with my product. I have repeat orders from dentists around the country.

with adequate profit margin that sells well into a niche can be just as lucrative.

When I was evaluating the market for my product, the TP Saver, the numbers appeared to show that there was a sufficient target market (parents with toddlers). But when I dug deeper, I found that the number was actually too low. Way too low! The number of toddlers that pulled the toilet paper was too small, the number of parents who were willing to purchase a product to address the problem was minimal, and the likelihood of reaching that narrow slice of the market was too big a challenge. Keep in mind that niche market items such as this can be very successful *if* there is sufficient revenue to justify them. In other words, we would have had to find a way to charge a lot more per unit for this item for it to be financially viable as a niche item. So, why did you launch the TP Saver, you might—with good reason—ask? Because I had not yet developed this methodology. Today, I would take a different approach, or select a different product to bring to market.

Often, when people do market research, they stop, as I did, after finding the answer to the first question. They say, "Oh, good! There are six million households with toddlers, which is plenty of people to buy my product." As you can see, these general data don't provide a realistic picture of the business opportunity.

In this example, we would go through the same exercise for each relevant market, such as pets and housewares, where we might sell our product (recognizing that each distinct market typically requires additional costs, such as packaging, marketing, sales, staffing, and knowledge). Then we add up the numbers for each market in the center.

Industry Data

Carefully gathering industry research data is a valuable step in forming the basis for moving forward with your product. The reliability and accuracy of source data are critical. This information is often also the hardest to find.

When developing data, you will first look for specific data that have already been produced. First, look for this kind of data using search engines and industry sources. Many industry publications (for example, *Kids Today* for the juvenile sector) can provide a wealth of information. Many industry groups sponsor and publish specific research data. Some examples are:

- The Juvenile Products Manufacturing Association (http://www.jpma.org)
- The International Housewares Association (http:///www.housewares.org)
- The American Pet Products Association (http://www.americanpetproducts.org/)
- The Direct Selling Association (http://www.dsa.org/)

Sometimes you hit the jackpot and find exactly what you are looking for. Other times, you need to pull together more disconnected data or to seek data on related items, especially if your product is totally new and innovative.

Use a search engine (for example, Google or Yahoo!) and search for variations on the "problem that your product solves + statistics," your product type, or the actual industry. For example, if we were developing a new type of yoga accessory, we would need to understand the yoga market. (See the search examples in Figures 1.6 and

1.7.) It took only two clicks to find incredible yoga industry data using "yoga statistics." It can be exciting when you find something after making a subtle change in your search description.

Not only did we find relevant data from a single search on "yoga statistics," but we also found additional industry publications like *Yoga Journal* that offer even more detailed market research to help you get a broader understanding of the yoga market.

Other sources that can increase your knowledge about the benefits associated with your product are blogs and posts from relevant

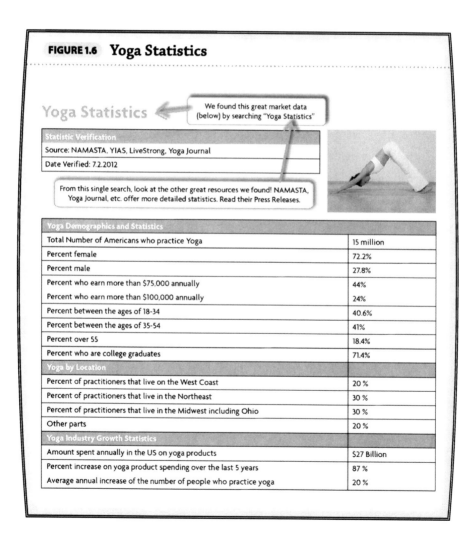

FIGURE 1.6 Yoga Statistics

Yoga Statistics ← We found this great market data (below) by searching "Yoga Statistics"

Statistic Verification

Source: NAMASTA, YIAS, LiveStrong, Yoga Journal

Date Verified: 7.2.2012

From this single search, look at the other great resources we found! NAMASTA, Yoga Journal, etc. offer more detailed statistics. Read their Press Releases.

Yoga Demographics and Statistics	
Total Number of Americans who practice Yoga	15 million
Percent female	72.2%
Percent male	27.8%
Percent who earn more than $75,000 annually	44%
Percent who earn more than $100,000 annually	24%
Percent between the ages of 18-34	40.6%
Percent between the ages of 35-54	41%
Percent over 55	18.4%
Percent who are college graduates	71.4%
Yoga by Location	
Percent of practitioners that live on the West Coast	20 %
Percent of practitioners that live in the Northeast	30 %
Percent of practitioners that live in the Midwest including Ohio	30 %
Other parts	20 %
Yoga Industry Growth Statistics	
Amount spent annually in the US on yoga products	$27 Billion
Percent increase on yoga product spending over the last 5 years	87 %
Average annual increase of the number of people who practice yoga	20 %

FIGURE 1.7 Google Search for Yoga Statistics

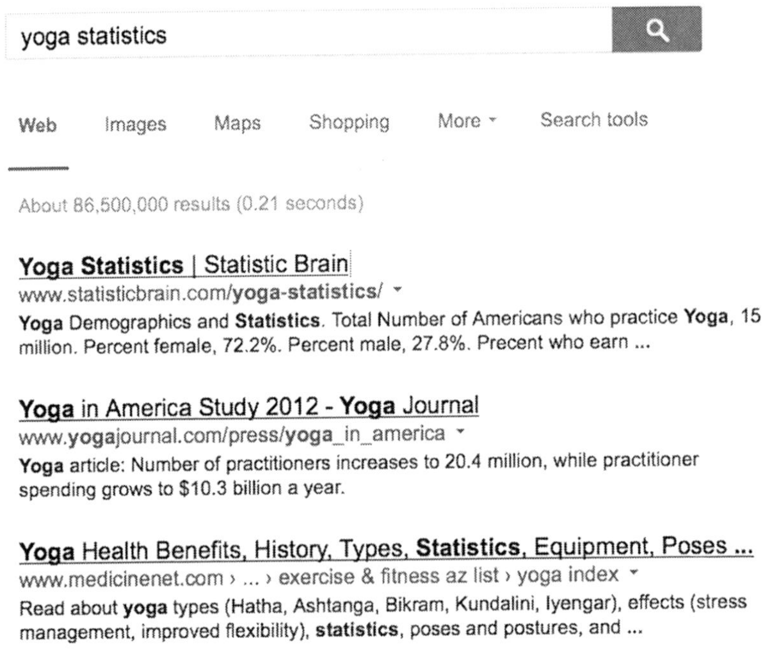

yoga statistics

Web   Images   Maps   Shopping   More ▾   Search tools

About 86,500,000 results (0.21 seconds)

Yoga Statistics | Statistic Brain
www.statisticbrain.com/**yoga-statistics**/ ▾
Yoga Demographics and **Statistics**. Total Number of Americans who practice **Yoga**, 15 million. Percent female, 72.2%. Percent male, 27.8%. Precent who earn ...

Yoga in America Study 2012 - **Yoga** Journal
www.**yoga**journal.com/press/**yoga**_in_america ▾
Yoga article: Number of practitioners increases to 20.4 million, while practitioner spending grows to $10.3 billion a year.

Yoga Health Benefits, History, Types, **Statistics**, Equipment, Poses ...
www.medicinenet.com › ... › exercise & fitness az list › yoga index ▾
Read about **yoga** types (Hatha, Ashtanga, Bikram, Kundalini, Iyengar), effects (stress management, improved flexibility), **statistics**, poses and postures, and ...

communities. In addition, you can make posts to communities yourself without disclosing your product design. For example, if you were working on a yoga product, you could use search engines to find relevant blogs and communities. If they have search windows on their sites, search on the need that your product solves. If you see nothing, create a post and see what you hear in response. For example, if you were developing a new yoga mat that had arm extensions, write a post that says, "Does anyone else have an issue with your arms coming off the yoga mat? If so, how do you address it?" Write the same kind of post on sites that are not as industry specific but that reach your demographic. For example, if it is a product for women, create posts on a mom blog like www.CafeMom.com, or on a women's forum like Yahoo!'s Shine, http://shine.yahoo.com.

Competition: Who Is Your Competition?

Competition is a reality in business. And the truth is that the more successful you are, the more likely you are to face competition. In other words, it is nearly unavoidable. However, because product development is expensive, it would be preferable for you to know about existing competing products and major competitors before you decide to invest in this business.

The good news is that *because* product development is expensive, it is not unusual for competitors to wait to see if you are successful

 Watch Video Message from Lisa Hoskins-Holmes and Karen Wildman

http://www.tamaramonosoff.com/karen-wildman-lisa-holmes/

Business partners (and, most important, sisters) Lisa Hoskins-Holmes and Karen Wildman, founders of Bheestie (www.bheestie.com), a line of products that removes moisture from electronic devices, describe their initial research.

It began out of our own personal need. We then polled friends and family to see if they had ever gotten their cell phones wet. Next, we were on the Internet searching on "wet cell phones" and "methods for drying wet cell phones." We quickly realized that almost everyone has either gotten her cell phone wet or knows someone who has. Our research also revealed that there are 300 million cell phones in the United States, and that one in three will get wet—that's 100 million wet cell phones! Then there are those other personal electronics: cameras, iPods, and so on. There was a huge need for our product idea.

I would also point out that another key point that would have been evident from this research, and highly relevant to their product's success, is the relatively high cost to replace new electronic products.

before they decide to develop and launch a competing item. This gives you some time to capture the market. And if you are able to do a good job, you could potentially box out the competition and create a brand that consumers prefer (see Chapter 9 for branding and marketing tips). This is the point when a lot of small companies sell or license their product rights to the competition.

When you find that you have an opportunity to launch without competition, it is highly likely that as soon as you start to secure large retail accounts or generate sales traction directly with consumers, major players will see an opportunity and consider going after this business as well.

For this reason, it is useful to know which companies make products that are in the same category and would therefore represent likely threats. For example, when I launched my TP Saver, it was the only item like it on the market. However, there are two or three major manufacturers that focus on items for baby safety. We watched them very closely after we launched. And, sure enough, after about 24 months, one of these companies launched an item that was directly competitive (with language on the packaging that was surprisingly similar). Keep in mind that we had a strong utility patent and a trademark, yet the competition was able to design around them and create a similar product with a similar name. Fortunately, we had had enough time during those first two years to generate our best sales and launch additional products as well.

It is time to put on your detective hat. The answers to these questions will help you get a sense of direct and indirect competition.

◆ What gave you this idea? In other words, what problem does your product solve?

◆ How are consumers currently solving the problem that your product solves?

◆ What products or processes will your product replace or eliminate?

◆ What advantages does your product have over others that are already on the market?

- What directly competing products are on the market?
- Which companies are making and distributing those products?
- How many companies will you be competing with?
- How large are they? What is their advantage?
- How well placed are they with your ideal distribution channels?
- Which channels have they not secured?
- Can you find out why they have not yet penetrated those channels?
- How well-liked are the similar products in the industry? By customers? By retailers?
- How will you differentiate your product from others that are already on the market?

Visit the websites of the companies you know that make items that would be directly related, as well as websites such as Amazon. com, Walmart.com, and QVC.com and retail sites that focus on your target audience. For example, if your item is a kitchen item, visit online housewares retailers and catalogs.

At each website, search using words that are related to your item to see what products show up. For instance, if your item is a child's shoe storage product, search using the words, "children + shoe + storage." As you search online, use different words and variations of words (grab a thesaurus or synonym finder to help you).

Visit retailers in person and note how much shelf space is given to items similar to yours and the depth of their presence. For the "shoe storage" example, we would visit the Container Store and speak to the associates to see whether they have this item, and if not, whether they ever have customers ask for this type of item. You should also ask which manufacturers would be most likely to produce something similar.

Also be sure to do these searches on the overseas sourcing web-sites as well, such as www.Alibaba.com and www.Globalsources. com. If you find something comparable on these sites, you may have found evidence of major competition. On the other hand, it may be that these companies do not yet sell in the United States and you have just found a fast path to manufacturing (which you want to take note of and will revisit in Chapter 5.)

Competition as Partners

Competitors can potentially become future licensing partners. Yes, you heard me right! If you have the next gold, shiny product to add to their existing product line, it may make sense for you and them to join forces rather than compete if they have a strong brand and distribution in the marketplace.

Chapter Wrap-Up

I hope this process has helped you sharpen your thinking about your product and clarify the true size of your target market. Understanding the competition is a practical step to help you prepare in advance for what you might encounter. Once you enter the market, you will be swimming with sharks. Learn what you can about them and be ready to swim circles around them.

Whether you decide to move full steam ahead, to make adjustments and proceed, or to switch to your next invention, good research is time and effort well spent.

If you do decide to move forward, it's time to pull out your hammer, tape measure, and glue gun, and turn this idea into something tangible. Building your prototype is the next step, which is covered in full in Chapter 2.

Forge on!

From Your Mind's Eye to the Palm of Your Hand

Video Message: Tamara Monosoff Introduces Chapter 2

http://www.tamaramonosoff.com/
tamara-monosoff-introduces-chapter-2/

Creating Your Product Design and Prototype

Even if you are a true Renaissance woman—functioning as equal parts attorney, engineer, manufacturer, and marketer (and mom!)—you will need help in communicating your vision to other people. Your invention team, which will consist of everyone who'll help you on your way to market, will make valuable—and often expensive—contributions to your product. The more clearly the members of your team understand your design vision and objectives, the better off you'll be.

It is also at this stage that it makes sense to begin research on the safety and regulatory requirements that you will need to comply with as you develop, and ultimately manufacture, your product. I will cover the prototyping process in some detail in the first part of this chapter followed by the process of assessing the safety issues relevant to your product.

At this stage, a prototype is the best way to communicate your unique invention. But what exactly *is* a prototype? And what will it accomplish? In a nutshell, a prototype is simply a three-dimensional version of your vision. It's typically a working model of your product, and it can be as simple as a silicon sticker or as complicated as a refined mechanical device, depending on your idea. It is risky to rely on the ability of others to imagine how your product idea will actually look, feel, and work. This chapter will discuss the ins and outs of building a prototype of your own.

Seeing Is Believing

The advantage of having a full-scale prototype is that it will enable you to avoid potential confusion when you try to communicate your idea. A prototype will also encourage others to take you more seriously. When you are meeting with any professional, from your own attorney to a potential licensing company, when you arrive with a prototype in hand, you separate yourself from the dozens of others who've approached him with only vague ideas in mind. Instead, you'll be viewed as a professional with a purpose, as opposed to *just* another inventor with a potentially good idea. Later, when you approach your test market and, after that, potential buyers, a prototype will also prove invaluable. There is simply nothing that brings a product idea to life like the ability to hold it in your hand and use it. And if your goal is to license your idea rather than manufacture it yourself, presenting an actual prototype can help you better articulate your idea's value. Though a drawing may be sufficient to sell an idea to a potential licensor, demonstrating that you have already worked through the design challenges and received valuable consumer feedback will further strengthen your case and help support your sales process.

Watch Video Message from Cheryl Hajjar

http://www.tamaramonosoff.com/cheryl-hajjar-amy-perreault/

Cousins Cheryl Hajjar and Amy Perreault are the creators of the Indigo Pixies (www.indigopixies.com), a family of multicultural fairies (dolls and accompanying picture books) that helps children build the confidence they need to overcome challenging developmental milestones, such as giving up their pacifiers (the Paci Pixie is their top seller). The cousins learned firsthand that even though they could visualize how they wanted their dolls to look, a sketch did not adequately communicate what they wanted the factory to create. Cheryl shares their story here.

When we first started the company, we wanted a prototype for a doll. We had a friend who did a lot of manufacturing in China, so we asked him if he could help us. We sent only a picture of the character without specific sizes and instructions to his manufacturer, and we thought we were going to get a perfect prototype that we could reproduce. Well, were we surprised by what came back! We had envisioned our character, the Paci Pixie, as a beautiful, light-haired fairy with a flowing purple outfit. We wanted her to beam beauty. Instead, we received a small stuffed doll that looked like something that came out of a horror movie. It had red clothing, and the stitching was coming apart on the sides of her face, almost like the character "Sally" from the movie The Nightmare Before Christmas! *This was perfect for that movie, but not for our products! We were green and did not have the slightest clue about what goes into designing and making a prototype, let alone the cost of making one.*

After many renditions, the Indigo Pixies have successfully found their way to Walmart.com, BarnesandNoble.com, Amazon.com, and many other online retailers.

This is a great story to illustrate how important it is to clearly communicate exactly what you want, whether you are working in the United States or overseas. The more detailed you can be, with clear instructions, specifications, and materials, the more likely you are to get a better result with your initial prototypes. Your vision can be understood by others only if you don't just assume that others will "get it."

Form and Function

Your idea works perfectly in theory. It's not until you start physically creating it that you'll encounter flaws in your thinking. That's why another great reason to develop a prototype is to test the functionality of your idea. You'll never know the design issues and challenges until you begin actually taking your idea from theory to reality.

In developing my own invention, for instance, I had to refine my design as much as possible prior to mass production. It was critical to observe the baby-proofing effectiveness of my prototype and have it evaluated for safety. Plus, it needed to be a preproduction prototype (see the next section), which is the last opportunity to tweak a product and make final changes before mass production in a factory. In addition, many retail stores wanted to see the final, finished product before they committed to ordering it.

Haste Makes Waste

If you feel tempted to skip creating a prototype, reconsider. Sure, you might be in a huge rush to get to market, but moving too fast risks compromising your design. Take the time and do your homework, learn as much as you can at this stage, and develop a prototype that performs well and looks good. You'll inevitably encounter some bumps in the road, but it's better than losing out completely by taking unnecessary or foolhardy shortcuts.

The Importance of Creating Your Prototype

1. A prototype enables you to test and refine the functionality of your design.
2. A prototype makes it possible to test the performance of various materials.

3. A prototype will help you to eventually describe your product more effectively to your team, including your attorney, packaging or marketing experts, engineers, and potential business partners.

4. A prototype can help communicate your idea's value to licensing prospects, potential investors, prospective consumers, and wholesale buyers.

5. A prototype is exciting because it makes your product idea *real.*

Just Your Type

There are many prototype formats, but the two most important for you are likely to be the presentation prototype and the preproduction prototype.

If you plan on licensing your idea rather than manufacturing it yourself (more on making this decision in Chapter 9), the presentation prototype is adequate for showing your idea to prospective licensors. But if you plan to manufacture the product yourself, you'll need a preproduction prototype.

The presentation prototype is typically less complex than the preproduction prototype. At times, digital drawings or even hand drawings of good quality will suffice when you are presenting an idea to a potential licensor. However, it's never a bad idea to create a three-dimensional prototype (see the discussion of 3-D printing later in the chapter) to better communicate your idea to all parties involved. While it should look and feel close to your vision, it doesn't necessarily have to include all functioning parts or be at the more sophisticated level of the prototype you need when you are planning to mass-produce the product yourself.

The preproduction prototype, on the other hand, must be a functional version of your final product. All moving pieces and parts (if applicable to your invention) must work, and it must be in the near-final phase of development. This is the kind of prototype I used when I developed the TP Saver.

Developing Your Prototype

This stage in the inventing process is possibly the period of greatest learning... and is also my personal favorite. I love the creative exploration that prototyping inspires. This is where your words and thoughts change from "Can I?" to "How will I?"

Of course, every prototype demands different materials and types of designers, and varies according to your product. Your product may incorporate a range of materials, such as plastics, textiles, metals, chemicals, electronics, software, and so on. Entire books could be written on developing products with each of these materials, so my intention here is to introduce basic concepts using the more common elements. We will focus on products that mainly fall into two

Watch Video: Tamara Monosoff
Interviews Justin Aiello

http://www.tamaramonosoff.com/justin-aiello/

Justin Aiello, owner of Aiello Design (www.aiellodesign.com), specializes in many of the early-stage aspects of designing and preparing a product in the hard goods categories. He tells inventors,

Simply put, the more complex a product, the more expensive it will be to develop and manufacture. Therefore, one of the most important principles in conceiving a new invention is, "Keep it simple!" I see a lot of inventors adding unnecessary technology (the "everything but the kitchen sink" syndrome) because they think it makes the product better. This will increase the product cost and in the end make it too expensive for consumers to purchase. Spend time brainstorming ways to simplify the invention, not to add bells and whistles. When you've thought through your concept, one of the best ways to obtain real production cost information is to have proper engineering documentation that includes all the details of each part of your product: geometry, size, volume, material, dimensions, color, finish, hardware, and assembly procedure, to name just a few.

categories: hard goods and soft goods. Hard goods refers to items made of plastic, wood, metal, rubber, and similar materials, and soft goods refers to items made of fabrics or textiles that are cut and sewn, such as bedding, curtains, towels, purses, bags, and clothing.

There is one universal truth to developing every prototype: trial and error. In the beginning, you probably won't know the ideal combination of design elements or materials. Plus, while going through the process, you may get a sudden burst of new ideas or concerns about your product's functionality. Be receptive to your results and open to change. This is one of the most creative parts of the process, and it is important that you let your thoughts unfold freely. Once

Watch Video Message from Heather Sonnenberg

http://www.tamaramonosoff.com/heather-sonnenberg/

Heather Sonnenberg, inventor of Lil' Cub Hub Convertible Carrier (www.lilcubhub.com), a diaper bag that converts into a sling-style baby carrier in just one zip, had her own stop-and-go experience when developing her initial prototype at home.

Oh my goodness, I had no idea what I was doing! I literally went to a craft and sewing store and bought random things— a snap gun, a hot glue gun, snaps, safety pins, and so on— and drew ideas on a pad and tried different ways of putting a prototype together. I took a sewing class so that I could learn the basics of sewing. I eventually tried a prototype manufacturer who wanted to charge me more than $8,000 for my first prototype. So instead, I shipped a sample to my mother and talked through some ideas with her, and she sewed my first prototype. This first sample was invaluable in that it helped me convey what I wanted the end result to look like when I showed professional sewing manufacturers.

Lil' Cub Hub Convertible Carrier was recently featured on *Los Angeles Morning News* on KTLA, is sold on Amazon and eBay, and is distributed under a private label in Australia.

you've explored a large number of ideas, then you will want to simplify your design.

While it may seem easier to hire a professional, developing your own prototype can be a cost-efficient first step that can help you better articulate your vision to a professional. If you can put something together at home first, I recommend that you do so.

Getting Crafty

Making a prototype by hand is a great way to start bringing your product to life. Remember, there are no rules! Give yourself permission to experiment. Look around the house and select materials that you can use to see if your idea works. Spend an hour wandering around craft and hardware stores just looking for materials. If you need a wire coil, pull it out of a spiral notebook. If you need durable yet flexible plastic, cut a piece out of a two-liter soda bottle. Use modeling clay or your children's modeling compound to make an initial form. There are no boundaries on what you can find and use. After you've exhausted the available supplies in your home, the next step is to go shopping! Look for materials in places that you've never considered, such as plumbing, or kitchen supply stores; computer stores; or toy stores. When I was developing the TP Saver, I was inspired by a hair-perm rod in a beauty supply store, of all places, which led to my final design.

Textiles 101

Textiles (cloth or fabric) are one of the materials commonly used in products. As with plastics, you can apply this information to your own prototype development.

When using any materials, try to be open to alternatives that you may not have originally considered. For example, you may be convinced that you want to use cotton. If this is the case,

Watch Video Message from Kimberlee Vaccarella

http://www.tamaramonosoff.com/kimberlee-vaccarella/

Kimberlee Vaccarella, inventor of the Bogg Bag (pictured here) was determined to design a beach bag for beach-loving people to use:

After years of buying beach bags that just couldn't handle my beach-loving family's needs, we thought there must be a better bag. We wanted a lightweight bag with holes (think Croc shoes) that would carry everything for a long day at the beach, but could then be hosed down and easily washed for our next adventure. I was a controller for a commercial real estate lender with a husband who was a police officer, and neither one of us knew what to do next when we came up with the Bogg Bag (www.boggbag.com). I wandered around a local craft store looking for something that I could use to attempt to make a sample. I came across some big foam sheets. I went home, cut them up, made holes, sewed the sides together and voilà, the Bogg Bag was born! Now Bogg Bags can be found at more than 125 specialty boutiques and surf shops and are available online at Amazon, ShopVault.com, and TheGrommet.com.

One of my most memorable moments, among many, that made me feel "rich" along this journey is when I was at work and my husband called me and said, "You need to come home right now!" I asked why and explained that it would be hard for me to leave work at that time. He explained that the first samples of the Bogg Bag had come in and were "the coolest thing he'd ever seen."

challenge yourself by asking, "Why?" Perhaps another material might work, such as a stretch material like Lycra. Or how about using mesh, canvas, nylon, or leather? What about taking a leap and trying neoprene (wetsuit material)? There are also higher-end, exotic, and green fabrics (bamboo) that might really make a splash when you hit the market. This is the time to ask, "What if?" and allow yourself the freedom to explore. When creating a product from textiles, you'll also need to consider possible attachments—"notions," such as buttons, elastic, zippers, fasteners, and appliqués (labels that can be ironed or sewn on). Visit www.britexfabrics.com/notions, www.joann.com, and www.nancysnotions.com/ and brainstorm different ways in which you can enhance your prototype. Keep in mind that anything and everything you add will increase costs in mass production.

Even if you are an outstanding seamstress and you've created a good-looking product with materials that work well, there comes a time when you'll need to hire a professional textile prototype devel-

Don't Assume that Professionals Will Think of Everything

Watch Video Message from Annette Giacomazzi
http://www.tamaramonosoff.com/annette-giacomazzi/

Annette Giacomazzi, founder of CastCoverZ! (www.cast coverz.com), the leading global manufacturer, e-tailer, and innovator of orthopedic soft goods, which are functional and fashionable products designed to cover casts, orthotic walking boots, splints, and braces; shared a lesson she learned from hiring contractors to produce her products.

What surprised me was that contractors (in my case, sewing contractors) wouldn't suggest a less expensive, even better way to construct our products unless they were asked. To avoid this, ask this question when interviewing contractors: "If this were your product, how would you make it?" Your goal is to listen for easier, less expensive ways to construct the item. Don't assume that just because they are professionals, they will think of this on their own. As a business owner, it's essential for you to think about creating the highest-quality products at the most affordable prices. If my production costs are lower, then I can pass these savings on to my customers.

oper. Textile developers will use your initial design to provide standardized specifications and to create patterns [similar to that of a computer-aided design (CAD) drawing when developing a plastic product] in preparation for a textile manufacturer.

A Fun Product to Whip Your Product into Shape

ShapeLock is a material perfect for making home prototypes. When the plastic pellets are heated in the microwave or with your hair dryer, this unique plastic formulation becomes pliable, kind of like clay, so that you can mold it any way you'd like. When it's cool, it becomes a hard plastic. You can test out your product design to see if it works. If it doesn't, just pop it back into the microwave and soften up the plastic again. You can reuse this plastic again and again until you come up with a winning design. The best part? It's only about $14.95 per container, and you can reheat it and reuse it again and again. Find it at www.shapelock.com.

Bringing In the Pros

Once you have developed your prototype as far as you reasonably can, it's time to consider hiring a professional to help you with the next steps. There are many avenues you can take at this stage. You may wish to hire professional prototype developers, engineers, and designers, but others may be able to help as well, including a handyman, a machinist, a student from a local industrial design college, or a manufacturer of similar products, for example. The complexity and materials to be used in your specific product will help drive this decision.

If you decide to go with a professional prototype developer, there are a few ways to find one. There is a free resource called ThomasNet (www.thomasnet.com), a one-stop resource with all the

What Will It Cost?

Plastic or Metal Prototype

- Engineer: $100 to $300 per hour.
- CAD drawings and product refinement for manufacturability: $1,000 to $10,000, depending on the complexity of the product. (The TP Saver CAD drawings cost $3,000.)
- Machinist: $50 to $100 per hour (varies by region).
- Hand-tooled prototype: $100 to $300, depending on the complexity of the product. (Each hand-tooled TP Saver prototype cost me $100.)
- 3-D printing (assuming that CAD drawings are complete): $150 to $500 (depending on the complexity of the product).

Textile Prototype

$500 and up (depending on complexity).

Safety Test

Sending your product to an independent safety testing lab will cost anywhere from $500 to more than $15,000, depending on the complexity of the product and the required tests. (TP Saver cost me around $800.)

Money-Saving Tips

- **Plastics.** Use ShapeLock or a similar product that will allow you to make the prototype by hand. Once you know that your product works, you can then hire an engineer to create CAD drawings, followed by a rapid-prototyping company that uses 3-D printing to produce finished-looking prototypes. Some rapid-prototype companies can also do CAD drawings.
- **Textiles.** Use a local seamstress, friend, or family member who can sew to flesh out as many of the issues as possible before going to a prototype developer.
- **Testing.** Speak to your manufacturer about which tests their safety lab plans to run; you may be able to avoid unnecessary testing. For example, if you have to test for the content of certain chemicals, but your factory can assure you that the product meets requirements, you may be able to skip this test (and the money you'd pay to have it conducted). Or, if one

test is only necessary to meet a European standard, e.g., packaging, but you don't plan to sell in Europe, that may be an unnecessary expense.

In addition, know the federal requirements in advance—for example, the choking hazard standard—and design your product in accordance with these requirements (explained later in this chapter).

---

information you need. It offers a database of 650,000 manufacturers, distributors, and service providers (including prototype developers) to choose from, broken down by state. Many of the following resources were generously recommended by the inventors featured in this book!

Take the time to evaluate each of these resources to find the right fit as I have not worked with most of them directly. Some of the resources are product development companies; others offer directories of product designers; and still others are prototype developers that have relationships with U.S. and overseas manufacturers. Most of these companies often offer the first consultation for free.

Resources for Hard Goods Designers and Prototype Developers

Core 77 Design Directory (www.designdirectory.com/)
Ray Tech Corp (www.raytechcorp.com)
Noble Plastics (www.nobleplastics.com)
Primordial Soup, LLC (www.p-soup.com)
T2 Design and Prototype (www.T2design.com)
Minnesota Rubber & Plastics (www.MNRubber.com)
Slingshot Product Development Group (www.slingshot pdg.com)
KDK Consumer Solutions (www.kdkcs.com/)
Aiello Design (www.aiellodesign.com)
Big Idea Group (www.bigideagroup.net)

Resources for Textile Designers and Prototype Developers

A. Rifkin Co. (www.arifkin.com)
Fiber Trim Sewing Company (http://fibertrimsewing.com/)
Me, Myself & I Textiles (www.mmitextiles)
Choices Apparel (www.choicesapparel.com)
Field Tex Products, Inc. (www.fieldtex.com)
Activewear, Inc. (www.activewearinc.com)
SJ Private Label (www.sjprivatelabel.com)

Check Out These Websites for Sourcing All Kinds of Materials Overseas

Alibaba (www.alibaba.com)—discussed in detail in Chapter 5, "Getting the Goods"
Panjiva (www.panjiva.com)

And, last but not least, search Google using keywords; for example, "textile developer + plush fabrics." A number of resources will pop up. And always check references before you sign any contracts.

Machinist Versus Engineer

A machinist is a specialized tradesperson who can create a prototype. Such a person is often skilled in using a variety of plastics and metals and can hand-tool a prototype for you at a fraction of the cost of an engineer. An engineer is a specially trained professional who is skilled in the technical aspects of designing and building. Engineers are typically trained in specific disciplines, such as mechanical, chemical, structural, electrical, and industrial design engineering. Although you can go directly to an industrial design engineer to make a prototype for you, a machinist will often quote you an hourly wage for her services.

There are definite pros and cons to both routes. Starting with a less costly machinist enables you to get closer to your preferred design before you have to pay more money to an engineer. However, an engineer can often help you come up with new designs or offer design alternatives that can help bring down mass-production manufacturing costs. An engineer understands the bigger picture and can produce the CAD drawings you will need if you are to move forward. By handling all steps of the process, from preparing the prototype to improving the design of your product, an engineer can help expedite the process of bringing your product to market.

The hottest thing on the prototype scene lately is a process called *3-D printing.* This process uses a machine that is programed to do additive manufacturing—a process by which a digital file is translated into a physical object by a 3-D printer. In other words, the printer reads your CAD drawings (more information on CAD drawings is given later in this chapter) and "adds" layer upon layer of liq-

3-D Printers May Become a Common Household Item!

Expert product developer Justin Aiello of Aiello Design gives us the lowdown on 3-D printing, how we can use it to our advantage as an inventor, and upcoming trends.

Stereolithography (SLA for short) is the technical term for 3-D printing. This is a method used to create parts from 3-D CAD files. In this process, the SLA machine uses a laser to solidify liquid resin in a tank. The laser is guided by the geometry contained in the 3-D CAD file. Everywhere the laser hits, the liquid resin turns solid. The laser moves around and slowly builds up the part one layer at a time. In the same way that an inkjet printer moves back and forth across a page to create a 2-D image, the laser moves around the tank to create a 3-D solid part.

SLA technology is constantly improving. The speed, accuracy, and quality of materials gets better with each passing year. There are now many types of printing materials available, each with different mechanical properties that come close to matching production materials. You can choose resins with good strength, rigidity, flexibility, transparency, and even rubberlike properties. There are also variations on the SLA process that utilize powder instead of liquid resin, where the laser fuses the powder together to create parts. In recent years, printing parts from powdered metal has also become possible. This process does not yet yield parts that are as high-tolerance as production parts, but it's just a matter of time.

The advent of 3-D CAD engineering coupled with 3-D printing technology has had a significant impact on the world of product development. Today prototype parts can be made faster and more cheaply than ever before. It's become an invaluable tool to create working prototypes for testing as well as for verification of part fit, form, and function before going into mass production. The performance of the part is directly tied to the expertise of the engineer who designed it. It's the same 3-D CAD files used for SLA printing that are used to create molds for production. And now, using this technology, engineers are able to find and resolve problems before going to production, instead of after.

As this technology continues to improve, it's predicted that 3-D printing will be able to go beyond just prototyping. It's possible that some day, 3-D printing will be used as a method of manufacturing finished goods. This would eliminate the need for costly injection molds and allow total design freedom to modify part designs on the fly. In the future, consumers may be buying the file rights to print out products right in their own homes. Shipping in goods made in other countries could become a thing of the past. As we speak, many manufacturers are selling 3-D printers targeted at home users. While these low-cost machines do not yet compare to the quality of large, expensive commercial-grade machines, they only have up to go.

---

uid plastic until presto—your product appears! This process enables inventors to have prototypes made quickly and inexpensively from CAD drawings by a large machine rather than an expensive injection mold. Rapid prototypes cost a few hundred dollars each, but they're a bargain considering the alternatives. When I first looked into the option of prototyping the TP Saver, for instance, I found that a high-quality preproduction prototype would cost more than $15,000. This included the cost of building an injection molding tool that would enable me to mass-produce my product. We were

Beware of Costly Flaws: 3-D Printing Perfection May Be Only on the Surface

Watch Video Message from Kimberly Meckwood

http://www.tamaramonosoff.com/kimberly-meckwood/

Although the new 3-D printing technology is dazzling and a great way to get a visual representation of your product into your hands, Kimberly Meckwood, inventor of the clever Click & Carry (www.clickandcarry.com), which allows you to carry multiple shopping bags at once without using your hands, learned an expensive lesson the hard way—3-D printing is not always perfect.

This part of the process was especially difficult. I made nine prototypes before settling on a winner. Each prototype was a few hundred dollars from a 3-D CAD printer. Each time I had the physical prototype, I would notice a necessary modification that needed to be made to produce the "perfect product." Once I settled on the "winner," I next had to have a steel mold created to see if the prototype would actually work. What I learned was that a 3-D CAD printed prototype is only for looks and area in space. I had the proper design and appearance secured, but there was no way of knowing if it would actually work. After paying $7,500 for the first mold, I found that Click & Carry did work. The bad news was that it held only 20 pounds before the end would bend and not remain in a secure position. At that point, I knew that it was back to the drawing board. It took me almost three months to figure out the problem and redesign the Click & Carry to have a "lip" on either side to keep the integrity of the design. Now the Click & Carry holds up to 50 pounds. Another flaw that was not proven in my 3-D printer prototype was the dimple that makes the click noise and secures the unit in place. We were not able to create the dimple on the 3-D CAD, and when I made the second mold, that issue was corrected. Now everything has been reworked and perfected. This was an expensive learning experience! Not only did I have to pay for two molds, but I had to apply for a second utility patent, since my product had changed. The good news is that my factory (Li & Y Manufactory: www.liy.com.hk) has been an incredible partner, that my product works and is helping people, and that I've recently sold 20,000 units so far!

at a point where we weren't quite ready to finalize our design, but we still needed a few high-quality prototypes of our product. I had a machinist hand-tool individual prototypes (hand-made prototypes almost always have imperfections). When I wrote the first edition of this book, rapid prototyping was brand new at the time, so a single prototype was very expensive. With advances in technology and the drop in cost, this option is more accessible. It's the perfect solution for this in-between stage of development because within a few days—rather than weeks or even months—you can have a finished-looking representation of your product in hand.

To locate companies that offer this 3-D printing service, do a Google search or visit these websites:

Sculpteo (http://www.sculpteo.com/en/)
Shapeways (http://www.shapeways.com)
Tech Shop (www.techshop.ws/3_D_Printing.html)

As of the writing of this book, the UPS Store is testing 3-D printers to make them accessible to start-ups and small-business owners. The test is being conducted in three markets: San Diego, California; Washington, DC; and Frisco, Texas. If consumers use the printers at these store locations, you can expect to see 3-D printers available for entrepreneurs to use at stores nationwide.

The Secret Formula

Yet another type of prototype developer is called a *formulator*. This is a chemist who helps create a new formula from scratch. A formulator is used for any number of inventive applications, from beauty products to cleaning agents to pet supplies to food and vitamins. (See Chapter 5, "Getting the Goods," to read stories about the ins and outs of manufacturing formulated products.)

Note that you will have to pay a formulator extra money if you are to retain 100 percent of the rights to your formula. Otherwise, formulators may sell your product to others under a different label.

Here are a few resources to help you get started exploring your options:

Formulator Sample Shop (www.formulatorsampleshop.com)
Sun Deep Cosmetics (www.sundeepinc.com)
Prima Fleur (www.primafleur.com)
Diamond Wipes (http://www.diamondwipes.com/)

Keep in Mind...

As you build and refine your prototype, you should keep a few manufacturing issues in mind:

• **Labor cost.** When you mass-produce, the general rule is that the less the "hands-on" labor required, the lower the cost. For example, during mass production of the TP Saver, a person must hand-knot the elastic on each end of the product, which drives up the cost of producing it. The Mom Invented® Good Bites Crustless Sandwich Cutter, however, consists of one simple molded piece. Once it is ejected from the injection-molding machine, it travels on a conveyor belt and drops into a box at the end. There is no additional labor required except for the person running the machine. Mass manufacturing is discussed in greater detail in Chapter 5. But for the purposes of developing your prototype, you should keep any labor-intensive issues in mind and avoid them if at all possible.

• **Safety requirements.** Be sure to research any regulatory requirements (see the next section) that are relevant to your product early in the prototype stage. This way, you will avoid unnecessary redesigns of your prototype. When I first designed the TP Saver, for instance, I was unaware of the federal choking hazard requirements. I had already completed my prototype when a consumer offered me some feedback, telling me that she would be concerned about her child choking on the cap. When I looked into it, I learned that there are federal safety standards that you must adhere to as a product

Watch Video Message from Kirsten Chapman

http://www.tamaramonosoff.com/kirsten-chapman/

Kirsten Chapman invented Kleynimals (www.kleynimals.com)— Clean Key Animals for babies. I'm sharing Kirsten's story here because it's a great example of her determination to create a safe prod-  uct. Even after her product prototype tested "safe," she decided to test again. Her results were surprising.

I was inspired by my youngest son's love of keys and put- ting anything and everything into his mouth. I came up with nontoxic, clean, 100 percent stainless steel keys that mimic the feel of real keys. I had developed a prototype based on a conversation I had had with the CPSC (Consumer Product Safety Commission) and the small parts requirements for toys. I found a split key ring that was 1.25 inches, which was the minimum for small parts. The first prototype was approved by the testing company. When I thought I was ready to launch based on this prototype, I sent the final product in for testing again. This prototype was rejected, as the ring was just under the 1.25 inches. What I did not realize is that there was a margin of error on the rings, and therefore some were slightly smaller. This meant that I had to rethink the ring entirely. I ended up with a larger-size jump ring, but I had to order 25,000 of them and then find someone to weld them for me at a decent price.

developer. Because I didn't know this earlier, I had to pay an engi- neer (who had not previously brought this up) to redesign and re- create his CAD drawings. Luckily, I hadn't manufactured any units yet, but it was still a costly mistake.

Regulatory and Safety Issues

Regulations and safety issues related to your product can be signifi- cant factors in your plans and design going forward. For example, I once met an inventor who had a great idea for a type of baby walker. She was not aware, until I told her, that baby walkers have been recalled in the United States many times, and that Canada has completely banned their sale because of safety issues. It is virtually impossible to secure product liability insurance for a baby walker. These hurdles would probably be insurmountable for a new product entrepreneur. So, as you work your way through these steps, think about the overall implications as well as the specifics related to your product.

As you begin evaluating safety issues related to your product, consider approaching it from this point of view:

- You don't want to harm anyone.
- You want to produce a high-quality product.
- You don't want to incur liability.

The way to accomplish this is to:

- Study the product
  ▷ Is there a federal regulation or test requirement?
  ▷ Is there a voluntary standard?
  ▷ Is there precedent or history?
  ▷ Common sense?

- Good design
  ▷ Design with safety in mind.

- Test
  ▷ Have your product tested by professionals to ensure safety.

- Insurance
  ▷ Purchase product liability insurance.

Federal Regulation

There are several ways to learn of the existing federal regulations. The Consumer Product Safety Commission is an important resource for companies that are developing new products. The CPSC is charged with "protecting the public from unreasonable risks of injury or death from thousands of types of consumer products under the agency's jurisdiction," www.cpsc.gov.

The first step is to visit the new Consumer Product Safety Commission website. The CPSC site has succeeded in putting data about federal regulations you will need at this stage all in one place.

Review the recalls on the home page and get a sense of the issues that are occurring that lead to product recalls (http://www.cpsc .gov/).

On the home page, look for a section labeled "Safety Guide" to review the various safety guides and identify a guide that is specifically relevant to your product (http://www.cpsc.gov/en/Safety-Education/ Safety-Guides/).

Next, you will go to "Business Education" and click "Get Started" (http://www.cpsc.gov/Regulations-Laws--Standards/ Statutes/The-Consumer-Product-Safety-ImprovementAct/#Classify YourProduct).

There are two forms that you should be aware of, although this has more to do with the actual stage when you launch your product. The first is for children's products and is called the Written Children's Product Certificate. The second is called a General Certificate of Conformity for non-children's items.

It will be important for you to know whether your item is considered a children's item. This web page will walk you through the process of classifying your product and will also provide the list of key substantive requirements just below the classification process. (That used to take hours to cobble together on the old CPSC website!)

1. From the home page, go to "Business Education" and click "Testing and Certification." After you land there, you will click "List of accredited test labs" (http://www.cpsc.gov/cgi-bin/ labsearch/Default.aspx).

2. At this point, don't concern yourself with the actual labs listed. When you have your product made, you and your factory will then choose a test facility. Instead, you want to scroll below the list of labs and read the list of items that labs are required to test for. *Note:* CFR stands for Code of Federal Regulation.

Often, you will see a reference to "#__CFR __#." This is how the federal government's regulatory code is referenced. For example, "16 CFR 1501.4" is a specific regulatory code relating to whether a product is considered a "small part" or to determine if it should be considered a choking hazard.

As you may have seen by now, "ASTM" shows up in a number of places. According to its website:

ASTM International, formerly known as the American Society for Testing and Materials (ASTM), is a globally recognized leader in the development and delivery of international voluntary consensus standards. Today, some 12,000 ASTM standards are used around the world to improve product quality, enhance safety, facilitate market access and trade, and build consumer confidence.

At ASTM, there are many committees comprising mostly industry people from different industry categories who come together to create standards for the development of certain types of products. These standards relate to both product quality and safety. Note that there is not a standard for every product or product type. However, if there is a standard that applies to your product, you will want to be aware of it.

1. Visit www.astm.org and click "Standards" on the left navigation bar. Once there, conduct searches relating to your product or its category.
2. In your first search, use the keywords search window. For example, if you type "crib" into the search window, you will see several standards relating to baby cribs.
3. You can also browse by "Interest Area." Each one has many standards relating to that area. For instance, "Sports and Recreation" brings up standards on items ranging from footwear to archery products to baseball bats.
4. You can also search by committee. Find the committee(s) that are most relevant to your product. If you select F15, the

committee on consumer products, you will see standards on products from baby monitors to candles to bedding.

5. When you find a standard, you will be able to read the summary of the standard. The actual full standards documents are also for sale at a fairly modest price.

Next, visit the test lab websites. We have personally used both www.intertek.com and www.bureauveritas.com for testing. When you go to their websites, visit the "Consumer Products" sections. There are many other labs as well. Spend some time on their websites and learn what you can about testing that could apply to your product. You will see references to some of the things you read about on both the CPSC and ASTM websites. You will already see your knowledge expanding quickly. Not only do their websites offer a wealth of information, but they can also provide consultations on what you need to be aware of for your specific item. They can provide answers to all of these questions:

- What Codes of Federal Regulations (CFRs) are applicable to your product?
- Are there any issues specific to your industry to be aware of?
- What are the labeling requirements for your product? Is a warning label necessary (for example, "This product contains small parts and is not meant for children" or "For Adult Use Only")?
- Are there packaging standards or requirements?
- How do all of these differ between the United States and other regions? (Europe has a number of different standards.) Make sure you understand this if you hope to sell anywhere outside the United States.

Once you have developed your product, you may need some testing to prove that it meets the pertinent requirements of your industry. For example, baby products have many requirements involving the content of chemicals such as lead, phthalates, and BPA. In addition, your product may need to pass the small-parts test, impact tests, or, for textiles, flammability tests. These labs conduct this kind of testing and certification. An initial discussion with a salesperson may be useful in finding out which tests the lab would recommend for your particular product and how much it will cost.

By now you will have identified the industry association(s) that are most relevant to your product. If not, type (your category + association) into a search engine. Visit the associations' websites and search on "product safety," "product regulations," "product standards," "recalls," and "product insurance." Some websites may have contact names of product safety committee members who will answer e-mail questions as well.

Finally, don't forget Google. Once you are there, type "your category + standards." For example, when you type "juvenile products + standards" and "juvenile product standards," numerous references having to do with standards that have been developed for certain (although not all) juvenile products appear.

Next, search with the following words and others that you come up with in order to alert you to problems in the area. Knowing information about these issues before you bring a product to market is invaluable.

- "Product type + recall"
- "Product type + label"
- "Product type + flammability"
- "Product type + small parts"
- "Product type + standards"
- "Product type + lead"

Be sure to note all the relevant regulatory requirements, standards, and safety issues that you have identified. Now that you fully understand the scope of safety issues with regard to your product, it's time to look into product liability insurance.

Product Liability Insurance

You may think that your product is safe—but it's better to be safe than sorry. Even the best manufacturers with top designers and retailers who sell high-quality products recognize the need for insurance to protect themselves against the unfortunate situation where the use of a product results in harm.

When you are thinking about product liability insurance, there are two main issues to research: requirements and costs.

Requirements

- ◆ Go to small retailers or e-tailers and ask what their vendor product liability insurance requirements are.
- ◆ Visit industry associations and related trade publications and look for articles and blogs on liability insurance requirements. E-mail their membership director and ask where you can find this information.
- ◆ If you see companies with products in the same category as your product, contact them and ask for their product development department. Tell them that you are an entrepreneur looking for advice and ask them about industry requirements.

Costs

- ◆ Contact insurance agents to get some cost estimates for product liability insurance for your product (or to hear about their experience with similar items). If you use the same broker who sold you your auto or life insurance, he is likely to be more helpful. Or when approaching a new broker, ask her if she can quote you for all three.
- ◆ Speak to manufacturers that make similar items and ask them where they purchased their liability insurance and how much they pay annually.

Some small retailers have minimal insurance requirements for their vendors (that's you), and some independent and online retailers have none. Most large retailers require proof of coverage of more than $1 million. Because Walmart is the biggest retailer, if you are in compliance with its requirements, you are likely to meet the requirements of most other retailers. Some retailers have "Vendor" or "Supplier" tabs on their websites that will list insurance-related information.

To see the insurance requirements for Walmart, visit www.walmartstores.com and click on the "Supplier" tab in the top navigation bar. Find and click on "Standards & Requirements." Once you are there, click on "Insurance Requirements." You will see that as of September 2013, Walmart has requirement levels for $2 million, $5 million, and $10 million in liability insurance coverage, depending on the type of product. In the same place, it also has a matrix that lists product categories to enable a vendor to determine the appropriate level of coverage. Most items fall into the $2 million category (http://corporate.walmart.com/suppliers/references-resources/insurance-requirements).

Note: When you speak to brokers and request an estimate, you can use the Walmart requirements as a basis for their estimates. They will be reluctant to quote you, as these rates vary. But if you ask them

Get Smart About Product Liability Insurance

If your goal is to sell your product to Walmart or another mass retailer, you will need a hefty amount of product liability insurance coverage. Make sure that you know what is required ahead of time. I recently spoke to an inventor who was heartbroken. She had successfully produced her product and gotten the attention of a mass retailer who was interested in purchasing her product, only to find out that because of the nature of her product, she couldn't get product liability insurance. Therefore, this mass retailer had to turn her down. Now she has 20,000 units sitting in her garage that she can't sell. Find out what insurance coverage you will need and how much it will cost *before* you bring your product to market.

The challenge (and cost) of securing product liability insurance varies dramatically depending on the nature of the product. Some items (for example, car seats for babies) are virtually uninsurable, especially if they are produced by a small, single-product company. While a policy for baby bedding can run more than $10,000 per year, insurance for some products is easy to get and relatively inexpensive (for example, $1,000 per year).

if they have ever issued similar policies before and how much they cost, you may get some helpful information.

State Regulations

Federal regulations may or may not supersede relevant state regulations. Some states do have supplemental enforcements on certain federal laws, and sometimes state laws are more restrictive than federal laws. It's valuable to know and understand any state regulations that relate to your product. The proper office to contact varies from state to state.

Labeling Requirements

To determine the labeling requirements for your product, you will probably need to follow the same process you followed for the other safety requirements. Follow the guidance of your trade association, the CPSC, voluntary standards, and common sense. Another organization, the American National Standards Institute (www.ansi.org), is also a resource. For instance, its voluntary standard Z535.4 addresses label formatting issues, such as font size.

Chapter Wrap-Up

Now that you've actually communicated your idea in 3-D and Technicolor, you've passed a big hurdle—congratulations! Your next step is to formalize your feedback through market testing and setting the "right" price for your product, which will be covered in the next chapter.

Market Research

Watch Video: Tamara Monosoff Introduces Chapter 3

http://www.tamaramonosoff.com/
Tamara-Monosoff-introduces-chapter-3/

Customer Feedback, Pricing, and Estimated Profit

In Chapter 1, you will have taken the steps to identify your potential target market. And the number of potential buyers may be substantial. But you need to be able to make decisions based on solid evidence that you gather from real feedback you hear from people. After you receive this feedback, you can expect to get your first glimpse of the business opportunity before you.

Nearly every day, I hear from an inventor who says, "I have the next million-dollar idea," or, "I know that every parent in America will buy this product." This type of enthusiasm is wonderful, and she may be right. The first thing I ask her is whom the product is specifically intended for and how many consumers are represented in this target market. Unfortunately, her answer is often silence. That is why Brad Kofoed and I developed the "How Hot is Your Product?" product evaluation system and why I put so much emphasis in teaching this process now. When organizing this book, I placed the prototype chapter ahead of this chapter, because a prototype is generally necessary, or at least extremely useful, when getting feedback.

This market research stage is the first time you will be sharing your product with others—hopefully, many others. (Before you do, read Chapter 4, "Protect Yourself.") Their feedback will enable you to gauge the financial viability of your product and to make critical refinements. This is the last step before you make a number of critical decisions and take some big steps.

Feedback: What Do People *Honestly* Think About Your Product?

The consumer market is fickle. People must see meaningful value before they will change their behavior or try new products. The best way to answer this *big* question about the targetable market for your specific product is to gather outside evidence and information.

How much people are willing to pay for a product (or service) depends on how much they need or want it. We liken this to the comparison between buying medicine and buying vitamins. People will spend almost any amount, at any time—irrespective of marketing—on medicine that will cure them. They need it. On the other hand, vitamins could be useful, but the need is not self-evident without a tremendous amount of information and marketing persuasion.

The fashion industry is a good example of marketing persuasion. Women don't necessarily "need" to have the latest handbag, sweater, or whatever, but fashion companies spend millions of dollars on marketing to create that emotional need. In other words, their goal is to convert a "want" to a need, often by marketing to your emotions. They will show you that by having their sweater, you will feel more beautiful, sexy, or hip . . . which will help to improve your self-esteem and how you feel about yourself. Therefore, wearing their sweater

Watch Video Message from Moschel Kadokura

http://www.tamaramonosoff.com/moschel-kadokura/]

Moschel Kadokura, a mother of triplets, was inspired to create her product, On-Task On-Time, out of sheer necessity (www.timelymatters.com).

Getting three 5-year-olds ready for kindergarten proved to be more than I could handle with simple charts and timers. I needed something that my kids could visually understand (being prereaders), plus get the concept of time passage.

Moschel's advice:

Build prototypes and fully test your product ideas with a good sample population before investing money in the final design. Get information from potential buyers about the use of your product and what they would be willing to spend. Get as much feedback and information as you can before making a big investment. Do not rely on friends or relatives to give you this feedback. You need a sample population.

will make you more desirable and successful in your life. The goal is to get you to the point where you feel you need to have that sweater, rather than feeling that it's something that would be "nice to have." As the local sports team starts to win, men (and some women) will suddenly *need* the jersey of their favorite player to feel connected to the team. If this sales messaging is still not clear, just watch QVC or HSN for 30 minutes. They have mastered this process.

Five Key Questions to Ask and Answer in the Process of Gathering These Data

- What problem is this product solving for consumers?
- What are the specific complaints online and in the market about the problem, and how common are they?
- How much money will people save by using your product?

- What are the key benefits of this product?
- Does your product fall into the need category, or is it a nice to have?

In this section, we are going to help you answer these questions by using people's opinions and statistics. Throughout this process, you will want to document:

1. The methods used to gather data (surveys and the like)
2. The process used for quantifying data (how did you tabulate the information?)
3. The breakdown of the results (summarize your findings)

In Chapter 1, you took the first step in this process by digging up any statistics you could find using search engines, industry associations, and the trade press.

In this step, you will select methods for gathering data directly from people. These could include informal focus groups, street interviews, e-mail blasts, or online surveys, as outlined here.

Each of These Methods Will Require Five Things

1. Preplanned questions
2. The identification of target subjects
3. A method for engaging subjects
4. A method for capturing data
5. A method for analyzing the data

When you are planning your questions, keep in mind that you will want to get both data that can be tabulated and input that is less structured. You cannot expect people to spend too much time, so you want to limit your questions. You can, however, make each question address both requirements by asking it in two parts: one part that gives you easily quantifiable numbers, and another that provides more subjective feedback and opinions.

Example

1. Do you find that _____ is a problem that you struggle with?

The benefit of asking the question in this way is that in the results, you can say, "X out of 20 people interviewed said yes."

2. How do you deal with this issue today?

This question provides a chance to get more subjective and descriptive feedback.

Informal Focus Groups

Convening an informal focus group involves getting a group of people together who will share their feedback in a comfortable environment with refreshments and snacks where answers can be clarified and discussed.

◆ There are many different ways to host informal focus group meetings. First, plan a get-together or a series of group meetings with friends and acquaintances that represent your target market, and ask each participant to bring someone you don't know. It's usually best not to hold these meetings in your home (maybe have a friend host the meeting), as the participants may not feel that they can be candid with their answers if they are guests in your home. Therefore, you may wish to tap into a group you belong to for participants (for example, a mommy's group, a religious group, or a club). You may also be able to get some time on the agenda within an existing group meeting. In addition, local libraries and civic or community centers will often rent rooms at a reasonable rate.

◆ Tell your participants that you value their feedback, both positive and negative. Let them know that you want them to be truthful and that you see negative feedback as a gift because it will help you understand whether it makes sense for you to develop the product and can inform important modifications.

◆ Have the participants sign a release form that states that they will keep the group discussion and product information shared confidential. (Sometimes a verbal agreement is all you can get. Just document the date and time.) (Go to www.TamaraMonosoff.com/Guides for a free release form.)

◆ List the questions you plan to ask, and listen to the responses carefully. Not only will you have the opportunity to get specific feedback about the product, but you may even hear great ideas for future additions to your product line.

◆ Ask one person to take notes for you or ask permission to tape or videotape the session. (Go to www.TamaraMonosoff.com/Guides for a free permission to tape or videotape form.)

◆ Ask another person to ask the questions and lead the discussion so that you are free to listen.

◆ Ask everyone in the group to provide an e-mail address (have people sign a sheet before they leave) so that you can send follow-up questions and a special thank you. Sometimes entrepreneurs provide a $25 to $100 gift card to some general, well-traveled, or online store (for example, Target or Amazon) as a gift for their efforts.

Street Interviews or Intercepts

By stopping people in their tracks (called intercepts) and quickly interviewing them about your product, you can get immediate feedback. These kinds of interviews are informal, and they can help you focus on key issues to help refine your product design.

Watch Video Message from Annette Giacomazzi

http://www.tamaramonosoff.com/annette-giacomazzi/

Annette Giacomazzi, founder of www.Cast Coverz.com, creator of fun and functional products that comfort orthopedic patients, says:

After developing some prototypes, I went to a mall and asked random people what they would call the product and how much they would pay for it. That was priceless research!

Watch Video Message from Meredith LaMirande

http://www.tamaramonosoff.com/meredith-lamirande/

Meredith LaMirande, creator of the Dropper Stopper (www.drop-perstopper.com), new mom, and Air Force wife, gives us a great example of juggling too many things, yet doing what it takes to get it right. After first overcoming design issues in order to ensure compliance with safety requirements, she wanted to develop a product that would work for anyone.

I was the crazy lady in Babies"R"Us going around testing my product on every stroller, highchair, and car seat the store carries. In addition, I was asking moms, friends, and parents for all the feedback I could collect.

♦ Choose a public place (for example, a supermarket, mall, street, post office, park, or wherever those in your target market spend time).

♦ When you stop people to interview, be sure to identify yourself immediately and make it clear what you are looking for (and that you are not selling them something). Speak warmly, and explain concisely what you are doing: "Hi. My name is Sarah, I am doing market research for a new product in the 'pet' industry. May I ask you a couple of questions? Do you have a dog?" And so forth.

If the person says no, be gracious, thank him, and move on to the next person. Interview as many people who fit your target customer profile as possible.

♦ Rehearse your approach and questions so that you sound organized.

♦ If you want people to fill something out, have a few questions pre-printed on a form with a clipboard. People are busy, so it may be more effective for you to ask them the questions and then quickly jot down the answers yourself.

◆ It's your product, so make sure you ask or do what you have to in order to get the information you need.

E-mail Blasts

E-mail is a powerful way to collect information. Create an e-mail campaign and send it to your network of family, friends, and business associates. If you plan to e-mail larger lists, use an e-mail marketing tool that helps improve deliverability and managing larger lists, such as www.mailchimp.com, www.constantcontact.com, www.verticalresponse.com, or www.madmimi.com. (Learn more about e-mail marketing campaigns in Chapter 8, "Blowing Your Horn.")

Send out a brief message with a request for information. Let people know that you are gathering market information about a product you are developing and that you need feedback from people who are experiencing the problem that your product solves. Note that you can do this without revealing your exact product design to anyone. Describe the consumer or target you are looking to speak with. (For example, "If you know any women who are currently planning a wedding, please forward.") Then include your questions in the actual body of the e-mail message so that it is easy for people to respond. In other words, don't send an attached document. Mention your deadline and, most important, express your gratitude for their help.

Online Feedback

Another quick and effective way to get information about your product is to post questions in online forums where you find your target customers spending time. However, make sure to be mindful of the rules and etiquette of the forum. Don't try to "sell" anything or you will be quickly ousted from the group. The goal here is to ask questions and to listen carefully to people's thoughts and opinions.

Note: Be mindful that revealing your product publicly before you have secured the intellectual property protection you plan to secure could have implications on your patent rights. So if you have not made patenting decisions or taken the steps you intend to take, but wish to use online methods, be sure to gather data based on the problem your product solves by mentioning other existing products in your post to give readers an example of what you are talking about, and gather "need" data without explicitly sharing your invention.

Conduct an Online Survey

There are great online survey tools available today that you can use to gather information about your product. With these tools, you can prepare surveys in minutes without any technical know-how. The survey tool platforms listed here will prompt you through the process, and at the end they will generate a link that you can e-mail or blast out via your blogs and social media networks to generate responses.

Here are just a few:

www.SurveyMonkey.com—The best-known online survey tool for easily collecting and analyzing data.

www.PopSurvey.com—A simple online survey tool with beautiful templates that's easy to use.

www.FormStack.com—This is not a survey tool; however, you can use it to create interactive forms to gather information that can be used like a survey. One thing I like about FormStack. com is that respondents are able to attach pictures and videos to their forms. Although you can gather information in an organized way using FormStack.com, it does not offer survey analysis, as the other tools mentioned here do.

Here are some sample questions to get you started. You can use these questions or variations of these questions that are specific to your product for any of the methods of gathering data previously mentioned.

- Have you seen anything like this before?
- How have you dealt with this issue without this product?
- Would you purchase this product? How many?

- If not, why not?
- What do you like about it?
- What would you change?
- What colors would you prefer?
- How much would you pay for it?
- Where would you expect to buy it? (Name specific stores where you shop.)
- How would you expect it to be packaged?
- How many would you expect there to be in each package?

Although these questions are designed to help you get started gathering information about your product, there are a number of ways to "ask" your potential customers for information. When going through this process, one goal is to figure out how to deepen your questions. In other words, you might ask:

- **Financial questions.** "How much would you pay for this product?" Then ask the opposite question, "What price would be too high to pay for this product?"

- **Questions that describe the needs of your customers.** "Describe any issues you face daily, weekly, or monthly that relate to [describe the need your product addresses]." "How big an issue is this for you?" "How have you dealt with this problem in the past?" "Have you discussed this issue with friends and family members?"

Even though research data are often deemed more reliable, we value what people tell us (through interviews, surveys, and the like), and we think that gathering both kinds of information is the best way to understand your market.

Retail Pricing, Production Costs, and Gross Profit Margin

For most consumer products, people are price sensitive. Understand that your realistic *profit margins* (how much money you actually get

Mom Market

Watch Video Message from Tamara Monosoff
http://www.tamaramonosoff.com/mom-market-survey-results/

If you want to sell to the "mom market," you will want to understand moms.

I collaborated with my friend Marta Loeb of Silver Stork Research (www.silver stork.com) on a survey project to gather research data on marketing and selling to the mom market. Together, we produced some statistical data that I have found to be invaluable. Since I want you to succeed, and I know that this may be a market that you sell to, I want to share the summary of those data with you here.

- **Moms can't *resist* purchasing items for which room in the house?**
  ▷ The kitchen.
- **How big a challenge is organization and storage for moms?**
  ▷ 58 percent of moms say that organization is a problem in her home.
- **What room(s) in the house is (are) number one in terms of organization and storage needs?**
  ▷ 50 percent of moms say the kids' bedroom.
  ▷ 50 percent of moms say the kitchen.
- **If mom had the "ear" of companies that sell housewares, what would she tell them?**
  ▷ Help me multitask.
  ▷ Make my life easier.
  ▷ Make it look more like "me."
- **What two rooms in the house does mom want to redecorate?**
  ▷ The family room
  ▷ The kitchen
- **Are moms shopping more or less?**
  ▷ 39 percent are shopping less, *but* when they do shop, they purchase more at one time!
- **How are moms shopping?**
  ▷ 52 percent do more comparison shopping.
  ▷ 69 percent researched online before buying in the store.
  ▷ 85 percent buy something for themselves when they shop.

◆ **Do shopping carts matter?**
  ▷ *Yes!* 65 percent of moms *buy more* when they use a shopping cart.
  ▷ 66 percent are *more likely to purchase impulse items* when they have a shopping cart.

◆ **Do bags matter?**
  ▷ 60 percent of moms have a strong preference for reusable vinyl or mesh bags.
  ▷ 44 percent of moms show a strong preference for paper bags with handles.
  ▷ Plastic bags were the least favorite among moms.

◆ **With so much available online, what brings moms into retail stores?**
  ▷ 80 percent need something immediately.
  ▷ 75 percent go to the store to see, touch, and feel items.
  ▷ 60 percent like to see a product outside of its package before they buy.
  ▷ 61 percent are looking for in-store sales or offers.
  ▷ 68 percent like or love to shop—they see it as "relaxing" and "time for me."
  ▷ 57 percent of moms want to get out of the house!

◆ **Does "nagging" from kids influence moms' purchasing decisions?**
  ▷ Apparently *not!* One out of two moms select items based on what *they* think their kids will like, not what the kids ask for.

◆ **What special considerations affect moms' purchasing?**
  ▷ Moms like and support companies that:
    – Offer coupons or discounts if you register online.
    – Give back to a cause or charity.
    – *Sell products created by a mom.*

---

to keep out of every dollar of sales that you earn) are based on a realistic retail price *before* you invest time and money into development, production, and marketing. There probably will be ambiguity in this process because, in theory, your product has not been made before.

Manufacturing companies with production and sales experience can typically leverage that prior knowledge to make these kinds

Watch Video Message from Michele Goodman

http://www.tamaramonosoff.com/michele-goodman/

Michele Goodman, inventor of Baseboard Buddy (www.baseboard buddy.com), embodies the stamina that makes entrepreneurs unique. After losing her apparel company in the storm of the recession through bankruptcy, she found herself cleaning her home to make her downtime productive. With little hope for a new career at her stage in life, given the withering of the apparel industry at that time, she hit upon a solution that would make the

process of cleaning baseboards easier. Reading about the process she followed from market research to prototype development to production to marketing is a classic story. Her determination to "show my son and his boys that even when the chips are down and you lose everything, you can start over" was her driving force.

of business calculations. However, *unless you have made products before, you are not likely to have that sort of knowledge. We are going to show you how to leverage the work of other experts to put yourself in a stronger position.* That way, you can realistically estimate production costs, sales prices, and profit margins.

Three-Step Process

1. Determine what the market might pay for your item.

▷ Find comparable products and note their retail price points. Use Amazon.com, Walmart, specialty retailers, and catalogs. This will enable you to get the highest and lowest market prices.

▷ To determine "comparable," consider items made of similar materials, bought by the same customer, and sold through the same venues. For example, if your invention is a new hand-held gardening tool made of steel, research various garden shears that are on the market.

▷ Write down the top and bottom retail price range that you find (for example, $10 to $7).

▷ Be conservative. In our experience, inventors tend to think that consumers will pay a lot more for their product than is realistic because of the newness or inventiveness of the product. This is rarely the case. If your item is a new lunch box and the market for lunch boxes is $5 to $15, at this stage it is not prudent to assume that you can sell yours for $25 without very good evidence.

2. Estimate production costs. This can be done in two ways. You may have already received estimates in the process of getting your prototype designed; which is ideal. Or, you may be able to get an estimate from the engineer you worked with on the prototype. If not, there is another method that I use. You can get an idea of the production cost of your item by looking at overseas factory production costs on items that you deem to be similar to yours.

First, visit global sourcing websites (www.alibaba.com and www.globalsources.com) and identify the overseas price of items made of similar materials with comparable complexity.

Next, in the search windows of these websites, insert items that you know to be similar (for example, gardening tools, jewelry, bibs, or sandwich boxes). You will be *amazed* at what you will find. Not only will you most likely find the item you are searching for, but you will also probably find a list of other, often related items produced by the same factory.

Now just start digging. These factories sell these items in bulk. In other words, they sell them to people like you ("manufacturers"), who will then sell them to retailers or consumers directly. Keep in mind that these factories are already in mass production, so your initial costs with small production runs are likely to be higher. Therefore, your own wholesale pricing (the price you offer to retailers) may be higher in the beginning until you work out all the kinks, problems, and challenges that most of us face in our initial manufacturing runs. Also, as you go through this process, make a note of the overseas pricing of items that you think are most comparable to your product.

Some factories may list their products but not the prices. You can request a quote from the factory. I have found them to be quite responsive to inquiries. One thing to consider is that, even though the pricing they list is "bulk" pricing, you need to note the volume levels they are referring to. In other words, the pricing they offer may be based on the purchase of 500 units or minimum order requirement (MOQ). In this case, you would want to request a quote for custom production runs of, say, 5,000 and 10,000 units in order to get a closer estimate of the production cost at future volumes. Keep in mind that some quotes may be listed in a different currency (many times it will be the renminbi [RMB], the Chinese currency), which you will need to convert.

The term *FOB* stands for "freight on board." This means the cost per unit when it is picked up by a freight carrier in China. It does not include the costs of shipping (often called freight forwarding) or other landing costs, such as tariffs to get the items back to the United States.

Sometimes entrepreneurs are stunned to find their exact product, or one that is even better, on Alibaba.com, already for sale at extremely low prices. If this happens to you, figure out whether there is a way to modify your product and improve upon those that are already available. If not, then you may want to let go of this idea and move on to your next one or, if you believe that there is an untapped market, just purchase theirs and distribute it.

3. In the table given here, there is a section for the tariff. A tariff is like a tax charged by the U.S. government for importing your product from overseas. Of course, if you produce domestically, this will not be a factor. For the purposes of this section, you can simply add in some amount to cover tariff and freight, say 5 percent each (or you can jump to Chapter 5, "Getting the Goods," and figure out exactly what your tariff will be).

At this point, you should be able to come up with an estimated retail price point and an estimated production price point.

You can do a quick check to gauge whether your product pricing model will work. To do so, multiply your estimated retail price point (use the lowest price you have found to be realistic) by 20 percent

Landed Cost Estimate

Cost Type	Costs
Production cost per unit	
Tariff	
Freight forwarding	
Other	
Total	

(or simply divide your lowest price by 5). For example, $10 (retail price)/5 = $2 (production cost requirement per unit).

How does that figure compare to your estimated production cost? If it is close, you are in good shape. If it is off, you will want to review carefully to see whether your pricing model will work.

In summary, when we evaluate the viability of an item that we hope to sell through retail, we like to see the production cost below one-fifth (or, even better, at one-sixth) the retail price that we believe price-sensitive customers will pay. You should be able to multiply your product production cost by 5 (or 6), and have the resulting number equal or be below your anticipated retail price. The reasoning behind this number is that when you sell wholesale (to other retailers), they will usually require at least a 50 percent ("keystone") margin, also known as a 100 percent markup. In other words, if the suggested retail price is $20, the retailer will ask you for a wholesale (sometimes called "keystone" price) of $10 (often with other costs that they charge, too!). Therefore, you need the 5 times (to 6 times) margin to make a meaningful profit. (For example, $20 divided by $5 = $4. Your production cost would need to be about $4 to make this product work.)

Note: Once you have done the math, validation of your assumed retail price by real consumers is important.

Here is an example of how this might look for a product that retails for $20.

You Sell Wholesale to Retailer		You Sell Wholesale to Distributor, Who Then Sells to Retailer	
$20	Retail price paid by customer	$20	Retail price paid by customer
$10	Wholesale price paid to you by retailer per unit	$10	Paid to distributor by retailer per unit
——		$7	Distributor pays you $7
$4	The production cost that you pay your factory per unit	$4	The production cost that you pay your factory per unit
You earn $6 gross profit margin (60% gross margin)		You earn $3 gross profit margin (43% gross margin)	

Note: When a distributor is involved, a retailer may not expect a full keystone markup. In other words, a keystone markup is any item selling at twice the price that it was bought for (that is, a retailer buys something from you for $10 and sells it to customers for $20). However, when a distributor is involved, the retailer may tolerate a smaller margin because the distributor needs to earn money, too. To calculate gross profit margin, divide the profit ($7 − $4 = $3 gross profit) by your sale price ($7), or $3/$7 = 0.428. To convert a decimal into a percentage, multiply by 100. Therefore, 0.428 × 100 = 42.8 percent, rounded to 43 percent.

By estimating your retail price and your production price, you have been able to come up with an estimated gross profit margin. Keep in mind that this is just for the production of your product. There are many other costs after production. These include marketing, rent, legal, bookkeeping, insurance, salaries, and many others. These are paid out of the gross profit you just calculated. The money that is left over after you pay these nonproduction costs is called your *net profit.* While this is not ideal, many new product entrepreneurs do not pay themselves a salary until they know whether there will be a net profit.

In the next section, you will take one more step in this financial analysis that will reveal what it will take to achieve your personal financial goals.

First, Review a Few Key Questions

◆ What is your personal income goal?

◆ How many units do you need to sell to achieve your financial goals?

◆ Can you realistically reach that many customers?

▷ If your personal income goal is $100,000 per year and you will earn $0.25 per unit gross profit, from which you will pay all your expenses and salary, conservatively you will need to sell between 500,000 and 1 million units ($0.25 × 500,000 = $125,000), depending on how low you can keep expenses. Some products, especially commodities (any marketable item produced to satisfy wants or needs), sell at that volume. But very few new products achieve that volume. Marketing and other costs tend to be high for new companies. On the other hand, if you earn $10 per unit gross profit, you could approach your $100,000 income goal by selling just 20,000 units. Hopefully, by now you have some insight into whether the customers who will pay that amount of money exist and whether you can find, sell, and distribute to them.

The following table gives an example of an item sold at $30 retail. You can use the outline for your own product to get some idea as to how to achieve your financial goal. When you create your own table, it is easiest to start with the retail price point and work backward.

Note: The gross profit calculation in this table was made by simply subtracting each number from the one above it to arrive at the gross profit. When you look at this number, you can determine whether this product will enable you to achieve your financial goals. Unfortunately, there is no set number that you can use to determine how much your expenses (marketing, selling, and so on) will be. In our experience, many start-ups keep administrative costs low by managing a lot on their own (administration, bookkeeping, staffing, and the like). For many of us, our warehouses and offices begin in our homes. However, we still have expenses like advertising, marketing materials, and trade shows, which are expensive.

Per Unit	Optimistic	Conservative
Retail price estimate (sold to consumer)	$30	$30
Wholesale price (sold to retailer or distributor)	$15	$13.50
Price paid by you to factory (your cost estimate)	$5	$6
Per unit gross profit	$10	$7.50
Unit sales per year (your market estimate)	50,000	20,000
Total gross profit	$500,000	$150,000

As previously mentioned, there are other ways to add revenue once your business is running, but ideally you will begin with a product that will meet your goals.

Blank Table

Here is a blank table into which you can plug your own numbers and preferred assumptions.

Per Unit	Optimistic	Conservative
Retail price estimate (sold to consumer)		
Wholesale price (sold to retailer or distributor)		
Price paid by you to factory (your cost estimate)		
Per unit gross profit		
Unit sales per year (your market estimate)		
Total gross profit		

This would be a good time to watch the 12-minute video tutorial on how to use our margin calculator to figure out the best price and margins for your product in a wholesale and retail scenario. As mentioned earlier, go to www.TamaraMonosoff.com/Guides.

Chapter Wrap-Up

At this stage in the process, assuming that you have figured out the true size of your market (Chapter 1), developed your prototype (Chapter 2), validated your business case with feedback from consumers, and determined product pricing that works (this chapter), the next step is to understand the tools and options that are available to protect your product.

Protect Yourself:
All About Patents, Copyrights, and Trademarks

I wish to acknowledge and thank business law and intellectual property attorney John Merchant of J. Merchant Law (www.jmerchantlaw .com) for his significant contributions to this chapter.

Video Message:
Tamara Monosoff introduces Chapter 4

http://www.tamaramonosoff.com/tamara-monosoff-introduces -chapter-4/

Disclaimer: The information in this chapter is not legal advice. It is intended as a guide only. You should seek professional legal counsel when making legal decisions.

PART 1:
What You Need to Know About Patents

There are many misconceptions about the role of patents in the process of taking a product to market. I'd like to share the following conversation to illustrate this point.

Inventor: *I am so excited to have your book. I have a new invention that I think will be the next million-dollar idea.*

Me: That's great! How do you know this product will be a hit?

Inventor: *I have never seen any inventions like it, and my friends agree. And, my sister's husband's brother is an attorney. He thinks it is a good idea too, but he said that I need a patent. I just don't know how to get one. Do you have any advice?*

Me: Sure. But first, who is the demographic target market for this product? How many of these people are there?

Inventor: *Every (fill in the blank) in America will want this invention, and I have checked at my local store and it doesn't have anything like it. But I just don't have the money for a patent. Do you know how to find investors to pay for a patent?*

Me: Did you speak with the local store owner about the problem that this product solves? Did you ask her if she thinks there is a need for this item? Have her customers ever asked for it? Has she sold anything like it in the past? If so, why didn't she continue carrying it? Did she have any suggestions or ideas about how to improve the look, feel, or function of your product? Did you find out how much she thinks an item like this could sell for in her store? If she couldn't sell the item, did she have ideas as to what other stores might be a better fit?

Inventor: *No. I saw an ad on television, so I know that before I do anything, I need to get a patent filed. I know that if I mention my idea, someone will steal it, since I don't have a patent.*

This example may seem extreme. But, I assure you that it is more common than you might think. *And, this is not the fault of the inventor.* There is a wildly common misconception that a patent is required in order to make money—that has been drummed into every inventor's psyche by advertisers and "experts" since they first heard about inventing. We even have an entire government agency division—the U.S. Patent and Trademark Office (USPTO)—that is devoted to managing patents. It appears that getting a patent is the answer. Perhaps it is... *but* not necessarily.

It is important to focus on whether a product is viable in the marketplace, not solely on protecting it. It is important to understand that the product is not necessarily the invention. The product may contain one or more inventive ideas, and those inventive ideas may give the product an advantage over other products, but it is important that you understand the viability of the product first. If you determine that it is viable, then you can focus on trying to protect those aspects of the product that give it an advantage, from a legal perspective, in the marketplace.

You may also notice that the inventor mentioned in the example believes that obtaining a patent will prevent the invention from being stolen. A patent can be an effective deterrent to those who might otherwise steal the invention, but it will not automatically prevent others from stealing your invention or otherwise trying to get around your patent.

To help you digest the information in this chapter more easily, I have divided it into two parts. Part 1 focuses on patents, and Part 2 covers trademarks, copyrights, and nondisclosure agreements (see Figure 4.1).

By the end of this chapter, you will have an excellent foundation for navigating and making good decisions in this process. I hope to make four things clear:

1. A patent is only a tool that may or may not be useful to you and is definitely not required.
2. A patent does not usually cover a product. It applies to some aspect(s) of that product.

FIGURE 4.1   **Basic Legal Definitions**

Before we dive into this section, we want to define a few terms for you. For the most part, we simply used Wikipedia definitions as they are relatively straightforward. *We did add some content where we thought it was necessary to simplify or expand the definitions:

Intellectual Property (IP)

"Creations of the mind..." For our purposes, when we say "intellectual property" or "IP," we are generally referring to those aspects of your product that are protected (or protectable) through patent, trademark and copyright filings with the www.USPTO.gov. Trade secrets are also considered IP.

Invention

A unique or novel device, method, composition or process. It may be an improvement upon a machine or product, or a new process for creating an object or a result. An invention that achieves a completely unique function or result may be a radical breakthrough. Such works are novel and not obvious to others skilled in the same field. *Wikipedia*

Patent

A patent is a form of intellectual property. It consists of a set of exclusive rights granted by a sovereign state to an inventor or their assignee for a limited period of time, in exchange for the public disclosure of the invention. *Wikipedia*

Novelty

Novelty is a patentability requirement. It means that your invention must be different from what is already known to the public.

Non-obviousness (or Unobviousness)

The is also a patentability requirement. It means that at the time the inventor came up with the invention, it would have been considered unobvious to a person skilled in the technology involved in the invention. This requirement is usually satisfied by showing new and unexpected, surprising, or far superior results when compared with previous invention (or knowledge) in the related area of technology.

Prior Art

Any knowledge that was made publicly available, anywhere in the world, prior to the filing date of the patent application. In order for an invention to be considered novel, it must have some physical or method-step difference over all prior developments and concepts available to the public anywhere in the world. Those prior developments and concepts are considered the "prior art" and usually consists of previously issued patents and/or published patent applications. But, publications and general prior knowledge of concepts related to the technology associated with an invention are also considered prior art. What exactly is and is not "prior art" can be the subject of debate during the patent process.

A Novelty Search (also known as a Patentability Search)

A "novelty" or "patentability search" is a prior art search to determine if anyone disclosed the inventive developments or concepts in a publicly available work anywhere in the world before a critical date (such as the date of filing). It is often conducted by patent attorneys, patent agents, or professional patent searchers before an inventor files a patent application. There are many reasons to perform a "novelty" or "patentability" search prior to filing a patent application including 1) to determine whether you can get a patent, 2) to avoid needless expenditures of work, 3) to help in preparation of the patent application, 4) to clarify an invention's novel features, and other helpful reasons.

A Validity (or Invalidity) Search

This is an exhaustive patentability search that is usually conducted after a patent has issued. This search compares the granted claims against the prior art to make sure that the claims are enforceable. This type of search is helpful for someone interested in enforcing a patent and is sometimes required by businesses interested in licensing a patent. The goal is to make sure the granted patent claims will not be invalidated using prior art as there is a chance that not all prior art was considered by the examiner during the examination process and any prior art (considered or not) may be used to invalidate a patent claim. There are other searches such as Infringement Searches, Clearance Searches and State-of-the-Art Searches that are not covered in this chapter.

*Source: Business Law and IP Attorney, John Merchant (www.jmerchantlaw.com)

3. Trademarks and copyrights can be used to help protect the product, but they are different from each other, and from patents, in how and what aspects of your product they protect.
4. Get advice from a professional who is willing to think strategically, as opposed to just filing a legal document.

What Is a Patent?

A patent is a grant from the government that gives an inventor the right to exclude others from making, using, selling, importing, or offering an invention for sale for a fixed period of time. In other words, a patent gives the patent owner the right to sue someone who is making, using, selling, or importing the patented invention(s). Patent rights are territorial. That means that a U.S. patent will grant the right to exclude in the United States only. A U.S. patent will not allow the owner to exclude others in other territories. Patents are also limited in duration (usually 20 years from the date of filing the patent application, but 14 years for design patents). The patent does not give the owner the right to exclude others after the patent term has expired.

To Patent or Not to Patent?

The process for determining whether to pursue a patent can be complex. Certainly your goals, your timeline, and your budget will be very important factors in making a decision.

Watch Video: Tamara Monosoff Interviews John Merchant—"What Is a Patent and When Do You Need One?"

http://www.tamaramonosoff.com/tamara-monosoff
-interviews-john-merchant-patents/

It is important to remember that patents cover only inventions and that not every product is an invention. An invention is any new article, machine, composition, process, or new use developed by a human. Many marketable products simply aren't patentable. For example, some very marketable product ideas aren't really new. Unbeknownst to you, another inventor may have thought of the idea before but never bothered to market it. Or it may be a fairly obvious improvement over what has come before. It can be very helpful to do some serious research to determine whether your idea is new or obvious given the "prior art" (see Figure 4.1) before you commit to the patent process. Understanding whether the aspects of your product that make it uniquely competitive in the market-place are based on patentable inventions is probably your first step in the process.

Some Benefits of Filing for Patent Protection

There are many benefits of filing for patent protection. One obvious benefit is that by filing a patent application, you may obtain "patent pending" status, which means that you have put your competition on notice that you may obtain a patent that covers an important marketable aspect of your product. This can, by itself, be a strong deterrent to someone who might otherwise try to steal your patent-able invention. Another benefit is that filing it gives you priority over subsequently filed patent applications. This can be very important not only in obtaining the patent, but in defending your right to use, make, or sell a product against others who may claim that they have prior rights. Many inventors obtain patents not because they want to enforce them but because they don't want competitors stopping them from using their own idea.

Filing a patent application may allow you to freely disclose, or even license, your product. One common strategy used by many inventors who are manufacturing and marketing their products themselves is to file one or more provisional applications on those aspects of their product that (1) are inventive, (2) are based on utility (as opposed to design), and (3) may be perceived as providing an advantage in the marketplace. They are then able to test the market-place for up to a year before they have to file a regular (nonprovi-sional) application. This is outlined later in the "Provisional Patent Application" section.

Investors and licensees are usually more interested in investing in a product that has patent pending status than in a similar product that does not. If you are trying to persuade someone to back your product, a patent application can help provide some reassurance. In fact, many manufacturers (prospective licensees) will not even look at an invention submission that does not have either a patent or patent pending status. Their rationale is that they may have seen or be working on the idea already. Also, patent applications (if written well) can be very helpful in explaining to others what your product is and how the inventive aspects of your product are an improve-ment over existing products.

It is important to keep in mind that you can file a patent applica-tion only if you have a good faith belief that your invention is patent-able. As an inventor, you will be required to file a signed declaration that says that you believe the invention is entitled to a patent. Filing a patent application based on an invention that you know is not patentable (for whatever reason) can have severe legal implications and can cause you to lose credibility in the marketplace.

The Real World

There are some realities that you need to consider. In the real world—which entrepreneurs must inhabit—there are significant limitations concerning patents. For one thing, no patent can guar-antee that a competitor will not steal your invention (or product based on that invention). Patented inventions are often infringed, and relatively few are ever enforced. One reason is that enforcing a patent is very expensive, and most inventors simply do not have the means to file a lawsuit. Another reason is that many patents are difficult to interpret. In other words, it may not be entirely clear from the patent whether a particular competing product is actually infringing, and for that reason, it can be too risky to pursue an infringement lawsuit. Additionally, some patents are easy to "design around." A competitor may be able to design a product that has all the advantages of the patented product (more accurately, of the invention upon which the product is based), but that doesn't actually infringe the patent. There are many examples of inventors obtaining patents (usually after much hard work and expense) that they cannot enforce.

Another reality is that getting a patent doesn't mean that your product will be successful in the marketplace. While it is generally true that some consumers may be impressed by a product that says "patent pending" and that there is a general impression (or misconception) in the marketplace that a patented product is a "better" product, there are many patented products that simply aren't very marketable. All a patent means is that some aspect of the product defined in the patent as the "invention" is a novel improvement. *A patent does not mean that the product will appeal to the consumer.*

Another reality is that the patent process takes a long time. Currently, there is an extensive backlog of patent applications sitting on the desks of patent examiners at the U.S. Patent Office. It may take two or more years before an examiner will have the opportunity to pick up and read the application, and it often takes another year of back and forth between the inventor and the examiner before a patent will be issued. That is a very long time in the marketplace, and market conditions can change drastically by the time you are able to obtain a patent. Many patent applications actually become obsolete (or irrelevant) before they are examined because the inventor has already modified the invention significantly to meet new market conditions. This is not that much of a problem for larger companies that have the money to file different applications to reflect the various modifications and improvements on a particular invention, but it can be a big impediment to an inventor with limited resources.

When we were manufacturing products, we filed some patents on various aspects of those products to gain a competitive advantage, but we often found that the cost of patenting outweighed the benefits. We also noted that our most successful products often had weak or no patent protection. We found that those products with patents were copied just as often as those without them. The value of a well-written, valid, and enforceable patent is really based on your desire and capability to defend it. At $400 an hour, hiring patent attorneys to fight a well-heeled infringer with an in-house patent attorney can get costly very fast. We often concluded that that same investment (that is, what we spent on attorney's fees and costs) could better be spent on outmarketing our competitors or on the development of our next new product.

What Has Changed in the Patent Law

Since the first edition of this book was published in 2005, my overarching philosophy about the role and proper priority of patents has not changed. However, there have been some major changes in patent law that warrant discussion here. On September 16, 2011, after much debate and lobbying, President Obama signed the Leahy-Smith America Invents Act (AIA). On March 16, 2013, the first-inventor-to-file provision of that law went into effect.

Under this new law, the United States, like most countries, now has a "first-to-file" system. In other words, the first inventor to file a patent application has priority regardless of whether she was the first to invent. Prior to this law, the advice commonly given to new

**Watch Video: John Merchant Explains
"First-to-File" Law**

http://www.tamaramonosoff.com/tamara-monosoff-interviews-ip-attorney
-john-merchant-new-first-file-patent-law/

inventors was to keep a bound notebook, signed by witnesses, noting the key aspects of the invention and the dates when they were developed. The reasoning behind this was that previous U.S. patent law essentially said that if two inventors filed a patent for the same invention, the person who could prove that he was the first to have invented it would have priority, irrespective of who was the first person to actually file the patent.

As you can imagine, the new law creates some additional urgency to filing as soon as you can to preserve your priority. And there are additional important wrinkles to the law that affect not only the filing schedule, but also the inventor's ability to obtain patent protection. An inventor who discloses her own invention will have a year from the date of disclosure to get an application on file. However, a prior disclosure of an invention by someone other than the inventor may serve as an absolute bar to filing. So, in effect, the new law determines priority by disclosure and filing. Although it is safer (in many instances) to wait to disclose your invention until after you file an application, early disclosure may be advantageous in situations in which there are likely to be competing inventors. For example, suppose you are working very hard on a new invention, and you know that a competitor is very close to independently coming up with the same thing. If that competitor discloses the invention before you do, the disclosure may be considered a bar to your obtaining patent rights. This is a more common situation in the academic setting, where early publication of research results can be important for maintaining funding and obtaining credit for research discoveries, but it is applicable to individual inventors too.

The point is that the new law is not just about filing first. Prior disclosure can make a difference and must be balanced against the possibilities of losing foreign rights. Sound complicated? Unfortunately, it can be. This and other nuances of the new law require inventors to carefully consider when and how they will disclose their invention in addition to when they will file the application. When in doubt, talk to a qualified attorney before you disclose your invention.

Generally, the move from a first-to-invent to a first-to-file system has created significant anxiety among inventors, and many inventors are pushing to get their patent applications on file as soon as possible so as not to be beaten out by competing inventors. As a result, fast filing of provisional applications has become more popular of late. Inventors should note that provisional applications are available only for certain utility-type inventions and not for designs. And, inventors need to be mindful of what they put in their provisional applications because the contents of the provisional application will serve as the basis for the nonprovisional application if they choose to file within the next 12 months.

While critics of the new law have complained that the current system favors large companies that have the resources to file many patent applications quickly (even if the invention is only in development), the new system is an attempt to keep in step with the rest of the world and to obtain better certainty among inventors on who has priority over a particular invention. Under the previous law, an inventor might be in the middle of the patent process before learning that someone else had indeed invented the same product earlier. In addition, priority claims often had to be litigated before who was indeed entitled to a patent on the invention could be settled. It is too early to determine whether the current system will help the individual inventor in the long run. Suffice it to say that all inventors must be aware of the need to file to establish priority in the invention through filing a patent application (and disclosing the invention prior to filing in some cases).

Patentability Basics

There is an abundance of helpful information at the USPTO.gov website to assist you in understanding the nuances of the new patent laws. My goal here is not to reproduce everything already listed there, but to help you recognize some key concepts and requirements. I encourage you to spend time on that site reviewing content, or to even consider visiting one of the USPTO resource libraries to learn more about your invention.

In order for an item to be patentable, there are a number of criteria it must meet.

- It must not already be patented by someone else.
- It cannot already be out in public anywhere in the world, whether that instance is patented or not.
- If you have sold it publicly or otherwise disclosed it publicly outside confidentiality, you must file a patent within one year of the disclosure. *Note:* If an invention is disclosed by someone other than the inventor prior to filing, that disclosure can be an absolute bar to filing a patent application. And, prior disclosure is allowed only in the United States. Public disclosure prior to filing (regardless of who is disclosing) can be an absolute bar to patenting in other countries.

Understanding Your Resources

There are a number of legal resources available to you when you are making important decisions about legal protection, including patent attorneys, patent agents, and patent search firms. There is more than one type of patent available (utility and design), as well as legal tools other than patents that may be more applicable to protecting those aspects of your product that provide you with an advantage in the marketplace, such as copyright and trademark protection. The following provides an overview of your options when you are pursuing legal protection. While it is meant to inform, it's not meant to advise. Again, your best bet is to obtain the advice of a legal expert before making any final decisions.

Know Your Patents

It is important that you understand the difference between a utility patent and a design patent.

This excerpt is taken directly from the USPTO website at http://www.uspto.gov/inventors/patents.jsp#heading-3.

What Can and Cannot Be Patented?

What *can* be patented:

Utility patents are provided for a new, nonobvious, and useful:

- Process
- Machine
- Article of manufacture
- Composition of matter
- Improvement of any of the above

Design patents are provided for new and ornamental design of an article of manufacture.

Plant patents are provided for asexually reproduced plant varieties.

What *cannot* be patented:

- Laws of nature
- Physical phenomena
- Abstract ideas
- Literary, dramatic, musical, and artistic works (these can be copyright protected). Go to the U.S. Copyright Office (http://www.copyright.gov/).

Inventions which are:

- Not useful (such as perpetual motion machines); or
- Offensive to public morality

To be patentable, the invention must also be:

- Novel
- Nonobvious
- Adequately described or enabled (for one of ordinary skill in the art to make and use the invention)
- Claimed by the inventor in clear and definite terms

Utility Patent

Utility patents apply to the utility of an invention—the structure and operation of the invention. They protect the idea of the invention regardless. For this reason, utility patents tend to be broad (that is, covering different arrangements—embodiments—having equivalent elements or characteristics). The most valuable utility patents cover those aspects of your product that make it uniquely competitive in the marketplace.

Like all patents, what is actually described in the claims is defined as the "invention." Utility claims are one-sentence descriptions (often in legalese) of what the inventor believes to be the unique idea. Be careful about equating a product with an invention. It is a misconception that a utility (or any) patent covers a product. As we have said many times before, products often contain novel inventions. For example, there may be specific claims granted by the patent that pertain to inventive improvements of a "stove" or a "cell phone," for example. But a patent on those inventive aspects will not prevent competing stoves or cell phones from being sold. They will prevent only competing stoves or cell phones with those inventive aspects. For my first product, the TP Saver, I obtained a utility patent on the unique functional aspects of the product, which was the way it prevents unrolling of the toilet paper. Unfortunately, even though I had relatively broad patent protection covering the specific utility aspects (and their equivalents) of my product, that did not prevent a competitor, who saw that I was gaining momentum in the market with my product, from "inventing" a different way to prevent kids from unrolling the toilet paper.

Assuming that all maintenance fees are paid, a utility patent will have a term of 20 years from the date of the patent application filing. This usually translates to about 17 years from the date of the patent grant.

Design Patent

Design patents cover the novel aesthetic aspects of an article of manufacture. They do not cover the utility aspects of the article.

However, many times the unique aesthetic aspects of a product do provide the competitive advantage in the marketplace. For that reason, design patents can be quite valuable. Also, it is possible to obtain a design patent on many products that also contain elements that may be the subject of a utility patent. In other words, design and utility patents are not mutually exclusive, although they cover different things. For many products that are not necessarily based on novel utility features, design patents are the only option. For example, there may be nothing new about the function of a particular automobile rearview mirror, but the specific design of the mirror is valuable property to an automobile maker who has a novel design that fits with a specific model of car. Or, there may be nothing particularly new about the function of a particular wine bottle opener, but the novel modern design of a particular wine bottle opener may make it the most wanted opener on the market.

If your product has elements that can be subject to a design patent, it can be very beneficial to pursue design patent protection in lieu of, or in addition to, utility patent protection.

Here are some advantages to using design patents as part of your protection strategy.

1. **Cost.** If you want a patent, but the cost of a utility patent is a deterrent, a design patent is less expensive.

2. **Legal threat.**
   a. Upon filing, the use of "patent pending" is acceptable. And unless you disclose, until the patent is publicly posted on www.uspto.gov, nobody will know that it is a design rather than a utility patent.
   b. The design patent rights are usually more likely to be granted than the utility patent application, which is more often declined.
   c. Surprisingly, many people working in the product or sales and marketing groups in manufacturers, who would be your potential threats (or licensing partners), don't know the difference between a design patent and a utility patent. I have often been asked, "Is the item patented?," but almost never, "Is it a design

or a utility patent?" Of course, there are exceptions to this as well.

d. While a design patent eventually becomes public, so it can be fairly easily designed around, a clever patent attorney can often file multiple design patents for the same product.

3. Satisfaction. Some people view the receipt of the USPTO patent certificate as a major achievement.

4. Support for utility patent filing. Many important technological developments that become products are protected by both utility and design patents. For example, there are numerous patents (both design and utility) covering the iPhone. The potential success of the overall protection plan can be enhanced by pursuing both types of protection.

5. Licensing asset. As outlined previously, the design patent can be used as your asset in a licensing negotiation.

Provisional Patent Application

The provisional patent application is one strategy that we have used frequently. First, let me reiterate that a provisional application simply provides a priority date. It is an application that describes your invention in enough detail to provide an adequate basis for the filing of a nonprovisional application. The provisional application is not examined by the patent office. It is not published. And the priority date is entirely dependent on your filing a nonprovisional application claiming the priority date of the provisional within one year of filing the provisional. I would like to emphasize that there are five

Watch Video: John Merchant Explains Provisional Patent Applications

http://www.tamaramonosoff.com/tamara-monosoff-interviews-john-merchant-ppa/

key benefits to using provisional applications as part of your protection strategy.

1. Time. If you have an invention, and for any reason, including those I have mentioned earlier, you wish to delay the investment of filing a utility patent, but are concerned that someone else may file a competing patent before you, a provisional application sets your filing date the day you file it. Once you have filed, you have 12 months' time to file your utility patent application. If it is filed within that 12-month window, the filing date of your utility patent is the date of your provisional application filing. The idea is that even if someone else files a patent or launches a competing invention during that time, your patent filing date will precede theirs.

2. Cost. The cost of writing and filing a provisional application is a fraction of the cost of filing a utility application. While we have always hired a professional to handle our provisional applications (see the warning regarding potential traps in the next section), that is not a requirement. In addition, the USPTO filing fees are minimal.

3. Threat. Once you file a provisional, it is within your rights to apply the words "patent pending" to your product packaging, presentation materials, and so on. Often this notation alone is sufficient to deter would-be knockoff companies. Unless you choose to disclose this, they have no way to know whether the pending patent is a provisional application or an extensive utility patent.

4. Licensing asset. As with an actual patent, if you find a licensing partner during this 12-month time frame and it is evident that this partner wishes to license your rights, and if you believe that a utility patent is plausible (based on legal advice from a patent attorney), you can "license" your provisional application, and the partner can then incur the costs of filing the utility patent. Or you could file it should your partner require it of you as part of your agreement.

5. Privacy. Although it takes many months before an actual patent application or patent itself is publicly listed on the USPTO website, eventually it will be available for all to see—and, if desired, design around. A provisional application is not made public. So, even though you are securing your filing date, there is no way for others to see what it is that you have filed. As with an actual patent filing, it is simply not public.

It is important to reiterate that a provisional is not a patent, does not indicate that the USPTO has granted you any rights, and does not ensure that you will ever be granted rights. It only gives you the right to file a utility patent application (not a design patent application) using the provisional filing. And, you get to use patent pending.

The 12 months that this gives an inventor to make a determination as to the patentability and viability of the product, along with the legal threat that patent pending offers, can be extremely useful to warding off competition while you test the market.

Watch Out for Potential Traps

Provisional applications provide many advantages. You should, however, consider some of the potential traps that inventors often get into with provisional patent applications. Although you are not required to follow specific formal preparation requirements, as you are with regular nonprovisional applications, you are required to include all the information that is necessary in order to explain and enable the invention. In other words, you have to include everything—you can't add new matter (such as additional important details that are required to make the invention work) in the nonprovisional if you don't already have them in the provisional. This can be a particular problem for inventors who attempt to prepare and file their own provisional applications because they sometimes neglect to include important details. The classic situation is one in which an inventor who is very enthusiastic about the potential marketability of a product based on an invention describes very carefully and thoughtfully all the things that the invention can do and why it is going to be successful, but fails to provide all the important details about what the invention is.

Remember, if an important detail isn't in the provisional, you can't include it later in the nonprovisional, and if the detail in the provisional does not adequately describe the invention, you may be prevented from claiming the priority date established by the provisional filing. In some instances where the inventor, relying on the priority date established by the provisional application, actually discloses the invention (by making it, selling it, offering it for sale, and so on), the disclosure could prevent the inventor from obtaining a patent based on the nonprovisional filing if it later turns out that the provisional did not include all the necessary information upon which to base a nonprovisional filing. Also, as stated previously, provisional applications are not available for design patents. The only way to establish priority for a design is to file a design patent application.

Fees, Fees, Fees

There can be numerous fees associated with obtaining a patent on an invention, depending on the type of invention and other issues that may occur during the process. But, generally speaking, there are three types of fees that you can expect to pay when seeking patent protection: (1) preparation fees, (2) filing fees, and (3) maintenance fees.

Preparation fees are fees that you pay to an attorney or other professional (whether that be a prototype engineer, agent, illustrator, or some other person) who is helping you prepare the patent application and the associated documents. Filing fees are the fees you pay to the patent office when you file the application. Maintenance fees are the fees you pay to the patent office after you have been granted a patent in order to maintain the patent's validity during the patent term.

Preparation fees vary greatly and depend, in large part, on what kind of invention you are trying to patent. If your invention is fairly simple (in terms of technology and scope), then the preparation fees can be very reasonable. You may be able to do much of the work yourself, and you may not need a professional illustrator, for example. If, on the other hand, your invention is in a highly technical area and/or is very difficult to explain (many moving parts, many embodiments, and the like), then you may need to hire someone with familiarity in the area of technology and patent law to help you prepare the application. That can be very expensive.

Filing fees depend on what type of application you are filing (utility, design, plant, or provisional) and the status of the filer. There are currently three status categories: (1) large entity, (2) small entity, and (3) micro entity. Small-entity status allows small businesses, independent inventors, and nonprofit organizations to file a patent application for a reduced fee (about 50 percent of the large-entity fees). An entity qualifies for small-entity status if its number of employees, including affiliates, does not exceed 500 persons. If the entity does not qualify for small-entity status, it is considered a large entity and must pay the regular fees. Micro-entity status is a new category added by the new patent laws and allows a further reduction in fees. Micro-entity status is really a subcategory of small-entity status that applies to small-entity filers who have filed fewer than a certain number of patent applications and have a gross income of less than a certain amount and/or have assigned their patent(s) to their employer, which is an institution of higher education. Most independent inventors will fit into the small- or micro-entity categories.

As you will see from the following chart, the USPTO breaks down the filing fees into subcategories covering three important parts of the examination process: (1) the filing fee, which is the fee you have to pay simply to file the application, (2) the search fee, which covers the examiner's search costs, and (3) the examination fee, which covers the examiner's examination of the application. Again, these fees depend on what type of patent you are filing and your filing status (small entity, micro entity, and so on). Here is an example of the current fee structure, as of this writing, as published by the USPTO on its website.

There are, of course, other fees associated with moving the patent application through the examination process. These are fees gen-

As of August 2013	Standard	Small Entity	Micro Entity
Utility patent	$280	$140	$70
Search fee	$600	$300	$150
Examination fee	$720	$360	$180
Design patent	$180	$90	$45
Search fee	$120	$60	$30
Examination fee	$460	$230	$115
Provisional application*	$260	$130	$65

*There is no search or examination fee associated with a provisional application.

erally associated with choices that you might make, such as fees for requesting an extension of time to respond to an examiner's rejections and fees associated with filing continuations (which are separate applications based on your initial application). Those fees are listed on the USPTO website. The basic rule of thumb when dealing with the USPTO is that if you are requesting something from it (an extension or something else), you are going to have to pay a fee for it. The USPTO is one of the few government administrative offices that actually make a profit.

The Time for the Process

Expect to wait a while. The time it takes for an application to move through the patent examination process and be issued (that is, granted) depends on the complexity of the technology. And, assuming that you are successful in convincing the examiner that you are entitled to a patent (and depending on many variables that I will not attempt to go into here), it can take six months to two years after that for the patent to actually be issued. Under special circumstances (for example, the presence of a terminal illness or being a certain age), you may be able to expedite this process by paying extra fees. The average time for receiving an issued patent on a utility application is two to three years from the date of filing.

Design patents generally move more quickly, and it generally takes between 18 and 24 months from the date of filing for the patent to be issued. The timing varies depending on the backlog and the type of technology. These estimates are based on current conditions at the patent office and the recent experience of attorneys we talked to.

Keep in mind that moving the patent through the examination process (called *patent prosecution*) involves a back-and-forth conversation between you (or your attorney) and the patent examiner. It is highly unlikely that the examiner will simply grant your patent without first issuing rejections based on prior art, making objections as to form, and/or presenting other issues that require you to submit a formal response. In most circumstances, some sort of amendment to the patent claims is required to get the patent issued. So much of the attorney time (and expense) associated with obtaining a patent occurs after you have filed your patent application.

A new utility patent filed on or after June 8, 1995, expires 20 years from the date of filing. Maintenance fees are subject to change and are due for a patent at 3.5 years, 7.5 years, and 11.5 years from the date of the granting of the patent. Check the USPTO website (www.uspto.gov) for updated fee schedules.

You do not have to wait until your patent is issued to start selling your product. Once your application is officially filed, you can mark your product and packaging patent pending, which makes it clear that obtaining a patent is in progress.

Finding a Patent Attorney

There are thousands of lawyers out there. Not all of them are qualified to help you protect your product. So, it is important that you understand some of the differences (and legal jargon) before you start looking for an attorney to assist you.

The overall field of law covering patents, trademarks, copyright, and trade secrets is called *intellectual property law*, and lawyers specializing in one or more areas of intellectual property law are called *intellectual property attorneys.* However, you need to understand that not all intellectual property attorneys cover all areas of intellectual property law; in fact, they may do specific work only within a particular area. Those attorneys who specialize in patent law tend to come in two flavors: (1) those who help inventors obtain patents on their inventions (called *patent prosecutors*), and (2) those who help enforce patent rights in court (called *patent litigators*). Patent prosecutors are distinguished by the fact that they must be registered to practice at the USPTO before they are allowed to prepare and file patent applications on behalf of inventors. This means that they have to (1) meet special training requirements (that is, have a certain level of knowledge in one or more areas of technology) and (2) pass the patent bar, which tests for competency in patent law. Patent litigators do not have to be registered with the USPTO, but they must, of course, be licensed attorneys and have an understanding of patent law. So, in other words, you will be looking for a patent prosecutor to help you file your patent. And, you will be looking for a patent prosecutor who has experience prosecuting patents in the area of technology related to your invention.

Interestingly, not all patent prosecutors are attorneys. There is a class of patent prosecutors called *patent agents* who also meet the criteria for practice before the USPTO. Patent agents can prepare and file patent applications on behalf of inventors, and they can work with inventors to move the application through the process (that is, prepare and file amendments, respond to examiner objections, and so on). However, they cannot enforce patent rights in court (or provide you with legal advice about patent enforcement) because they are not attorneys. And, they are limited to patent prosecution—they are not licensed to provide legal advice about any other area of intellectual property protection.

Also keep in mind that not all patent prosecutors like working with individual inventors. There are many reasons for this. One reason is that individual inventors tend to be unprepared and/or have only one invention to patent. It is much easier (and generally more profitable) for patent attorneys to work with larger businesses that have research and development departments that are very familiar with patent prosecution, have prior experience working with the attorney, and provide the attorney with a steady stream of work. Another reason is that many patent attorneys who service larger businesses are prevented from working with potential competitors of their current client base because there is a potential legal conflict. So, you will be looking for patent attorneys who work with individual inventors and smaller businesses. Your patent attorney (or agent) can be located anywhere, but it may be helpful to use someone local to you. Patent prosecutors can be found by geographic region by visiting the USPTO website (http://www.uspto.gov). There are other resources as well that can be used, such as Legal Zoom (www.legalzoom.com) and your local bar association referral system.

What to Expect in the Patenting Process

Once you find an appropriate attorney (or agent), you'll probably want to know how to prepare for your first meeting, how long the patent process will take, and how much it will cost.

Meeting with Your Attorney

Prepare in advance. Patent attorneys are among the most highly trained—and expensive—attorneys you will meet. Whether you are going to an initial free consultation or paying for the attorney's time, show up knowledgeable. The last thing you want is to pay a patent attorney $400 an hour to explain how the patent office works, the different kinds of patents, and other basics. So the message is to be prepared. Not only will this enable you to maximize the return on your time and financial investment, but the perception you make matters. And if you are prepared, you will set yourself apart from many of the inventors that the attorney has probably spoken with before. This matters because these attorneys need to make decisions as to whom they are willing to work with. If you are focused and serious, they will instantly determine that your project will be one that you will manage well. Here is what I recommend you do to prepare in advance of your meeting:

1. Know the basics as outlined in this chapter. In addition, spend time on the USPTO website and read its summaries. Visit the other patent resource websites as well so that you have a number of perspectives and descriptions of processes, time frames, and insights.

2. Do your own patent and trademark research (as outlined later in this chapter). Print out patents that seem most similar to your product. Highlight possible differences and document the patent numbers of all the patents you have found that are similar.

3. Know what you are asking—and not asking—of this professional. I have consistently found that patent attorneys are experts in patent law, navigating the obstacles of the USPTO, drafting legal documents, and potentially litigating patent infringement cases. They can typically advise you on the likely patentability of your product (after some research), file your patents, and manage the process.

4. I have also found that most patent attorneys are not really competent to advise you about the viability of your product or your business. Appropriately, a "good" invention, in the eyes of a seasoned patent attorney, often means one that is patentable, not one that you will be successful in marketing and selling. By now, you know that my definition of a good product has little to do with its patentability and everything to do with its marketability.

Patent Research

Now that you have a good understanding of patents, I want you to take some time to research the patents in existence that relate to your product.

Watch Video: 10 Tips to Make Your Patent Research Easier

....

http://www.tamaramonosoff.com/tamara-monosoff-offers-10-tips-make
-patent-research-easier/

10 Tips to Make Your Patent Research Easier

These 10 tips are the key elements of this section. Tips 1 to 6 provide basic knowledge of the search tools, and Tips 7 to 10 require deeper digging, reading, printing, and note taking.

Patents can be found at:

- U.S. Patent and Trademark Office (http://www.uspto.gov)
- Google Patents (http://www.google.com/patents/)
- Patent Storm (http://www.patentstorm.com)
- Patent Genius (http://www.patentgenius.com)
- Free Patents Online (http://www.freepatentsonline.com)

The following steps will show you how to use these sites and what to look for. (Go to www.TamaraMonosoff.com/Guides to see a video tutorial.)

1. When you are using patent search sites, there is usually a search window. In this search window, type in the most descriptive word(s) possible, including the function of your product (that is, what it does) to help you get started. My preference is Google Patents, as I have found it the easiest to use. For example, when I go to http://www.google.com/patents and type in "garden trowel," a large number of patents are listed.

2. Once you find patents for items that are similar to yours, you will see that most of the sites offer an image of the patent filing (see Figure 4.2) and an option to read the text. *Look at the photo first.* I click on the images, as I find it easier to determine how closely related this patent is to my idea by first viewing an image.

FIGURE 4.2 **Example of a Patent Image**

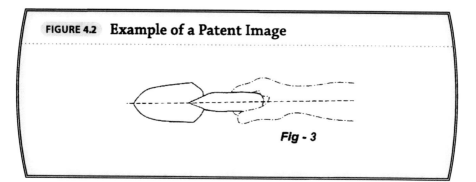

Fig - 3

3. Look at the patent number (see Figure 4.3) and figure out whether it is a utility or a design patent. If the first character in the patent number is a D (see Figure 4.4), it is a design patent.

FIGURE 4.3 **Find Patent Number**

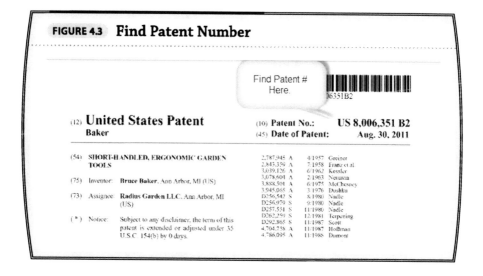

A design patent protects only the precise design of the product. A utility patent covers the function, task, or process that the product achieves. In the example in Figure 4.3, there is not a D listed in the patent number, which means that it is a "utility" patent.

4. Look at the date issued (see Figure 4.5). If it is a utility patent that was issued more than 20 years ago, you know that this patent

FIGURE 4.4   The Letter D Indicates a Design Patent

The letter "D" at the beginning of a patent # indicates that this is a Design Patent.

(12) **United States Design Patent**   (10) Patent No.:   **US D504,889 S**
Andre et al.   (45) Date of Patent: ** May 10, 2005

(54) ELECTRONIC DEVICE

(75) Inventors: Bartley K. Andre, Menlo Park, CA (US); Daniel J. Coster, San Francisco, CA (US); Daniele De Iuliis, San Francisco, CA (US); Richard P. Howarth, San Francisco, CA (US); Jonathan P. Ive, San Francisco, CA (US); Steve Jobs, Palo Alto, CA (US);

D396,452 S * 7/1998 Naruki D14/424
D451,508 S * 12/2001 Iseki et al. D14/341
D453,333 S * 2/2002 Chen D14/374
D458,252 S * 6/2002 Palm et al. D14/343

OTHER PUBLICATIONS

Andre et al., U.S. Appl. No. 29/180,558 entitled "Electronic Device", filed Mar. 17, 2004.
"HP Compaq Tablet PC tc1100", downloaded Aug. 27,

has now expired (the term of a design patent is 14 years). This is good news and bad news—good because the idea is not owned by someone else and you can use it, and bad because it is now in the public domain and therefore is not something to which you are likely to be able to claim patent rights.

FIGURE 4.5   Find the Date when the Patent Was Issued

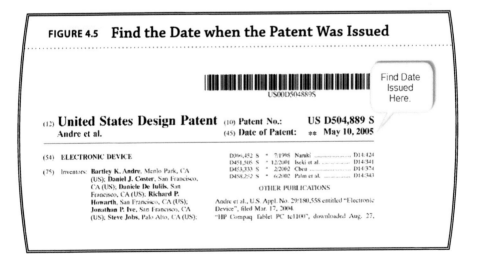

US00D504889S

Find Date Issued Here.

(12) **United States Design Patent**   (10) Patent No.:   **US D504,889 S**
Andre et al.   (45) Date of Patent: ** May 10, 2005

(54) ELECTRONIC DEVICE

(75) Inventors: Bartley K. Andre, Menlo Park, CA (US); Daniel J. Coster, San Francisco, CA (US); Daniele De Iuliis, San Francisco, CA (US); Richard P. Howarth, San Francisco, CA (US); Jonathan P. Ive, San Francisco, CA (US); Steve Jobs, Palo Alto, CA (US);

D396,452 S * 7/1998 Naruki D14/424
D451,508 S * 12/2001 Iseki et al. D14/341
D453,333 S * 2/2002 Chen D14/374
D458,252 S * 6/2002 Palm et al. D14/343

OTHER PUBLICATIONS

Andre et al., U.S. Appl. No. 29/180,558 entitled "Electronic Device", filed Mar. 17, 2004.
"HP Compaq Tablet PC tc1100", downloaded Aug. 27,

5. *Note:* I have found Google Patents to be the easiest to use, as there is no additional download needed.

6. When reading a specific patent, read the section called "claims" (see Figure 4.6). This is the most relevant section of a patent document. This is where you will find the "how," the part of the invention to which other people have been granted the rights. Keep in mind that a utility patent is filed not on a product, but on specific claims about that product.

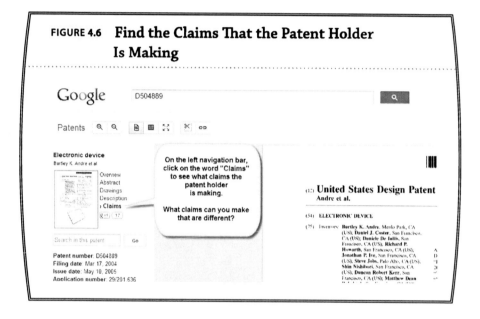

FIGURE 4.6 Find the Claims That the Patent Holder Is Making

Here's an example of using a "gadget" as a product. A patent often does not prevent others from producing their own gadgets. But if your gadget is fastened using a unique and novel way of fastening, your claim would enable you to defend your right should someone attempt to copy your fastening method.

7. When you find a patent that is related to your product, you have discovered the first bread crumb in a trail that you should follow to get closer to the patent(s) that are similar to your product invention. Once you find relevant patents, record the patent numbers, as you will want to use this process in more than one patent search engine, and some may produce different results.

8. Within each patent filing, you will find a section called "Citations" or "Patent References" (or "Field of Search" in some patents that are less detailed). These sections list the other related patents that the attorney or agent who filed the patent you are reading used to show that this filing was unique. As you review this list, click the link or copy and search the patent numbers for the others that appear most closely related to yours (see Figure 4.7). After doing this for a while, you will gain an incredible amount of understanding of what is out there today and how professionals have written the claims.

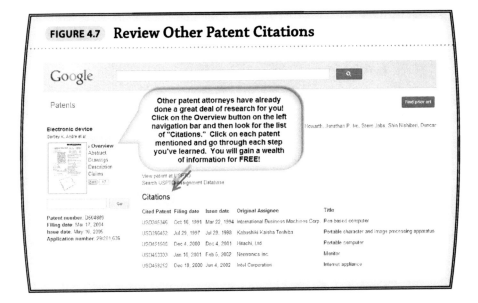

FIGURE 4.7 Review Other Patent Citations

9. As you follow step 8, print or note the patents you believe to be closest to your product so that you can save yourself time if you later hire an attorney. You can present your own research, helping to expedite the attorney's efforts. You will have a more intelligent and efficient initial consultation because you won't be burning precious time as the attorney explains basic patent concepts to you. This will save you money and earn the respect of your attorney.

10. There is a temptation to read the summary of the invention and skip the claims, as these often sound legalistic. Read the claims.

These are the keys to what may be patentable about your product. Print and highlight those that seem to overlap the most with key aspects of your product idea. From what you learn, you may be able to modify your method to further differentiate your product. (This is the kind of discussion that is worth having with a creative patent attorney and designer.)

While I strongly encourage you to take the time to do this patent research on your own, there are firms that you can hire to do specific searches for you. In fact, if you ultimately decide to file a patent, a formal search will be required. These can be done independent of a patent filing as well, and there are firms you can pay a few hundred dollars to conduct a search, such as www.walsh-ip.com, www.neustel .com/psearches.htm, or www.legalzoom.com.

Go to www.TamaraMonosoff.com/Guides to view the patent research video tutorial.

Give Yourself Credit

Make sure that your name is included on the patent. Sometimes helpful husbands or partners will "take care of" the patent for you and mistakenly leave off your name as the inventor, including only their own because they are filling out the paperwork. Note that you will *not* have an opportunity to add your name later.

PART 2:
Other Intellectual Property Tools

In some cases, you will want to take advantage of trademark or copyright protection in addition to—or instead of—patenting your invention. Part 2 provides an overview of the fundamental differences among patents, copyrights, and trademarks (or service marks).

Copyrights

When you want to protect a traditional idea or invention, a patent is most appropriate. However, when you want to protect published or unpublished literary, scientific, or artistic work (in a full range of expressions), a copyright registration is generally the way to go. In some cases, your attorney may advise you to use both forms of protection.

Whether your creation is literary, artistic, or dramatic (think of a painting, a play, a song, a unique dance, a photograph, or something similar), copyright laws grant the creator the exclusive right to reproduce, prepare derivative works, distribute, perform, and display the work publicly. Copyright protection is effective upon creation of the work. No additional filing or effort is necessary to have earned copyright protection as long as the work fits the definition of a copyrightable work. With regard to products, copyrights usually apply to unique designs or logos (such as the unique designs found on stickers or artwork that is affixed to the product itself). The arrangement of marketing materials can also be subject to copyright. As the definition of copyrightable materials is complex, I invite you to review the helpful materials found on the U.S. Copyright Office website at www.copyright.gov.

Term

Copyright terms depend on a variety of factors, including when the work was first created and whether the copyright was renewed. Generally, a copyright term lasts from the date of the work's creation to 70 years after the death of the creator.

Advantages

The benefit of a copyright is similar to that of a patent, in that it gives you legal protections against infringement and provides a warning to those who might otherwise feel unhampered in copying your work. And, it can be sold or transferred to others, as is the case with this book. While I own the copyright upon its creation, I have the ability to transfer that right to McGraw-Hill, which then reproduces and sells it.

There are also major protection benefits of a copyright. Unlike with a patent, there *are* "copyright police." If you've ever rented a video, you have seen the FBI warning at the beginning that warns you not to violate the copyright. While an individual must rely on the state to prosecute a case of copyright infringement (rather than suing the perpetrator himself), the benefit is the penalty. Unlike civil penalties relating to patent infringement, copyright infringement has an even greater deterrent—possible jail time.

Preparation and Advice

As mentioned earlier, the creator of a work covered by copyright has no obligation to do anything to earn the protections of U.S. copyright law or to use the © on your copyright notice. However, your copyright must be registered before you can file a lawsuit to enforce your rights. And there are reasons to take the steps necessary to register your copyrights even if you do not want to enforce your rights in court.

Providing notice of copyright on your work at the time of its creation is fairly easy to do. Write your name, the year, and a © on your work (created by putting the letter c between parentheses, which tells your Word program to automatically create that little circle around your c). Although this is not required, it does eliminate the defense someone might use that she was not aware that someone had claimed a copyright on the work. For example:

© 2013 Tamara Monosoff

Copyright registrations are managed by the Copyright Office, which is part of the U.S. Library of Congress (not the USPTO). A basic filing fee at the time of this writing is just $35.00.

Registration is something that you can do on your own. However, some people have it done by an attorney to ensure that all possible issues are addressed. Whether you are doing it yourself or using an attorney, you will need to have clear evidence of the history of your work. Ancillary information, such as whether anyone else was involved in creating the work (an employee or a work-for-hire agreement, for instance) can be helpful to your attorney.

Timeline and Cost

As of this writing, a standard copyright registration application takes approximately 3 to 4.5 months to be issued by the Copyright Office. This timeline can be expedited for additional fees.

For additional information, visit the Copyright Office website or contact the office:

www.copyright.gov
U.S. Copyright Office
101 Independence Avenue SE
Washington, DC 20559
(202) 707-3000 or 1-877-476-0778 (toll free)

Trademarks

Watch Video: John Merchant Explains Trademarks

http://www.tamaramonosoff.com/trademarks-can-used-advantage/

What's in a name? As you probably know, a clever or attractive name can mean the difference between a successful product and one that sells poorly or not at all. It is therefore always a good idea to consider protecting any trademark rights pertaining to your product. Basically, trademarks are source indicators. While patents and copyrights preserve the rights of the inventor or author of an original work, trademarks are focused on preventing consumers from being confused as to the source of the goods and services. A trademark is described by the USPTO in the following way:

> A trademark is generally a word, phrase, symbol, or design, or a combination thereof, that identifies and distinguishes the source of the goods of one party from those of others.
>
> A service mark is the same as a trademark, except that it identifies and distinguishes the source of a service rather than goods.
>
> Source: *Basic Facts About Trademarks*, USPTO, p. 1.

A trademark can be a name, a phrase, a logo, or even a distinctive package design, color, or sound. You're probably familiar with many different types of trademarks: iPod is a trademark of Apple; Band-Aid is a trademark of Johnson & Johnson; and Kleenex is a trademark of Kimberly-Clark. No one else may use these trademarked brand names. This is why even though everyone looks or asks for "Band-Aids," a generic term such as "adhesive bandage" is used on the packaging of manufacturers other than Johnson & Johnson. Having this type of trademarked brand equity is a big advantage in the marketplace.

A service mark can be the name of a company (and commonly is), but it is not restricted to that. Some examples are 24 Hour Fitness and all its "branded class" formats, various car washes and their different "branded" levels of service, and banks with their levels of service. Apple is actually both a trademark *and* a service mark in numerous different classes of goods and services.

Trademark is a complex area of the law, and understanding the nuances can be critical in making the right choice of mark for your product. It is important that you educate yourself and even consult a trademark attorney before choosing to invest in a particular name for your product or service. It is important to know, for example, that trademarks do not apply to generic or merely descriptive names. You cannot obtain trademark protection for the name "apple" if your product is apples, but you can if your product is computers. There are weak and strong trademarks. Trademarks that are purely made up, such as the name Kodak for camera equipment, are considered very strong, and thus they are easier to enforce against similar marks. Trademarks that are descriptive (though not generic or merely descriptive), such as "Fast Oil Change" for oil change services, are weak. There are plenty of similar names that are allowed in the marketplace. So, it helps to consider the availability of trademark protection and the strength of the mark before you decide on a particular name for your product.

As in copyright, your rights to a trademark attach at the time of use. You don't have to register your name to have some trademark rights. But, it is generally very beneficial to register your trademark for purposes of enforcing (and defending) your trademark rights. To do this, you will need to submit a trademark registration application and go through the process.

The Trademark Office organizes registrations of marks into classes, with each class pertaining to a different type of product or service. If the mark is used to sell products in more than one class, it may be necessary for you to register your mark in more than one class in order to obtain adequate protection against potential infringers. But whether or not a mark infringes on another will depend on more than the class. Remember, trademark law is focused on preventing the consumer from being confused as to the source of goods and services. Thus, your ability to register your mark and/or enforce it against similar infringing marks depends largely on those factors that would be relevant to a consumer in the marketplace and the likelihood of confusion. Whether similar marks are being used for similar products is only one factor. Another factor is whether the products containing similar marks are marketed in the same way to a similar group of consumers. It is best to consult a trademark attorney to determine whether there are any conflicting (that is, confusingly similar) marks already registered before you choose the mark you want to use for a specific product or service.

The ® symbol on a packaged product means that the trademark has been registered, and it signifies that the owner of the mark has certain exclusive rights to its use in the marketplace. A ™ symbol is different in that it has no real legal effect. It simply serves to provide notice to potential infringers that the owner considers the mark to be a trademark (which is, nevertheless, helpful in many situations). While some trademarks are issued through your state, the federally registered ® offers the greatest protection because it's protected nationwide, whereas state registration may not confer that broader protection. The mark can be registered both in a state and with the federal government. Check the USPTO website to determine the cost of filing a federal trademark application. You can check with your state secretary's office for information about filing for state trademark registrations. Federal registrations provide a greater geographical scope of protection and are more expensive than state registrations. However, the mark will qualify for federal protection only if it is used in interstate commerce (that is, in more than one state). Many local marks are protectable only through state registration. Again, it is helpful to review the USPTO website and/or talk with a trademark attorney to determine what may be the best approach for you.

Why I Like Trademarks

There are a lot of reasons to like trademarks.

- First, you can easily search and claim trademark rights without any permission or expense (as with copyrights).
- Second, your mark can be a very effective tool for protecting what may be one of the key reasons your product is competitive in the marketplace.
- Third, filing for trademark registration at both the state and the federal level is relatively inexpensive compared to the cost of patent protection. And, it is not even that expensive to have trademarks professionally done, especially if you use an online resource.
- Fourth, it is much easier to defend your use of a mark if you have a trademark registration. It is a competitive marketplace, and it is relatively certain that if you have a good idea, competitors will want to do something similar. You wouldn't want a

competitor to register a similar name and then send you a letter telling you that you are infringing on its registered mark. So, it makes sense to register your mark as soon as you begin using it.

Even in situations in which I have elected to forgo patent filings, I have always leveraged trademarks to the extent possible.

Some Details to Consider When Using Your Mark

As with a copyright, you can, and should, start using your "mark" as soon as possible. And, to denote your claim of ownership of that mark, you can, without federal or state registration, simply start by using the trademark ™ or the service mark ﹕ after your mark. The raised ™ is easily produced by placing the letters "tm" inside parentheses, which then automatically raises the letters. Word does not do this automatically with the sm for service mark. But one trick to achieve this, wherever you want the service mark to appear, type "2120," then press "alt x," and voilà, an ﹕!

You will want to do trademark searches to ensure that you are not infringing on other marks, but the point here is that federal and state registration of your mark need not prevent you from demonstrating your use of the mark and claim of ownership. Once your mark becomes registered, you simply switch the ™ to an ®. Take notes and screen shots or photos of your first use of your mark in commerce to be used in your future applications.

Preliminary Search

Just as you would when filing a patent, it's imperative that you determine whether there are prior registered marks that might be considered confusingly similar to yours and thus prevent you from obtaining a registration. While it's not mandatory that you do this before filing a trademark (the search is included in the cost of filing), it is a very good idea to do a prior search. You may find that there are too many similar marks already registered and decide to change your mark. Remember, though, you need to search for similar marks (including spelling, sounds, foreign translations, and, in some cases, design elements) and not just look for exact matches of the mark you are considering.

You'll need to conduct a search not just for federal trademarks, but also for state registrations and common law (that is, nonregistered) usage. Any mark that is currently being used (registered or not) may affect your rights.

To first search for federal trademarks, follow the steps here:

Step 1: Go to the U.S. Patent and Trademark Office site (www. uspto.gov), and under the heading "Trademarks," click on the "Search" button.

Step 2: Start with the "Basic Word Search." A form with an empty field will open up. Type the name of your goods or services into the "Search Term" field and click on "Submit Query." It will bring up a list of similar names, or the exact name if someone already has the trademark. If the record of the name you searched comes up, don't lose heart right away.

Step 3: Scroll to the bottom of the page to check whether the mark is *live* or *dead*. If it is dead, you may still have the opportunity to use this trademark yourself.

It is also wise to search state registration databases. Each state maintains its own trademark database. However, not all these databases are online.

Keep in mind that your mark may pertain to more than one class of goods and services. For example, if you sell T-shirts and jewelry with a particular logo on it, you may want to register your mark in both the class pertaining to clothing (class 25) and the class pertaining to jewelry (class 14). Filing fees are calculated on a per class basis, so a single mark registered in two classes requires double the filing fees.

There are a total of 45 classes—34 product classes and 11 service classes (for service marks). If you don't know the class you wish to register in, you can leave that designation blank and the examiner will determine one for you. But it's helpful to know the classes so that you can make choices. Locating a simple, clear list of classes on the USPTO website is surprisingly difficult. However, there is a simple list provided by Legal Zoom here: http://www.legalzoom. com/trademarks-glossary/trademark-class-classification.html.

It's important to note that during the examination process, an examiner may cite a previously registered federal trademark, a previously registered state trademark, or even a common law mark (that is, one that is not registered) as being "confusingly similar" to your mark and thereby reject your application. For example, if you are trying to obtain a federal registration for the mark XYZ and someone in California has been using XYZ as a trademark (either registered with the state or unregistered) for the same type of goods or services, the Patent and Trademark Office is likely to refuse to register your use of the XYZ mark. Nevertheless, you may still be able to use and register your XYZ mark in your home state or area, as long as your territorial use does not overlap or interfere with the other person's territorial use of the XYZ mark. Or you may be able to use the XYZ mark for products in a different class. Trying to compete using the same mark is *not* recommended. If you are successful and the other mark is still being used, you will not be able to register your mark, or to use it where the other person's product is being sold.

Common Mistakes and Advice

Most first-time inventors don't realize that they can begin using a trademark symbol immediately, prior to actually filing any formal documents. Use actually helps you establish certain priority rights and can be helpful in obtaining a registration. You also avoid having to file a subsequent declaration (with a fee) establishing use if you use your mark prior to filing an application. However, you can file an application for trademark registration prior to actually using the mark in interstate commerce. Many companies will file for registration first because they want to be assured that they will be able to register the mark before they commit the associated marketing resources. For example, if a company was planning on selling thousands of units of product under a certain trademark, it generally wants to have confidence that it will be able to register the mark. So, the company might actually go through the entire process of obtaining the registration before committing to a particular mark.

If you do use your mark before you submit a registration, be sure to note the date you first did so and copy or photograph the specimen showing first use. This will be helpful when you file your state or federal trademark application.

Time and Cost

The federal USPTO electronic filing fee for a trademark at this time is $325 per mark per class if you use your own description of goods and services and $275 per mark per class if you use one of the predetermined descriptions provided in the trademark description index. Note that the filing fees are per mark per class which means that if you have a single mark, but you register it in two classes, the filing fee will be double what it would be if you filed in only one class. The same goes for state registrations—fees are generally calculated on a per mark per class basis. The general rule is that if you use the mark in interstate commerce, you would be better off filing for a federal registration. If you use the mark only in a single state, state registration is a viable alternative.

Some people choose not to file for registration at all. As I have outlined previously, trademark rights are automatic and apply generally to local areas where consumers are familiar with your mark as the source of certain goods and services. Such common law rights (that is, rights based on prior use within a certain locale) can be helpful in defending your ability to maintain use of the mark against subsequent users, but it is very difficult to assert enforcement rights against infringers of your mark without a registration. There are many complexities associated with defending and enforcing trademarks that go beyond the scope of this chapter. Suffice it to say that if you are investing in a mark by placing it on your product or spending marketing dollars to spread the name to consumers, then it is probably worthwhile to pursue registration of the mark, either federally or through state registration.

I have typically done the following myself:

1. I research the federal trademark database and use search engines to look for others who are using the same names in commerce.
2. If I see no apparent conflict, I begin using the mark immediately and put ™ next to it. Then I record the date when I began using it and file this with a screen shot or photo of this first use.
3. I file for federal registration once I know it is worthwhile.
4. When the federal mark is issued, I change the ™ to ®.

A federal trademark registration usually takes between 12 and 18 months to issue, assuming that you don't have any significant delays associated with having to overcome rejections from the examiner or opposition from third parties. The time frame is broken into two stages: (1) examination and (2) publication. It usually takes between four and eight months for the examiner to examine the application and issue an initial response (the examination phase). And once the mark passes the examination process, it will be published for six months to allow others to object (the publication phase). Assuming that there is no opposition within that six-month publication phase, the mark will be issued.

Nondisclosure Agreements

Contractual agreements, usually in the form of nondisclosure agreements (or NDAs), can be very helpful in protecting your inventions in a number of situations. Generally speaking, an NDA

Watch Video: John Merchant Explains Nondisclosure Agreements

http://www.tamaramonosoff.com/john-merchant-explains-non-disclosure-agreements/

is a contractual agreement that prohibits the disclosure and/or use of the invention that is being disclosed. If, for example, you need to discuss your invention with someone in order to get it built or documented, an NDA can help ensure that the recipient of the information will keep it confidential. Many consulting agreements and employment agreements actually have NDA language built in. Another common use of an NDA is during the initial marketing process. If you are interested in determining whether another individual or entity is interested in your invention, having an NDA in place beforehand can be critical.

A disclosure of information covered by an NDA does not count as a disclosure for patent purposes (foreign or domestic), and NDAs are generally effective in preserving trade secret information. If the discloser breaches the NDA by revealing or using the invention, it can be subject to contract damages and in some cases misappropriation of trade secret damages, in addition to any damages that might be available by proving patent infringement (assuming that you are successful in obtaining a patent covering the invention).

There is really no "standard" template for an NDA, and the terms of agreement can differ substantially, depending on the specifics of the technology being disclosed or the norms and realities of a particular industry. Sometimes the terms of the agreement will restrict the receiver of information from disclosing the received information to others without permission. Sometimes the terms of the agreement will also restrict the receiver from using the information. It is preferable, of course, to have both. Some NDAs are one-way agreements, while some are mutual in that both parties are both disclosing and receiving information. Regardless, you should make sure that the terms of the agreement are clearly written and that you understand them. Specifically identify the confidential materials and the names of the parties. Have the receiving party sign and date the agreement, and give a copy of the signed NDA to the receiving party, and also prepare any extra copies that may be needed if any other persons in the receiving party's organization are to sign also.

You should note that if the person with whom you enter into an NDA steals or copies your invention, your NDA will be of little value unless you have the funds to hire an attorney to sue the breaching party and/or your case is strong enough for you to get an attorney to take it on a contingent-fee basis.

Forms for nondisclosure agreements, as well as examples of many other helpful contractual legal documents, can be found for free simply by doing a Google search. Websites such as www.lawdepot.com and www.docstoc.com provide such forms. It is a good idea to check with an attorney to make sure the agreement is appropriate for your intended use.

NDAs Aren't Always Effective

It is important to reiterate that entering into an NDA does not guarantee that the receiving party will not steal your invention or disclose it to others. All agreements are subject to potential breach by the parties, and the specific terms of any agreement can be contested. Clauses within NDAs can be subject to interpretation by the courts. For example, noncompete clauses are limited in certain states (even if the language in the agreement says otherwise). In practice, you are likely to find that some people (or companies) will simply refuse to sign an NDA. This is often the case if they see little incentive to make a legal commitment for which they could later be sued. It can be a bit awkward to request an NDA signature from someone who is offering free input. When you cannot get someone to sign an NDA, ask that he agree to keep your conversation in confidence and then document this verbal agreement. This is not the best practice, but it is sometimes the best you can do. You might even send the recipient a letter confirming your agreement that the conversation was in confidence and requesting that he contact you in writing within a certain period of time if he disagrees with you. Something is better than nothing. The most important thing is to make sure that the receiving party understands and agrees that the information is "confidential" and that he agrees not to use it without your permission.

One of the ironies of the use of an NDA by inventors is that when an NDA is used for the purpose of showing a prospective licensee her invention, this targeted licensee is presumably a company that makes or sells similar items . . . in other words, very possibly a potential competitor. Even in the case where the potential licensee is willing to sign the NDA, it is uncommon for it to sign a noncompete clause because it doesn't want to be contractually precluded from competing against you (it is a competitor, why should it?). So, often the only NDA you can get in this situation is an NDA that binds the potential licensee to not sharing your idea with others. And, in that case, the agreement does not prevent the other company from making your product. The fear of being knocked off at this early stage is generally overblown, but it is important to understand the real protection, or lack thereof, provided by an NDA.

Taking On the World

U.S. patents provide rights only in the United States. If you want to prevent others from making, selling, using, or importing your invention in another country, you will need a patent granted by that country.

It makes financial sense to focus on the U.S. market first because it often offers the largest economy and largest potential market with spending power. This is generally true, although it is not necessarily true for certain products (inventions) that are more popular in other countries. Thus, you may also become interested in pursuing international markets and thus in securing the protections that are available in other countries. I took these steps for my first product, the TP Saver, but I have never done so since. At this point, I would need to have a very compelling reason to incur the added expense of foreign protection before I felt it was justified. It bears repeating that this is an area where you will want a professional's help, but I will address some key considerations for protecting yourself when going global.

Loose Lips

There are fundamental differences in intellectual property protections throughout the world. For example, the United States is the only major developed country in which an inventor has a year from the time an invention is publicly disclosed to actually file a patent. In the rest of the world, once an invention is disclosed publicly without a nondisclosure agreement or a patent filing in place, the patent rights are lost (there is an exception relating to the PCT Treaty covered in the next section). That doesn't mean that you can't sell your product in those countries; it just means that you won't be able to file for a patent. It's good to be aware of this when pursuing international options. As outlined earlier, the America Invents Act (AIA) has changed the U.S. law so that it is now more in line with the rest of the world regarding the first-inventor-to-file approach.

Proper Protection

To file for patents in most foreign countries (those that are members of the Paris convention), an inventor has one year from his first U.S. patent filing (provisional or nonprovisional) date to do so. There's one option that can buy you more time: applying through the Patent Cooperation Treaty (PCT). This will preserve your right to file patents on the same invention in other countries for a period of time. It also provides centralized filing procedures and a standardized application format. While there is a lot of information about the PCT process at www.uspto.gov, I would highly recommend that you consult an experienced patent attorney if you wish to go down this path.

While a PCT application is commonly referred to as an "international application," it is important to note that there is no such thing as an international patent. Patent rights are country- or region-specific. A PCT application simply preserves your rights to file in other countries or regions for a period of time. It will never become a patent itself. In order to obtain patent rights in a particular country or region, you still must file for a specific patent in that particular country or region, even after filing a PCT application.

A PCT application is not mandatory; you can file in each country individually without using the PCT process. But this process may be helpful under certain circumstances. As mentioned earlier, I filed a PCT application for the TP Saver. I wasn't ready to spend the money to file individual patents in separate countries, but I wanted to protect my rights to do so in the future if I felt that there was a need at a later date. The PCT gives you that option. It was expensive, costing approximately $7,000 at that time, but after much thought, I felt it was worth the investment. Today I most likely would not.

International Copyright Protection

Unlike patents, copyrights are a bit easier to protect; they're recognized by all treaty member countries (most of the world, with very few exceptions). However, rights to sue for copyright infringement vary by country. In the United States, generally speaking, you must register your copyright with the copyright office before you can sue someone for infringing on your copyright.

International Trademark Protection

International trademark protection is as complex as international patent protection. There are two routes you can take to protect your trademark outside the United States:

1. File in individual countries directly.
2. Use the Madrid Protocol. This protocol includes filing an application similar to the PCT application for patents. It's a little bit more efficient than a PCT application in that filing one application gives you trademark registration in multiple countries (the International Bureau handles filing in individual countries). However, each country will conduct its own examination of the trademark.

Chapter Wrap-Up

Patents can be very valuable tools, and you should consider them. But it is my opinion that having a patent is not essential for taking a product to market, and the inability to afford one should not be a deterrent to your progress. You'll find that a significant number of products sold are not patented. Often the urge to get a patent is driven by the fear of competition and by misinformation spread by (1) those who do not understand the process of taking a product to market, or (2) people who stand to profit from your patent filing. This is a good time to get comfortable with the fact that you are entering a competitive industry. Intellectual property laws and documents can be useful tools. However, they are only tools, and they are sometimes minimally effective in preventing competition. So, use them strategically if it makes sense, and tactically if possible. Again, remember that what you are trying to protect are those aspects of your product that provide you with a competitive advantage in the marketplace.

Consider your attorney's advice, but the final decision about whether to pursue intellectual property protection rests with you. While there are a number of do-it-yourself publications and other shortcuts that you can take during the patenting process, I highly encourage you to use a qualified expert should you decide to file for intellectual property protection. It can be expensive or even impossible to correct mistakes that a professional could have helped you avoid in the first place. Once you've made your filing decision, it's time to move on to your next important step: manufacturing. All the fundaments and resources are covered in the next chapter.

Getting the Goods

Video Message: Tamara Monosoff Introduces Chapter 5

http://www.tamaramonosoff.com/Tamara-Monosoff-introduces
-chapter-5/

Manufacturing

Now that you know that your product doesn't exist, you've made a successful prototype, and you've completed your market research, you're ready to move forward and manufacture your product. Even if you plan to license your idea to someone else, it's still useful to understand what goes into the manufacturing process and to determine the costs and manufacturing parameters of your own product. This will put you in a strong position to negotiate the best deal for yourself. (Learn more about licensing and negotiating in Chapter 9.)

This chapter goes into depth about choosing the right factory—including the pros and cons of domestic versus overseas manufacturing. It covers information on tariffs, freight forwarding, and customs, should you decide to manufacture overseas. Without a guide to follow, I learned a lot the hard way during the manufacturing stage, and

I'd like to help you avoid making the same mistakes I made. Other entrepreneurs mentioned in this chapter have also shared their stories about the ups and downs of manufacturing.

In this edition, not only are there new invaluable design and material sourcing directories (also mentioned in Chapter 2), but, most important, *proven* factory resources both in the United States and overseas that have been carefully vetted and generously shared by the entrepreneurs featured in this book.

We will discuss the manufacturing of "hard" and "soft" goods (see Chapter 2 for a detailed discussion), and there are new sections on producing environmentally friendly "green" goods and some of the ins and outs of developing food products. My aim here is to shed light on the manufacturing and importing process, give you a framework, and share as many resources and steps as possible to save you time, money, and untold frustration. By the end of this chapter, you will be on the right path. It will help you make your next big business decision—which manufacturer will produce your first run.

What Is Manufacturing?

Manufacturing is simply the process of making things. Companies manufacture nearly everything that we consume in our daily lives, right down to the food we eat. The manufacturing process can include any combination of industrial machinery, raw materials, and human labor. We are so accustomed to having and using these items every day that we don't even think about the effort it took to produce them.

Who's the Manufacturer in This Scenario?

There's a confusing use of terminology in the industry that I want to clarify before we start. While you think of the "manufacturer" as the factory with which you contract to produce or fabricate your product, it's important to note that retailers—to whom you will sell your finished product later—will refer to *you* (and your company) as the manufacturer. For purposes of this chapter, we'll still refer to the factory as "the manufacturer." But later, think of your factory as an extension of your company; together, you are the manufacturer.

Pinpointing the Right Manufacturer

There are countless types of manufacturers, producing adhesives, electronics, chemicals, hardware, machinery, tools, metals, plastics, rubber, and textiles, to name just a few categories and materials. The key is narrowing your search to an appropriate organization—one that specializes in the materials from which your product is made, in the volumes that you need, and at a price that is within your budget. For instance, you wouldn't approach a manufacturer that specializes in plastics to make a luxurious pillow.

To begin narrowing down factories, visit resource directories like www.thomasnet.com and www.IQSdirectory.com, where you will find a network of thousands of factories to choose from domestically. You can search by materials (vinyl, wire, cotton) and by state (see Chapter 2 for other useful resources).

In earlier chapters, you used Alibaba.com to gain information about production costs and competition. Now you can use this resource to find a factory. Try searching Alibaba (www.alibaba .com) and a similar website called Global Sources (www.global sources.com).

Americans as a Resource Around the Globe

There is an American Chamber of Commerce (AmCham) in most countries, which can be a great resource. The purpose of these offices is to serve Americans by helping to facilitate positive business relations between American businesses and the countries within which these AmCham offices reside. When my husband was offered a job in Hong Kong, I found the country's American Chamber of Commerce. I showed up at its office (I had not started Mom Invented at the time) and was welcomed graciously by the American staff. They introduced me to other women's business organizations (both American and Chinese), and I joined both, which eventually led to wonderful opportunities. The point is,

Dripsters Invented by Dawn Firsing-Paris

Watch Video Message from Dawn Firsing-Paris
http://www.tamaramonosoff.com/dawn-firsing-paris/

Dawn Firsing-Paris is the inventor of Dripsters (www.dripsters.com), a compressed sponge in the shape of a bulls-eye or star that absorbs ice pop drips. As the ice pop melts, the sponge absorbs the drips and begins to puff up—no more sticky hands or floors. Dawn's business was up and running quickly after she spotted what she needed on Alibaba.

The biggest obstacle was finding a manufacturing company that understood what I wanted and could make what I needed. I went to Alibaba.com, typed in the words "compressed sponges" in its search box, and instantly found several sponge companies. I e-mailed them all and worked it from there. I made my own prototype and sent it to China, and through e-mail and photos I was able to communicate the product line and specifications, although communication was not easy.

I would have preferred to find a manufacturer in the United States, but I couldn't possibly make them here because the price was too high. Even though it was relatively simple to find a sponge manufacturer overseas, I had issues with the ink that was to be printed on the sponges. Knowing that the ink in China is lead-based, I did more searching in the United States to find an ink manufacturing company. I didn't want kids or anyone else's kids to be exposed to lead. I found One Stroke Ink (www.OneStrokeInk.com) in Kentucky that made ink that can be cured onto a sponge. I had the ink made and shipped to my sponge factory in China.

reach out to anyone and everyone, as you will never know what you discover until you do.

To find specific contacts, visit www.uschamber.com, click on the "International" button, and locate the "AmCham Directory." You will then see a world map. Click on the area of interest on the map (for example, South America), and it will bring up all the AmCham office locations by country. (See more on choosing a U.S. or an overseas manufacturer further on in the chapter.)

There is another resource available through the U.S. government (www.export.gov) that encourages Americans to export their goods to other countries. If you develop a product that makes sense for global markets, go directly to the Sales and Marketing page (www.export.gov/salesandmarketing). The government offers a surprisingly large number of support services, including making business introductions to experts, suppliers, and partners in 80 countries.

There are other ways to find a manufacturer, including a more general Internet search using Google. I was recently mentoring an inventor who said that she wanted to make her product out of the same durable foam that Croc shoes are made from, yet she didn't know what that material was called or how to find it. In about one minute, I typed "footwear foam material" into Google and found out that it's called ethylene vinyl acetate (EVA). A list of suppliers with pricing then popped up, and I could see that it is readily available and inexpensive. Google quickly becomes an entrepreneur's best friend!

Word of mouth is also one of the best ways to ensure that you are working with someone reputable, so I recommend asking friends. (I often hear stories like, "Oh, yes, my good friend's husband does injection molds and works with overseas factories.") You will never know unless you ask. Also ask fellow inventors, prototype developers, suppliers, attorneys, and engineers to share their resources.

Once you have identified several companies that seem appropriate, start by visiting their websites so that you are better informed about their services *before* you call or e-mail them. I suggest that you interview at least three manufacturers before settling on one to partner with. Knowing the right questions to ask to compare and contrast different companies is important. Here's a list of questions to get you started:

1. What types of products do you make?
2. Do you have reference customers that I can contact?
3. What is your strength (textiles, plastics, metal, or other materials)?
4. Do you have minimum requirements? What is the smallest manufacturing run that I can do for my first order?

Sasquatch! Pet Beds

Watch Video Message from Tony Deitch
http://www.tamaramonosoff.com/tony-deitch/

Tony Deitch, the inventor of Sasquatch! Pet Beds (www.sasquatchpetbeds .com), "The World's Most Unique Pet Bed—It's Shoe Shaped," shares how he found a manufacturer that could produce such a large product (Sasquatch! Pet Beds measure 26 inches long by 10 inches high by 13 inches wide).

This was a very worrisome part of the process, as you never know what your business relationship with your manufacturer will be (that is, quality control) until you begin to work with that firm. We had done a lot of online research until finally our comfort level was strong enough to decide to try out MFG (www.MFG.com), which allows you to submit products (confidentially) to go out to bid. Our product is so big as an injection mold that not many manufacturers initially responded, as they were not able to make the tooling for the mold in the necessary size. (Big!) We wanted to make it domestically; however, we had no manufacturer from the United States even connect with us. We did, however, have a Chinese manufacturer who was honest enough to tell us that while he would have loved to make our product, it was too big for the firm's expertise in tooling, so he referred us to another manufacturer in China that could make it. So we had that firm make samples from our drawings, loved the quality, and have developed a very cordial relationship to this day!

5. Do you charge extra for samples? How long does it take you to produce samples, and when can I expect to receive them?

6. Is product packaging included in your pricing? Or do you outsource or subcontract the packaging?

7. If your product involves plastic, do you make injection molds? If so, how long will it take to produce a new mold? Note that a company typically won't offer a price quote at this point without seeing either a prototype or computer-aided design (CAD) drawings.

8. If your product involves fabric, do you make textile products? Do you work with my particular textiles (for example, cotton, canvas, silk, and neoprene)? If not, can you recommend any alternatives? How do you want product designs communicated? Do you expect a professional pattern, or will a hand sketch suffice?

9. If you are contacting an overseas manufacturer, ask if it complies with any particular standards. For example, is it ISO certified? (This is an international standard that applies to good business processes.) Or has it been inspected and approved by any other bodies or private companies? (Walmart and Target are both known to inspect and certify overseas manufacturers for their compliance with human rights and quality control standards.)

10. How much do you charge for your services? How do you break down your costs (for example, cost of mold, per unit cost, and packaging)?

11. What are the payment terms?

12. How do you handle damaged or defective product runs? Is there a percentage of product that must be damaged before you refund my money or do a new production run?

13. Can you assure me that you will not sell my product to others?

I offer these questions because, as a novice, I learned some tough lessons. Having specific questions in hand would have helped me a great deal and might even have enabled me to avoid the terrible experience I had with my first manufacturer. When I received the first 30 cartons containing thousands of packaged TP Savers, I eagerly ripped opened the first carton—only to find that the product packaging was falling apart. Although the production of the product itself was excellent, the plastic on the blister package (which houses the product and is glued to the backing card) was not adhering properly. Because we were launching our product at a trade show just three days later, my husband and I stayed up nearly all night gluing the blisters onto the packages. (It wasn't pretty!) We ended up gluing 1,500 pieces by hand. In addition to this "little problem," I discovered that the hang-hole on the package was centered. This seems logical; however, because of the design and weight of the product, the package hung crooked on a peg. The last thing retailers want is a package that hangs incorrectly on their store pegs. Therefore, I was also forced to hand-punch an additional hole on the top of each package in order to distribute the weight properly. Needless to say, I let go of our first manufacturer.

On a positive note, it was a valuable lesson learned—I found out what to ask and what to watch for. This enabled me to approach the second company with a few more questions and a lot more sophistication—proving once again that if you understand the process and know the facts, you can make sound business decisions.

Fringe Benefit

One of the benefits of using a manufacturer that specializes in your industry or in similar products (say, toys) is that the manufacturer will probably be familiar with labeling, safety, and other regulatory requirements. This is information that you've probably also uncovered when researching safety requirements in Chapter 2. Be sure to address and plan for these safety issues with your manufacturer.

First Things First

Before you actually choose a manufacturer and go into production, there are a number of additional issues that you'll need to address: communicating your design to the factory and deciding between domestic and overseas production.

Video Message from Randy Bieniek

http://www.tamaramonosoff.com/randy-bieniek/

Randy Bieniek is a pet artist who was commissioned to paint original pet paintings of cats and dogs using their real names and stories.

My children and neighbor kids always wanted to see who I was painting and got a kick out of my 3-D style. They always wanted to hear the "story" that went along with each painting. I manufactured note cards, and this morphed into creating eight dog-themed children's games called Zazzy Pals (www.zazzypals.com).

When I was trying to figure out how to manufacture all the different pieces of the game (as well as the packaging), I first asked others who were in the game business, became a member of the American Specialty Toy Retailing Association (http://www.astratoy.org), went to its trade show, and became a member of the Georgia Inventors Association. The most valuable information came from the Chicago Toy and Game Group (http://www.chitag.com) conference, where I arrived with my prototype, was able to consult with the "big dogs" of the industry, and asked for the names of game manufacturers.

I interviewed several game manufacturing companies based in the United States that source in China. After I first sourced in the United States, I realized that I could not be profitable with that plan, sorry to say. I got four formal "bids" for my game, did a lot of research (not entirely based on price), and talked to people who had used the two manufacturers I narrowed it down to. I had "sourced" all the "pieces" of the game and packaging myself (through alibaba.com) and had various samples sent to me, so by the time I actually got the formal bids, I had a good idea of what things should cost and figured in another $1 to $1.50 per unit that the American "middleman" (the game manufacturer) would need in order to make some profit. I quickly realized that it was going to take several factories (eight, to be exact!) to produce this, and I did not know whom I could trust, despite what "they" told me via e-mails. I ended up working with a New York company called Design Edge (www.DesignEdge.net) that knows the ins and outs of toy production, given that it does design work for Mattel and Hasbro.

Design, Drawings, and Prototypes

Depending on your invention, the best and most commonly used tools to communicate product design to your manufacturer are CAD drawings and an actual prototype. (CAD drawings work well for items that involve plastic or metal, but do not apply to textiles.) No matter where you've decided to manufacture, I recommend that you have these tools developed in the United States, to facilitate easy communication and get the ball rolling on a local level.

Though you may be able to take some steps directly with the manufacturer, creating a CAD drawing or an actual prototype with an engineer or a prototype developer is likely to save time and possibly avoid costly errors, especially if you're working with an overseas factory.

Although it is not necessary to fly to China or any other country to manufacture successfully, doing so gave Danielle the confidence that the production issues were in order. She used a creative combination of sourcing both in the United States and overseas and now sells her clothing line at high-end fitness and yoga studios nationwide.

Note: Other proven textile manufacturing resources are www.topwell-asia.com (overseas) and www.fibertrimsewing.com (United States).

The Great Debate

One of your big decisions during this process is to decide whether to produce your product domestically (in the United States) or overseas. Nearly every entrepreneur featured in this book had hoped to manufacture in the United States. A few were able to pull it off because of the nature of their product. However, the majority (including me) were not—even when they made great efforts to do so.

Talking strictly from a business standpoint, there are benefits and disadvantages to both. From a political standpoint, the issue often inspires heated debate. In this section, I will discuss this issue mainly from a business perspective; see my own story and decision-making process in the sidebar "More than Meets the Eye."

Research Pays Off!

Video Message from Danielle Dobin
http://www.tamaramonosoff.com/danielle-dobin/

Danielle Dobin left her job as a corporate lawyer and real estate developer to pursue her dream. She wanted to create flattering, luxury activewear and lifestyle clothing for women. Her dream came true when she launched her gorgeous product line, Apifeni (www.apifeni.com). Danielle did her design and sourcing homework. She started attending fabric trade shows, asked representatives of various mills for their contacts, attended sourcing conventions (she highly recommends: TexWorld [www.texworldusa.com], MAGIC [www.magiconline.com], and Outdoor Retailer [http://www.outdoor retailer.com]), visited resource websites in the United States like Fashion Center (www.fashioncenter.com), and then explored overseas websites like Panjiva (www.panjiva.com) and Piers (www.piers.com).

I conducted a lot of research. We work with a number of factories in the United States and abroad. Fashions Unlimited (www.fashions-unlimited.com) in Baltimore is an established full-service sewing contractor. Mi Ger Underwear Co. in Taiwan (http://miger.taiwan trade.com.tw) is a great source of seamless designs of all types, from shapewear to T-shirts. If you are going to produce abroad, you will have to research the tariff involved with importing, and you will need to use a customs forwarding agent to arrange shipment (these topics are covered later in this chapter). *Keep in mind that while sewing costs are much lower abroad, tariffs and shipping costs can be significant. Be sure to include this in your total cost of goods so that you are truly comparing apples to apples when you look at U.S. and Asian production costs.*

I decided to fly to China to meet one of my current suppliers. I wanted to meet the factory owners, approve the conditions for workers myself, and gain my own comfort level with the quality we could expect from our sewing contractors.

More than Meets the Eye

While companies are often vilified for "outsourcing American jobs," I can tell you that this issue is much more complex than this simple statement suggests. I have no intention of inflaming anyone who has strong views on the subject, and I'm not inclined to argue the issues in depth here. However, new inventors are often conflicted about the issue and come to me for advice.

This is what I tell them: developing and launching a product is expensive. The combined costs of design and development, production, transportation, distribution, and marketing are substantial—before you have paid yourself a nickel in salary. For example, 10 years ago, I sought out U.S. manufacturers to create a simple injection mold for my first product. A highly reputable U.S. company told me that it would cost $15,000 to produce. I then found that I could purchase the same mold in China for $1,500 or less. Because of my financial constraints at the time, the first option meant that I would have to abandon the project altogether. But if I pursued the overseas option, I could afford to give it a try. In the end, I was actually able to produce the mold—and my entire first run—for less than half the cost of the U.S. mold alone!

It's true that by producing my products in China, I have helped pay the salaries of hardworking Chinese workers rather than deserving American workers. However, since the time I launched my company, I have also spent thousands of dollars employing American workers who provided technical design, wrote my patents, created my packaging and branding, developed my website, handled my bookkeeping, set up my computer system, managed my warehouse, handled my shipping, and the list goes on. Had I abandoned the project, none of these additional dollars (at least five times the amount of money I've spent on manufacturing) would have found their way into the pockets of any American workers. And I would have forfeited my own income, as well.

One more point to consider: Americans are price-conscious, which means that purchasing decisions dictate where products are made, not the other way around. This is evident by the fact that most Americans shop at Costco, Sam's Club, Walmart, Target, QVC, Kmart, Dollar Store, and other discount chains every month. They have clearly shown that low prices drive their purchasing decisions. Take 10 minutes in any of these stores and read the "Made in" labels of the products displayed in the store, and this will validate the point that we—the customers—expect high-quality, low-cost products. Therefore, as a manufacturer, you will need to make this decision based on what your customers demand. As a small business, production will be your largest cost and the single biggest factor in your profit margin potential.

Some people might see this as focusing on profit rather than living by a moral code. Obviously, I disagree with the very basis of this position, but I am not looking to convert anyone. If you feel strongly about manufacturing in the United States, then by all means, do so. Many American factories are coming up with new ways to compete with overseas manufacturers on cost, and because of labor and fuel cost increases in China, they may just provide an option that benefits your bottom line.

Domestic Manufacturing

There are definitely benefits to working in the United States. Since there is no language barrier and there are minimal time zone challenges, working with an American company can reduce the frustration factor. In addition, delivery time frames are shorter, there is no involvement with customs and freight forwarding, and order minimums are generally lower. Plus, it can be comforting for a beginner to work with another party that is subject to the American legal system, with all the caution and understanding that goes with it.

While American factories have taken steps to compete on price with overseas factories, they are typically at a disadvantage because of the higher cost of U.S. labor and materials. But even though the production costs may be higher, you should still evaluate all factors to determine whether it might still make sense to manufacture in the United States. For instance, if you want a relatively small manufacturing run, paying more early on to a U.S. company might make sense, because you can receive feedback and evaluate demand before saddling yourself with a huge inventory. (Overseas manufacturers often require larger manufacturing runs.) In other words, if you order 200 units and your product is selling well, you may want to increase your run to 400 units for the next order, and so on. Once you see that there is strong interest in your product, you may then consider lowering your production costs by producing larger quantities overseas—which will increase your profit margin and your overall income.

Taking Matters into Your Own Hands

Video Message from Natalia Ortiz
http://www.tamaramonosoff.com/natalia-ortiz/

Even if you think you've got everything sorted out, things can change at a moment's notice, and your flexibility and problem solving need to go into high gear.

Natalia Ortiz, owner of Two Hippos (www.twohipposstore.com/)—a company dedicated to inventing and manufacturing high-end textile children's products—took her situation to an entirely different level. She started out with her first product called the Wall Bumpi—a bed rail bumper so that kids don't fall out of their beds. After her U.S. manufacturer closed down, rather than seeking out another, Natalia took matters into her own hands.

Making my prototype wasn't hard for me—I went to the local craft store and had fun. My husband cut out the different shapes of foam until we found the one we liked and then had a seamstress make the cover. For me, the difficult part was finding someone who would manufacture it for me. I wanted to stay in the United States because I wanted complete control. I looked for months to find the right company that would take me on as a small business. This was very frustrating at times, but I finally found it! We worked together for two years until the company closed. I then purchased its industrial machines, hired its seamstress, and rented a small office space to start making the products.

Grandmother Solves the Never Ending Search for Flip-Flops

Watch Video Message from Mary Ellen Hathorn
http://www.tamaramonosoff.com/mary-ellen-hathorn/

Mary Ellen Hathorn was motivated by her grandchildren to invent My Pair Tree (www.mypairtree.com), a flip-flop and sandal organizer. She had to learn how to create an injection mold and all the intricacies of manufacturing a product.

My grandchildren inspired me to invent the flip-flop holder. Every outing that we planned to the park or the ice cream store began by searching everywhere for missing flip-flops. I feel very fortunate to have built a business with one product that has been on the market for six years without knowing anything when I started. I found a local injection molding company in my area for the plastic parts, Noble Plastics (www.nobleplastics.com), and shopped online to purchase all the other pieces, which I initially put together myself. Now I'm speaking to Noble about taking over the full production of my product to streamline my business so that I can focus on sales.

What Is an Injection Mold?

If your product is to be made out of plastic, your initial professional prototype will most likely be hand-tooled by a handyman, a machinist, an engineer, or a 3-D printer. This prototype will help you create a functional product. The TP Saver went through eight hand-tooled renditions before it was perfected and ready to take to the next stage. It was at this point that I needed an injection mold to allow for mass production. A *mold* is a block of steel with a cavity that is created in the shape of your product. A machine is programmed electronically with the specifications from your CAD drawings to cut the cavity out of the steel (this is why good design specs are so important!).

Once you have your steel mold, plastic pellets are put into the mold and heated until they melt, turning into hot liquid. This hot liquid then settles into the mold, forming the shape of your product. When it has cooled and hardened, the product is ejected from the mold and the process is repeated until you have completed the number of parts you are manufacturing. A single mold can be designed so that many parts can be produced at the same time. This is sometimes referred to as a *family mold*.

Manufacturing Beyond the Borders

There are, of course, also benefits to manufacturing overseas, but to many people, this prospect is daunting. Given the differences in language, culture, currency, time zones, and distance, this fear is rational. However, because you're working with people who are economically motivated to make the process work, the greatest challenge is less a meeting of the minds than it is of logistics.

The greatest benefit from manufacturing overseas is, as I mentioned earlier, cost. Labor and materials are simply less expensive. And if you can produce your product for less money while maintaining high quality standards, you will have a better profit margin in the end (that is, if your product sells!). The greatest disadvantage of overseas manufacturing is that it adds another level of complexity to your business. In addition to understanding all the manufacturing issues, you'll also need to understand the fundamentals of freight forwarding, tariffs, and U.S. customs payments. Moreover, communication issues can be frustrating, and you must trust your vendor implicitly because there are so many more unknown factors. And, your vendor must trust you as well.

But be reassured: thousands of companies have good experiences with manufacturers in foreign countries. This is evident by the predominance of products on our shelves that were made abroad.

Watch Video Message from Karen Walker

http://www.tamaramonosoff.com/karen-walker/

Karen Walker, the Canadian inventor of SwaggerTag (www.swagger tag.com)—identification tags that not only keep track of your gear but reflect your personality—took the leap and found a manufacturer in China.

Finding an overseas manufacturer was a challenge at first. There's so much to learn, and it's very easy to run into trouble when you speak different languages and are halfway around the world from each other. Fortunately, my manufacturer was recommended by someone who had really done his research for his own product. This manufacturer has proven to be great to work with, and extremely helpful with both the prototype and manufacturing process. It helped to fine-tune my 3-D artwork to ensure that the units were well designed from both an end-user and a manufacturing perspective. And, I've learned how important it is to have a strong relationship with your manufacturer, and that's possible with Skype, e-mail, and the imperfect aid of translation software.

Regrettably, the stories about positive experiences attract much less media attention than scandals and corruption. The bottom line is that when you're choosing a factory to work with—either at home or abroad—you should use good shopping practices. Look at the factory's body of work, speak with references, and make sure that you understand and clearly agree on the expectations for the job and the terms.

Once you learn the steps and have all the systems in place, working with an overseas manufacturer is as simple as any of the other processes that you put into practice when you are running a business.

Note: Other *proven* plastic and rubber manufacturing resources are:

Li &Y Manufactory (www.liy.com.hk) (overseas)
Xiamen Cuten Nicety Accessories Industry Co.
  (http://cuten.en.alibaba.com/) (overseas)
MN Rubber (www.mnrubber.com) (United States and overseas)

If you do take the overseas route, note that there are a few international-specific issues to understand, like tariffs, freight forwarding, and customs brokerage, which are discussed next.

Totaling Your Tariffs

You'll probably have to pay a tariff when you import the product you've manufactured overseas. A *tariff* is basically the tax you pay to bring items into the United States. A specific tariff is assigned to your goods when they go through customs. It's important that you know in advance the amount you will be taxed, so that you can include this figure in your overall budget. The most efficient way to find this information is by visiting the website of the U.S. International Trade Commission (www.usitc.gov) and using the "Tariff Search Tool" to find the Harmonized Tariff Schedule.

If you are considering using different types of materials for your product, make sure to check out each of them on the Harmonized Tariff Schedule. For example, one of our Mom Invented products is made out of high-impact polystyrene, and the other out of polycarbonate. By clicking on plastics, I learned that I will be taxed 6.5 percent for the value of the goods that contain styrene and only 5.8 percent for the value of the goods that are part of the polycarbonate family!

Calculate the Production Cost for Your Product

Earlier in this book, there was a process for figuring out the estimated production cost of your product to see if it was financially viable for you to move forward in developing it. Now this is where the rubber meets the road. You have your CAD drawings or your textile blueprints, and now it's time to figure out exactly how much your product is "really" going to cost to produce by getting quotes from factories.

Now, add in the actual tariff. If your production cost is $2, add ($0.01 + 2.8%) = $2.06, which is the number that we found from www.usitc.gov. You may not think 6 cents is a lot, but it adds up when you're doing production runs in the range of 100,000 units. The cost of a production run for 100,000 units (we've received orders of this size from store chains and online catalogs) is $206,000. In that case, 6 cents ended up equaling $6,000 to pay the tariff.

You must also include freight forwarding (shipping from China, for example, to the United States). We typically add another estimated 10 percent to cover overseas and local freight (10 percent × $2 = $0.20 per unit). The price of freight, of course, will vary greatly depending on the size, weight, and nature of your product. So using a $2 per unit production cost, we would add $2 + $0.06 (tariff) + $0.20 (freight) = $2.26 per unit so far.

After your product has "landed" at the warehouse in the United States, domestic freight and distribution costs become sales costs and are not calculated as part of your gross margin. Generally speaking, as discussed previously, if your production costs are below 20 percent of the retail price, you will earn enough gross profit to cover your warehousing costs.

Use the chart on this page to determine the landed cost of your product.

Cost Type	Costs
Production cost per unit	
Tariff	
Freight forwarding	
Other	
Total:	

Now that you have your actual production cost per unit, multiply that number by 5 to get a sense of what the bottom end of the ideal retail price point will be if you intend to sell through retail channels.

Creating Your Calendar

There is often a lag in shipping when you are utilizing an overseas manufacturer. However, it's not usually because of simple distance. It's more often the result of a lack of knowledge about how the different steps in the manufacturing, shipping, and delivery process are related. For that reason, you need to establish a clear list with all of these steps, each of which has its own time requirements. It's also important that you know which steps are dependent on the completion of prior steps and which ones can be done simultaneously. For example, the production of your product may be able to coincide with the printing of your packaging. Once you know this, you can take your interdependent list of tasks, add up the number of days each task will take, and forecast a delivery date. Transportation and customs clearance may affect your time frame. Also, pay close attention to holidays in other countries. Chinese New Year, for example,

Watch Video Message from AnnDee Beckerman

http://www.tamaramonosoff.com/anndee-beckerman/

AnnDee Beckerman, founder of Infinity Headbands (www.infinity headbands.com), a line of interchangeable fashion hair accessories, shares some of her many "surprises" launching her business, ranging from language barriers with her factory to problems with production and packaging. However, her stamina has paid off. Today she is running the business from her home and outsourcing her wholesale fulfillment orders to MacDonald Training Center (www.mac donaldcenter.org/), a nonprofit organization that employs and empowers people with disabilities.

falls in February and lasts for two weeks; a period when *nothing* happens. Make sure to build enough time into your calendar to accommodate these holidays so that you don't disappoint customers who are waiting for your product. When I started out, this came as a surprise to me, and I lost sleep over late shipments resulting from unexpected holidays.

Freight Forwarding

Freight-forwarding companies are service providers that offer help with transporting goods overseas and in the United States. *Freight forwarding* refers to moving cargo from one location to another using every kind of transportation available: air freight, shipping, rail freight, and trucking. Freight-forwarding companies also oversee logistics management, customs brokers, and export documentation.

A quick Internet search will reveal many companies that offer this service. However, if you feel more comfortable going with a well-known brand name your first time around, FedEx offers door-to-door service from countries around the world to the United States through its FedEx Trade Networks (www.ftn.fedex.com/us/). UPS also offers freight-forwarding services (http://www.ups-scs .com/support/freight-forwarding.html). Note that using freight-forwarding companies can be expensive, so shop around if you're not going to go with the big brands. I've used Transworld Shipping (http://www.twship.de/) successfully, but there are less expensive companies to choose from. And once you choose a preferred company, save money by going with a "consolidated" shipment, which means that you'll share a large container—and thus share the costs of shipping—with other importers. In industry terms, this is called *LTL* (less than load container).

Customs Brokerage

Just as when you cross international borders and must show your passport for clearance, the products that you import must also pass muster in order to enter the United States, going through U.S. Customs for approval. Though some freight-forwarding companies offer their own customs brokerage services, you may need to contract with a separate customs broker to handle the paperwork and help clear your shipment at the port when the vessel containing your shipment arrives.

This all sounds complicated, but I have found that between your factory, your freight carrier, and your customs broker, they know how to handle the process and will help you each step of the way.

There are certain documents that are required if your shipment is to clear U.S. Customs. The following are the basics; your particular product may require more. A customs brokerage firm can help you determine whether this is the case.

- **Packing list.** This document outlines the contents of your shipment, including the number of cartons and a description of your goods. It's prepared by the factory that manufactures your product and is given to the shipping company.
- **Bill of lading**. This outlines the contents of your shipment, and is prepared by the shipping company and given to you. It should exactly match the manufacturer's original packing list. In other words, if 22 cartons left the factory in Xiamen, China, the same number should be listed on the bill of lading headed for Long Beach, California.
- **Arrival notice.** This is a document prepared by the shipping company that announces the arrival of your goods. This will be sent to you upon the shipment's arrival. When you receive this fax, be prepared to send a payment immediately so that the shipment can be moved right after it clears customs. Delays in moving your goods will often result in penalties, unless the shipping company has the capability of warehousing your goods. Be sure you know the logistics of this before your shipment arrives at the port.
- **U.S. Customs bond.** Your customs broker can prepare a customs bond. This document is required by U.S. Customs

for any shipment over $2,000 in value, so that it's provided with "insurance" for payment upon arrival. For instance, if U.S. Customs has difficulty getting payment from you, the importer, it wants to be assured that someone will pay the duty and any fees. It's a relatively simple (one-page) application.

Your customs broker will ask you for copies of these documents and will be physically present to shepherd your shipment through customs. It's also possible to do your own customs brokering; for an outline of the process, along with the appropriate forms, go to the U.S. Customs and Border Protection website (www.cbp.gov) and click on the "Forms" button on the navigation bar. However, this experience can be frustrating and challenging. You may find yourself at the docks without proper documentation or information, which can delay taking possession of your goods. I believe a customs brokerage firm is well worth the money. These firms handle absolutely everything and usually charge about $200 to $400 per shipment. This amount is paid in addition to the U.S. Customs bond. Your tariff is also due at this time.

Cost-Cutting Measure

A common mistake when you're manufacturing for the first time is to believe that you'll need only one shipment per year. However, if your product is wildly popular and you need more inventory, you'll soon need additional shipments. Note that you are charged duty on every shipment. It is also mandatory that you purchase a U.S. Customs bond. Your choices include single entry bonds, which are currently charged at $5.50 per $1,000 in value with a minimum of $55.00 and are purchased for each individual shipment. Or you can purchase a continuous bond that can be used for ongoing shipments at a minimum of $50,000 coverage for a fee of $475.00. If you anticipate more than one shipment per year, I recommend the continuous bond because it allows for unlimited shipments throughout the year.

Manufacturing Know-How

Now that you've weighed the pros and cons of domestic versus overseas manufacturing, and you've evaluated your choices and hopefully chosen a partner, there are a number of issues concerning materials, labor costs, samples, specifications, and packaging that you need to be aware of as you go through the production process.

Making the Most of Materials

In talking about doing your market research and developing your prototype (Chapters 1, 2, and 3), I mentioned that you should pay particular attention to materials. Once again, you'll need to do some research on pricing, suppliers, durability, and quality. Be aware that some regions or countries have better access to, and pricing on, certain types of materials. Therefore, keep an open mind. You can turn to your manufacturer for advice and expertise, but don't always take your initial information at face value.

Luxury Activewear by Apifeni and the Green Cycler— the First-Ever Kitchen Precomposter

Danielle Dobin, founder of Apifeni (www.apifeni.com), the luxury activewear and clothing line for women (mentioned earlier in this chapter), asked her fabric supplier a simple question,

"Can we work together to develop eco-friendly high-performance materials?" I learned that the supplier was already working on creating fabric made from recycled plastic bottles. The fabric is beautiful and feels like thin, silky material that is cool to the touch. It is nothing like what you would expect. I knew immediately that we needed to design a collection around this recycled poly material because it fit so well with our company's mission of social responsibility.

Thinking Green

Consumers are now paying close attention to green materials and will even pay a little extra if they can see the health or environmental benefits. Retailers, buyers, and distributors are responding to consumer interest. I've been asked directly by buyers if I have new organic products to show them. This will also potentially create new sales and media opportunities for you as well. So, as you are exploring materials for your new product, think on a broader scale and ask

The Green Cycler Is Green Inside and Out

Video Message From Gail Loos
http://www.tamaramonosoff.com/gail-loos/

Another great example is the Green Cycler (www.thegreencycler.com), created by single mom Gail Loos. Not only does this beautifully designed kitchen precomposter (think high-end yet affordable kitchen appliance) help us compost easily, but Gail also did everything possible to use green materials in her manufacturing process. Gail explains,

We use recycled plastic in the production of Green Cyclers. We also use repurposed or recycled materials whenever possible in our packaging and user materials. For example, we use large plastic bags that were previously headed to the landfill in huge quantities to cover Green Cyclers inside their boxes. With the exception of those recycled plastic bags, all of our other packaging uses recycled paper and 100 percent compostable components. Our other primary product is ZeoPacks, which are super-green recyclable filters made from volcanic zeolite crystals, which, as it turns out, are nature's super-effective odor magnet. I was aiming to create an odor filter that could be recharged and reused indefinitely to replace single-use charcoal filters. Happily, we've accomplished that goal. Not only does the Green Cycler make composting inexpensive, practical, and a completely natural solution for feeding our organic gardens, but the U.S. Environmental Protection Agency says that composting is a critical step toward solving our current environmental crisis.

suppliers and factories what "green" materials you could consider for your product. The range of possibilities may surprise you!

Many new alternative materials and manufacturing solutions are becoming available every day. With some thought and effort, and with the guidance of others, you can often find creative solutions. When you are interviewing manufacturers to produce your product, ask them if they are working with green materials. Another excellent resource is CleanGredients.org, which works in partnership with the U.S. Environmental Protection Agency. For $150, you can add your name to its mailing list and access a phenomenal amount of information about already EPA approved green materials. Learn more about the benefits of joining CleanGredients.org in the sidebar.

Learning About Labor

The cost of labor can significantly influence your production costs. Just as they do when you get your car repaired, labor costs can often dwarf the cost of materials and parts when it comes to manufacturing your product. For instance, a typical U.S. manufacturing shop will charge anything from $25 to $100 an hour for labor. Say it takes exactly two minutes to assemble your product. If you go with a shop that charges $25 an hour ($0.42 per minute), your per unit labor cost

Benefits of Joining CleanGredients®

CleanGredients is a unique partnership between GreenBlue, the U.S. Environmental Protection Agency (EPA), and industry that benefits suppliers and formulators alike in a number of important ways.

CleanGredients builds on market demand for "green" products.

CleanGredients directly links chemical suppliers and formulators through an online database. Existing resources identify "known bad" chemicals; CleanGredients identifies preferable alternatives and provides supplier contact information, links to websites, material safety data sheets, technical fact sheets, and more.   Source: CleanGredients.org.

is 84 cents. If you go with a shop that charges $50 (a typical figure for excellent-quality work), your two-minute labor cost per unit is $1.67. Obviously a 100 percent difference in labor can change your profit margin significantly.

Getting Samples

Before you mass-produce your product with your chosen manufacturer, you'll want to examine samples of the product with the final materials you've selected. This will give you a true picture of what the final product will look like, and it will raise a red flag about any last-minute design flaws or issues with the materials. When I was testing the TP Saver sample, I used all my strength to try to break the product. When I couldn't, I was satisfied.

Do good-quality samples ensure that the quality of your entire production run will be maintained? Not necessarily. Even if you see high-quality samples, there are no guarantees that the quality will be maintained. However, if you have an initial sample that you both agree to, you have something to fall back on if a substandard run is later delivered. Be sure to get in writing what your recourse is, should you receive poor-quality product. For instance, if the factory ships you 40,000 units of damaged goods, what are your remedies? An honest company will have no problem signing such an agreement, because it stands behind its work. This is especially important when you are manufacturing overseas, because you can't visit the factory to oversee production yourself.

Manufacturing and Printing Specifications

Before you send your manufacturer the first purchase order, the go-ahead for it to mass-produce your product (sample available at www.TamaraMonosoff.com/Guides), make sure the company has the proper specifications that explicitly spell out the details that you and the manufacturer have agreed to. These specifications are in the form of a manufacturing and printing specifications (MAPS) document that contains details in categories relevant to your project (for example, printing and packaging, product quality and traits, and packing and shipping).

Specifics that you may wish to include in the printing category, for example, are the trim size and card stock of your packaging, and digital art that details your packaging designs, colors, front of backing card, back of backing card, and press proofs.

For the product itself, you'll want to clarify details like color, style, material used, process notes, and numerous other items. For packing, you'll want to pinpoint how many units should go into an inner carton, how many inner cartons should be included in a master carton, and what will be printed on the outside of your cartons. And shipping information should include all delivery requirements.

Unfortunately, many people do not take the time to create MAPS documents for their manufacturer. But I highly recommend that you do so, in order to have an organized record of the entire process, as well as the terms you both agreed to. Once your manufacturer agrees to the terms of your MAPS document,

What Are Pantone Colors?

The Pantone Matching System is the worldwide standard for color reference. By referring to Pantone color guides and mixing formulas, designers and printers across the world and across language barriers can clearly communicate exact color requirements and expectations. You can purchase your own Pantone Formula Guide by visiting www.pantone.com.

There are many variations of each color, and each color is assigned a number. The Pantone standard ensures that everyone is on the same page. For instance, if I simply told my manufacturer that I want my product to be red, he could choose whichever red he liked—it might be an orange-red, pink-red, or blue-red, while I expected a fire-engine red. Choosing a specific Pantone color can eliminate any miscommunication. Pantone also offers color chips that you can rip out of a chip book and send to your manufacturer.

you'll be able to send your first purchase order to officially start the process.

Proper Packaging

First-time inventors are often so consumed with the production of their product that they leave the packaging decisions until the last minute. But packaging is an integral part of your process, and you need to give it special consideration. In many cases, the packaging is more complex than the development of the product itself. After all, you have less than three seconds to get consumers' attention when they are walking down the aisle of a retail store, so the package needs to "interrupt" their thinking and draw attention to itself. Add to this the size (the dimensions of the package itself) and other retailer expectations, and the process becomes even more challenging. For instance, various retailers will have their own packaging preferences. After interviewing both independent stores and big-box stores like Walmart for my own product, I chose to adhere to Walmart standards so that my product would be accepted easily everywhere.

Your packaging should clearly communicate the name and function of your product. Every word counts and you need to communicate the contents of the package and its features and benefits in the quickest way possible. If the consumer doesn't get it, she just won't buy it.

Once again you can learn from my own mistake. When I began developing my own packaging for the first time, I hired a marketing company. The graphic designer was very artistic, and I loved his packaging design! But after launching the TP Saver, I found that people liked the package—but had absolutely *no* idea what was inside. The package was not clearly communicating the contents or function of my product to consumers, and this was a potentially fatal mistake for sales. Even though the packaging was pretty, it just wasn't effective.

While a graphic designer is required to produce retail-ready packaging, not every person who calls herself a graphic designer is an expert in this specialized area. When you interview graphic designers request samples of product packaging that they have done.

People read from left to right. The company's brand should appear at the top left, the name of the product in the center, and the function of the product beneath the title. The features and benefits should be communicated in quick and easy-to-read bullets. With

FIGURE 5.1

Designed by an artist rather than a retail packaging expert, my original TP Saver packaging was flawed. While it looked nice, the logo was not effectively placed to maximize brand recognition.

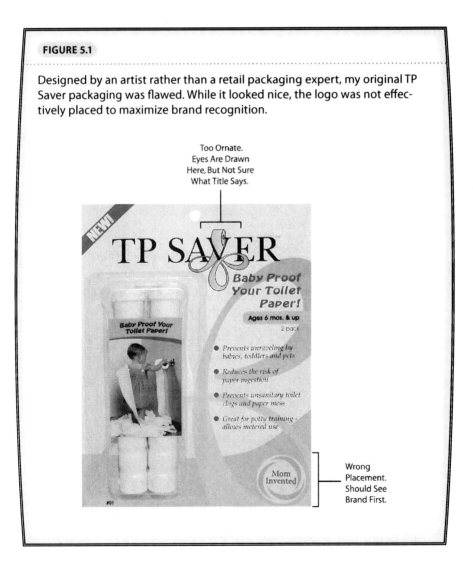

these key points in mind, the new designer was able to transform my package into something that both consumers and retailers understood and responded well to.

There are many options when it comes to packaging, and your choice depends on your final product and how it will be displayed. Your packaging may consist of anything from a cardboard box that's displayed on a store shelf to a blister package that's displayed on a hanging rack—with countless options in between. This is a decision

FIGURE 5.2

This is what my new TP Saver packaging looked like after being redesigned by a retail expert. Note that the Mom Invented logo was moved for better brand recognition.

that will be made in collaboration with your expert team (designer, printer, and factory) and is based on several factors, including the shape of your product, its size and weight, how it will be shipped, and how it will be displayed.

Manufacturers (both in the United States and overseas) typically outsource the printing portion of the packaging. In other words, the packaging is often printed off-site and then returned to the manufacturer so that it can insert the product and finalize the packaging for delivery to the client. The packager will use the designs your graphic artist created when producing the final packaging.

Warehousing

Unless the shipment is scheduled for delivery to your home or you've already contracted with a fulfillment house, you'll need to make arrangements for the storage, or warehousing, of your products. Many shipping companies also offer warehousing options, which can simplify the process for you. Each service has a separate fee, so be sure to get a proper rundown of costs. Make sure you understand all the steps you need to take to get your items from the manufacturer to your warehouse, and how much each of these steps will cost.

You may also choose to find your own warehousing options. Perhaps it's a monthly rental at an established self-storage facility. Or perhaps a friend or family member has an unused garage or storage capacity that he'll lend you. Once again, your options will be largely dictated by the size and amount of your inventory. If it's 10 boxes, a homegrown solution may work, but if you're beginning to store thousands of units, you'd probably rather go with a commercial storage facility that can monitor shipment inventory and pickup. As I mentioned earlier, companies that specialize in warehousing and fulfillment can be found online. Another great option is to work with a manufacturer that has extra space and staff already in place.

Shipping and Warehousing in the United States

Outsourcing the warehousing function gives you more time to spend on sales and marketing—and helps you avoid the challenge of storing boxes in the living room! Compare the costs of multiple vendors. The costs of line items vary from warehouse to warehouse. Some warehouses may simply charge a percentage of your order. Be prepared for the following potential costs:

- Setup fee
- Receiving-packages fee
- Storage fee by square or cubic foot or by pallet
- Stacking or shelving fee per box
- Fee for removing item from shelf to fulfill an order
- Packaging fee and box fee (if warehouse must break open an existing box)
- Shipping-label fee

Filling Your Orders

Your next decision will be whether to stock inventory and ship it to your customers from your home, or to hire a fulfillment distribution and warehousing company. Many inventors start out doing the shipping themselves, as I did, packaging their product on the kitchen table. However, when you grow, it is nearly impossible to keep up, and it is critical to the success of your company that you provide excellent customer service. The last thing you want to do is upset your retailers by sending out late shipments. Packing products is surprisingly time-consuming, as it also demands the proper shipping documents. To find an appropriate fulfillment house, search the Internet or ask other inventors whom they recommend.

Amazon to the Rescue

Fulfillment by Amazon (www.amazon.com/FBA) is now offering warehousing and shipping services for small businesses. It goes beyond any other fulfillment house that I have ever seen. It posts your product on Amazon and handles the orders, shipments, and customer service.

Domestic Shipping Tip

For shipments of less than one pound, the U.S. Postal Service Priority Mail is about the best value a small business can find. At the time of this printing, you can get two- to three-day delivery, a free box, and online tracking for $5.05 (with the Postal Service's box) anywhere in the continental United States. You can track all your packages at www.usps.gov/clicknship. Also, the Postal Service will ship you as many free boxes as you want—at no charge—*and* preprinted labels with your company name. Call 800-222-1811 to order preprinted labels and boxes.

Watch Video Message from Annie Pryor

http://www.tamaramonosoff.com/annie-pryor/

Annie Pryor, inventor of Mommy Genius Drying Racks (www.mommygenius.com)—a kitchen countertop accessory that provides the perfect place for baby bottles, dish towels, storage bags, and much more—says that FBA has been a lifesaver.

I am using Amazon's fulfillment services to ship my drying racks. I send a few large boxes of drying racks to Amazon warehouses each week. They ship the drying racks to the customers when they get an order. It is so much easier, less time consuming, and less expensive to use Amazon than if I were shipping each order myself.

What's Food Got to Do with It?

Over the past decade, I've heard from entrepreneurs that although they were able to benefit from the first edition of this book, food and formulated products (household cleaners, shampoos, food, and vitamins) are an entirely different category of manufactured goods that have a different set of standards and regulations at both the federal and the state levels.

While entire books have been written on the topic; like Gordon Fuller's book *New Food Product Development: From Concept to Marketplace*, I thought you would benefit from hearing a few stories directly from the women entrepreneurs who have navigated this labyrinth.

Spoonful of Comfort

Watch Video Message from Marti Wymer
http://www.tamaramonosoff.com/marti-wymer/

Marti Wymer created Spoonful of Comfort (www.spoonfulofcomfort.com), which sends chicken soup as a special gift to friends and family members who may need a little extra tender loving care. Marti tells us who inspired her to start her business.

My business was inspired by my mom. In October 2007, I received a phone call from my mother telling me that she had been diagnosed with lung cancer. I was shocked, scared, and panicked. The hardest part about hearing the news was that she was living thousands of miles away. I was so upset and felt so helpless being so far away. I needed to "do something." I looked into sending flowers or fruit, but nothing seemed appropriate. I wanted to show

Continued

her how much I cared, and in some way comfort her. I immediately thought of
chicken soup—it's what she (like many mothers) used to make to comfort me.
And the idea for Spoonful of Comfort was born.

Just six weeks later, I lost my mother. During her final weeks, she got lots of
soup and other comforts from many of her 11 siblings and close friends. In her
honor, it is my goal to help others who have sick loved ones. It is my promise
to make and deliver a Spoonful of Comfort to your loved ones with as much
care as if I were sending it to my own mother.

**Tamara: What hurdles did you need to overcome to bring a food product
to market?**
Marti: To be completely candid, it was a nightmare! The difficulty finding this
information almost shut the business down before I even got started! What
is so tricky about the food industry is that there are so many different regulations depending on the type of food you make and where and how you are
distributing your product—in state or out of state. I wish I had an easy, clear-
cut answer for you, but I don't.

Here are a few places one should start:
- Local Department of Health
- Food and Drug Administration (FDA.gov)
- U.S Department of Agriculture (USDA.gov)
- Industry websites and trade magazines for contacts and consultants.

Tamara: How do you keep your food product from spoiling?
Marti: We freeze our product and ship it using insulated shipping liners and
gel packs.

Tamara: How did you figure out how to do that?
Marti: Trial and error at the beginning! Now that we are beginning to see
significant growth, we felt it necessary to contract with a supply chain consultant. Since then, we have hired cold chain logistic specialists to help with our
packaging. Companies that manufacture and supply insulated boxes are great
resources and can help you through the process. Shipping companies like
FedEx and UPS also have awesome resources that I should have used more!

Tamara: Did you hire a food product formulator?

Marti: I did not. I just had my chef make up a good recipe. We are in the soup business, and so we had a few iterations of our soup recipe done by our own highly qualified chef.

Tamara: What has surprised you the most about bringing a food item to market?

Marti: Food is a *very* tricky item to bring to market, as it is so subjective. People have such individual and different tastes that it can be tricky to please everyone.

Tamara: Is there anything personal about the experience that you would like to share?

Marti: Every day I am in business, I get to think about my mother. I have built the business as a result of her death. Of course, I hope we have a very successful business that continues to grow, but at the end of the day, it's been so pleasing to help others provide this unique approach to gifting.

If you want to learn more, visit www.spoonfulofcomfort.com.

A New Way to Take Your Vitamins!

Watch Video Message from Hallie Rich
http://www.tamaramonosoff.com/hallie-rich/

Hallie Rich invented alternaVites (www.alternaVites.com) as a response to the more than 100 million Americans who have difficulty swallowing pills (including kids). Hallie created an alternative so that everyone can take their vitamins.

Tamara: What inspired you to start your business?

Hallie: I am the third generation in my family to be part of the vitamin industry as formulators, manufacturers, and marketers. Over the years, the most

Continued

common question I was asked was, "What vitamins do you take?" and my answer had always been the same: "None; I can't swallow pills." I had to admit to everyone that I couldn't benefit from the vitamins that I not only spent years promoting, but also passionately believed in. Since I wasn't experiencing any of the benefits that so many studies report or that I had personally witnessed, I became very aware of the fact that vitamins can't help you if you can't take them. When I discovered that I was not alone, and that everyone had reasons for why they didn't take vitamins, I was motivated to create alternaVites, a new type of multivitamin that would fit into everyone's lives and finally eliminate both the reasons and the excuses people have for not taking their vitamins.

AlternaVites is the most versatile vitamin, since you can sprinkle it on your tongue, where it melts in your mouth (think pixie stick!), or you can mix it into yogurts, smoothies, shakes, and puddings—whatever you prefer! It's available for both adults and kids. AlternaVites is available in amazing and delicious flavors, is free of sugar and gluten, is vegetarian and certified kosher, and is available in convenient stick packs that make it both portable and convenient!

Tamara: What hurdles did you need to overcome to bring a food product to market?

Hallie: Bringing a supplement product to the market is difficult at best, but not impossible. Despite rumors and innuendos, the dietary supplement industry is heavily regulated. Rules and regulations must be followed. From development and manufacturing to marketing and distribution, all aspects of each product must comply with the laws that govern the dietary supplement industry, which is overseen by both the FDA (Food and Drug Administration) and the FTC (Federal Trade Commission). This includes, but is not limited to, the sourcing of raw materials, determining the appropriate and proper nutrient levels for the formula and age group, following good manufacturing processes (GMPs) and guidelines, and adhering to label requirements. Finding reliable and trustworthy manufacturers, regulatory attorneys, and research and development personnel with which to align yourself is key.

Tamara: How do you keep your food product from spoiling?

Hallie: Dietary supplement products have expiration dates on them, which are supported by careful stability testing, evaluation, and analysis. Once that time frame is established, the expiration date is added to the label for customer reference to ensure potency and freshness. If you are using properly sourced nutrients and ingredients, expiration dating should be a couple of years from the date of manufacture. More so, the label should still meet its nutritional breakdown at the time of expiration.

Product integrity is the key to Rich Vitamins, which is further evidenced by the fact that alternaVites and alternaVites Kids are both packaged in daily-dose stick packs. Not only does this packaging type provide convenience and portability, but it acts as a secondary barrier that can help to protect the product against elements that have the potential to degrade vitamin products over time, like heat, light, humidity, and air.

Tamara: Did you work with formulators?

Hallie: Yes, we did work with formulators and food scientists. It was very important to me to use someone with experience not only in the supplement industry, but with food and flavors as well.

Tamara: Is there anything personal about the experience that you would like to share?

Hallie: Starting my own company has also offered me the ability to help in a greater context as well. It has always been, and continues to be, important to me, and therefore to my company, to give back. That is why Rich Vitamins donates a portion of our sales each year to support charities, most often cancer charities. This is a cause that is particularly close to my heart, as my father (who was not only my mentor in the vitamin industry but was also regarded as a pioneer in the field) passed away from cancer a few years ago.

To learn more about alternaVites visit: www.alternavites.com.

Mom to the Rescue with Natural Remedies

Watch Video Message from Carolyn Harrington
http://www.tamaramonosoff.com/carolyn-harrington/

Maty's Healthy Products (www.matyshp.com), which include All Natural Cough Syrup, Baby Chest Rub, and Vapor Rub, were all created because Carolyn Harrington was on a mission to improve her daughter's health.

Seventeen years ago, Carolyn Harrington's daughter was born with severe heart defects that required two open-heart surgeries before she reached the age of five. Carolyn got to work doing research on natural ways to help her daughter regain her health and keep her healthy. It soon became a passion. Over the years, she developed natural remedies for her family and friends. Then her husband suggested that she take the remedies to market so that others could benefit. That's when Maty's Healthy Products was born. They were launched at the Natural Products Expo in 2009, where they were a hit, and they can now be found in 32,000 retail outlets around the country.

Tamara: How did you come up with the recipe for your cough syrup?

Carolyn: When we decided to start the business, I had to gather all the knowledge on the remedies I used, and I worked hard to come up with the first production formula. We were all excited about getting started, and we got all the ingredients for what I thought would be the home run formula that would save the world. My family all gathered around the kitchen to watch the making of our first batch. I just knew that this was it, the next big idea. Everything went smoothly, and the time came to taste the cough syrup. We each took a taste, looked at each other, and nearly spit it out. It tasted awful. We were shocked, and we went to bed that evening all discouraged. Then, in the middle of the night, I came up with an idea that changed the formula enough to allow it to taste good without jeopardizing its effectiveness. The rest is history.

Tamara: Do you manufacture your products yourself?

Carolyn: We searched for contract manufacturers on the Internet and began speaking with everyone we knew for a referral. We interviewed many of them and finally decided on one. We also use our contract manufacturer for distribution. The manufacturer does all the fulfillment out of its warehouse. Fulfilling orders to retailers is very complicated and requires more shipping expertise than would be needed to ship to an end user.

Tamara: Did you seek out a professional formulator to assist you?

Carolyn: Yes, but not to formulate the product. We hired a formulator to help with issues of product stability. We also use a consultant to help with questions we have about different ingredients. The best way we found to locate professionals is to ask people who we already worked with: our suppliers, our comanufacturer, and sometimes even customers. People in the industry have connections that they are usually willing to share.

Tamara: Did you have to get your formula safety tested?

Carolyn: We do extensive testing on our products. For every ingredient that enters our manufacturing facility, we do what is called an identity test to ensure that the ingredient we received is what we ordered. We also require a certificate of analysis, provided by the supplier, before we can receive each ingredient.

Then for our cough syrups, which are ingested, we do additional testing once the formula is compounded. This test ensures that there is no contamination and that there is proof of the substance's integrity before it is bottled.

For any tests we do on our products, we send them out to an independent lab, which ensures the integrity of the tests.

Tamara: What about the Food and Drug Administration? Did you have to follow any regulations?

Carolyn: Since ours are all-natural products, we are regulated by the FDA differently from drugs. The FDA regulates them as a postmarket regulation, which means that they must live up to their label claims and, of course, be safe for use. If there are any complaints in the marketplace, the FDA steps in and investigates. This is similar to food products.

Continued

The FDA also requires the products to be made in a GMP-compliant facility. There are strict codes of manufacturing that any facility must adhere to, and the FDA audits facilities frequently, including ours.

One of the first things we did when we decided to produce our cough syrups was to locate a good FDA attorney. He helped us with constructing labels for our products and also helped us with regulation issues.

Tamara: Did your retailers require proof that your product adhered to these regulations?

Carolyn: Each retailer has us fill out extensive forms and sign documents confirming that our products are made in a GMP-compliant facility and that they meet any FDA regulations.

To learn more about Maty's Healthy Products, visit www.matyshp.com.

This Stay-at-Home-Mom Turned Her Passion for Honey Bees into a Buzzing Business: Bee True Products

Video Message from Blythe Weston
http://www.tamaramonosoff.com/blythe-weston/

Like the other women mentioned in this section, Blythe Weston started her business because of someone special in her life. She has three beautiful daughters, but at age seven, her daughter Brinly was diagnosed with cystic fibrosis, a genetic and progressive lung disease. This inspired Blythe to begin a personal journey to find ways to boost her family's immune system. And she found one solution buzzing in her backyard.

Blythe: I got my first beehive and started beekeeping four years ago. These amazing creatures give back so much to our environment. In addition to honey, bee pollen is an amazing super-food that has been used for centuries! Bee pollen contains at least 22 amino acids, 18 vitamins, 25 minerals, 59 trace elements, 11 enzymes or coenzymes, 14 fatty acids, 11 carbohydrates, and approximately 25 percent protein. It is extremely rich in carotenes, which are metabolic precursors of vitamin A. It is also high in B complex; vitamins C, D, and E; and lecithin. I have created infused natural bee pollen blends in a variety of flavors: Chocolate & Chai, Honey Hemp Toasted Oat, and Spiced Pumpkin.

Tamara: What was the most challenging part of bringing your Bee True Products to market?
Blythe: I've worked very hard on my recipes to make bee pollen more delicious. But one of the biggest challenges was finding a commercial kitchen and the right information about food licenses, liability insurance, and regulations and requirements. I started out by contacting my city's health department and learned that to sell my products locally, I would need to take a class to get a food manager's certificate. I also learned that I would have to pay extra taxes in the city in which the food is manufactured. You also must have your business established as an LLC or sole proprietorship in order to get your liability insurance. This information is typed on the insurance card that you have to show when you rent a commercial kitchen. One website that was invaluable and offers online classes to obtain the relevant certificates is www.learn2serve.com. You type in your city anywhere in the United States and the page with your local information, requirements, and available classes will pop up.

Tamara: How did you resolve the issue of finding a commercial kitchen?
Blythe: I looked for a long time and found commercial kitchens to be very expensive, and then I came up with a great solution at a fraction of the cost. I volunteer at my daughter's middle school PTA, and I learned that its concession stand met all the requirements that I needed. The best part is that the money that I pay for rent is donated directly to the school. It's very cheap ($50 for unlimited use each time).

To learn more about Bee True Products, visit www.beetrueproducts.com.

Chapter Wrap-Up

You may be surprised by all the elements of manufacturing beyond the assembly line—factors like materials, labor, packaging, shipping, and warehousing. But with an awareness of all these factors (and the potential costs associated with them), you'll be able to plan and budget more effectively in anticipation of receiving your final product. When you receive your first shipment, you'll have a sense of accomplishment that you never imagined. As your business takes off, you may need extra funding to manufacture larger shipments. In the next chapter, you will see that, now more than ever, there is a plethora of funding opportunities available for you.

Get Funded! Creative Ways to Fund Your Business

Watch Video Message: Tamara Monosoff Introduces Chapter 6

http://www.tamaramonosoff.com/tamara-monosoff-introduces-chapter-6/

It's a fortunate (and exciting) time to be an entrepreneur now that there's an abundance of additional funding resources. Today is unlike any other time in history, given the emergence of crowdfunding, which makes finding money and building public awareness of your business easier than ever. In this chapter, we'll explore new ways to fund your business—crowdfunding, online loans, microlending, and peer-to-peer loans—along with traditional forms of funding: personal savings, friends and family, grants, government-sponsored Small Business Administration (SBA) loans, angels, and venture capital (VC) funding. Just recognize that (more often than not) funding your business will require a creative combination of resources to get it off the ground and growing.

What's New in Funding?

Crowdfunding is one of the "hottest" (and fastest) new ways for entrepreneurs and small-business owners to raise money. Instead of having to appeal to and appease traditional investors, crowdfunding campaigns are funded by the general public. Crowdfunding gives entrepreneurs the chance to attract large numbers of Internet-connected people from all over the world to donate or invest money in their project or business with the help of social media networks.

There are two different methods of crowdfunding available. As an entrepreneur, you need to fully appreciate the difference between the two before diving into your first campaign.

1. Contribution crowdfunding (sometimes called "donations" or "rewards" crowdfunding) allows business owners to accept money in exchange for an "incentive." For example, if you're creating an app, you would give your donors the app and mention their names on your website in return for their donations.

2. Investment crowdfunding allows you to sell an ownership percentage (equity) of your business.

Each crowdfunding platform appears to have its own unique personality and focus. Some focus on nonprofits and social causes; others focus on businesses and retail product development. In this chapter, we'll focus on the platforms that fund businesses like yours. Be sure to scrutinize each platform carefully to develop a sense of the categories and types of businesses that successfully receive funding from it so that you can determine which resource best fits your product, project, or business. Choosing the "right" environment for your business will give you a better chance for success.

Key Advantages of Raising Money with Crowdfunding

• **Raise money quickly.** Traditional methods of raising money (bank loans) require three years of financials and tedious paperwork, and even then, lenders may refuse to fund your business. By contrast, crowdfunding campaigns usually last just 30 to 60 days, and if your idea is a hit, you can reach your funding goals within days!

◆ **Get cash without giving away the farm.** If you choose a *contribution* method platform, you'll maintain ownership of your company without giving away control, selling equity, or losing future revenue. In the case of the TV show *Shark Tank,* investors take a large piece of the farm, the farm animals, and, oh, by the way, you are no longer the farm owner but a "cowhand"—this is more of a standard equity investment. (See the end of this chapter for the advantages of TV shows like *Shark Tank.*)

◆ **Financial risk gets shared.** Crowdfunding lowers your personal financial risk because the risk is shared by contributors. But know this: when people contribute, they expect you to be organized, set achievable goals, and follow through on your promises.

◆ **Built-in marketing tool.** Another significant advantage of crowdfunding is that it is also a phenomenal marketing tool. As soon as you've launched a campaign, you'll see firsthand the reactions that people have to your product, project, or business. The reactions that you get to your idea are priceless because you can quickly find out whether your business idea is something that's worth pursuing or (equally important) whether it is something that you should let go of and move on. *Note:* This is another reason why choosing the right crowdfunding platform for your business is so important. In other words, if you have a technology gadget, don't choose a platform that focuses on art.

◆ **Prove your business concept for future funding.** A successful crowdfunding campaign shows future investors that you have something that's worth funding. If your campaign meets or exceeds your goals, you're far more likely to get financial support from outside investors to grow your business later on, if you need it. Investors can see how well received your business is by the general public, which confirms that you're on the right track (lowering the perceived risk inherent in investing), so they'll be more likely to offer funding.

◆ **The crowd speaks the truth.** Launching a crowdfunding campaign invites immediate feedback from the public. Experts insist that, when launching anything new, small businesses and entrepreneurs must perform market research to validate the market for their products or services. While you will have tackled this in Chapters 1 and 3, crowdfunding is another way to engage a crowd and to invite and receive valuable feedback and ideas (the good, the bad, and the ugly).

◆ **Build loyal fans and followers.** A successful campaign means that you've convinced people that your business is worth backing. Your contributors become your biggest support system because they're personally invested in your success and will help you spread the word about what you're creating. They will tell their friends, family, and business and social networks about you and their investment. *Note:* Your transparency, integrity, and follow-through are paramount when it comes to building and maintaining your support network.

◆ **Get free publicity.** To succeed with a crowdfunding campaign, you'll be working tirelessly to get the word out to your social networks: blogs, Facebook, Twitter, Google+, Pinterest, and any other venues you use. Often this visibility will spark the interest of traditional media (TV networks, newspapers, and magazines). But you can (and should) proactively contact the media directly. Media professionals are always looking for engaging feature stories. Search Google for relevant reporters and journalists who cover stories related to your business. It amazes me how accessible many of them are on Twitter. Make your tweet compelling, and be sure to include the link to your crowdfunding campaign.

New Crowdfunding Resources Are Emerging at Blinding Speed

Simply Google "crowdfunding success stories" to watch videos showing how people successfully orchestrated their campaigns.

Note that the specific terms outlined next are those published at the time of this writing (fall 2013). You should carefully review and understand all business terms specific to the crowdfunding sites before you use them.

◆ **Kickstarter** (www.kickstarter.com) is probably the best-known crowdfunding platform because it was among the first. Since 2009, Kickstarter has helped raise $649 million for projects that focus on art, movies, books, comics, dance, photography, music, and games (to name just a handful). At Kickstarter, entrepreneurs set a funding goal and a deadline. When visitors like a project, they can pledge money to make it happen. *Note:* Funding on Kickstarter is all-or-nothing. Projects *must* reach their funding goals in order to receive any money. If you meet your financial goal, Kickstarter takes 5 percent of the money raised plus payment processing fees. According to Kickstarter, "All-or-nothing funding might seem scary, but it's amazingly effective in creating momentum and rallying people around an idea."

◆ **Indiegogo** (www.indiegogo.com) considers itself the "world's funding platform." Its platform is open-ended, "available to anyone, anywhere, to raise money for anything." Indiegogo features social tools to help you get the word out about your campaign. The financial arrangement with Indiegogo is that you can keep the money you raise even if you don't meet your financial goal. If you fail to meet your goal, Indiegogo will keep 9 percent of the funds you raise (plus an additional 3 percent for credit card transaction fees). If you meet your goal, Indiegogo takes just 4 percent of the money raised. This tactic encourages you to focus on successfully getting the word out and generating excitement about and interest in your campaign. (*Note:* If you're a nonprofit, Indiegogo offers discounted rates.)

◆ **Crowdfunder** (www.crowdfunder.com) is a crowdfunding platform with a laserlike focus on raising funds for businesses, specifically, U.S.-based social enterprises, technology start-ups, and small businesses. Crowdfunder connects your business to its network of entrepreneurs and investors. It offers two models. You can select an *equity share* (where you give a percentage of your company shares to investors) or a *contribution model* (where you give incentives to funders, such as a copy of the finished product, a T-shirt, or recognition of some kind). The businesses that have the most success getting funding on Crowdfunder have financially viable or profitable businesses with social impact goals. Its unique CROWDFUNDx initiative connects local investors with local entrepreneurs in cities across the United States. It takes 5 percent if you meet your funding goals plus payment processing fees.

◆ **CrowdSupply** (www.crowdsupply.com) is a new crowdfunding platform that may be ideal for product entrepreneurs. CrowdSupply focuses on helping product developers bring new products and brands to the marketplace. It offers features and services tailored to the needs of product entrepreneurs. If a product is successfully funded, it offers support services—warehousing and shipping (also referred to as third-party fulfillment)—and "investors" in the campaign can preorder the product. After the product has been successfully brought to market, CrowdSupply becomes an online retailer and will purchase your product at wholesale, in essence taking on the role of a more traditional retailer.

◆ **Fundable** (www.fundable.com) is an online fund-raising platform specifically for small businesses. It is similar to other business-focused platforms (like Crowdfunder). There are essentially three steps to getting started: (1) create a free business profile, (2) choose whether you'll offer funders equity in your business or rewards, and (3) get the word out about your campaign. Fundable is different in that it charges a $99 monthly flat fee that applies only during your active funding campaign; most important, it doesn't charge percentage fees on the money you raise. This means that all the money you collect is yours. But for rewards-based funding, a 3.5 percent fee is deducted from the entire funded amount by WePay, its merchant processing partner. (This is a standard credit card processing fee, deducted directly by WePay, not by Fundable.)

◆ **RocketHub** (www.rockethub.com) is a crowdfunding site that welcomes art, science, business, and social good projects. One of its notable differences is its partnership with the A&E TV network. So not only do you have an opportunity to get a spot on TV, but there is also the potential for A&E to fund your project. Another point of differentiation is that RocketHub offers crowdfunding education, including a curriculum and tools to give you a better chance of successfully raising the funds you're seeking. With RocketHub, you keep the funds you raise whether you reach your funding goal or not. If you reach your goal, you pay a 4 percent commission fee plus a 4 percent credit card handling fee. If you don't reach your goal, you pay an 8 percent commission fee on the money you raised plus a 4 percent credit card handling fee.

Kids Have Amazing Ideas Too! Piggybackr Crowdfunding for Kids

Children have some of the best ideas. This is why I want to share a crowdfunding platform that is dedicated to supporting kids' projects. The Piggybackr platform is simple to use; it takes just a few minutes to set up a project profile page. The best part: there are young coaches available to support each child as he navigates the crowdfunding process.

The impressive, enthusiastic management team at Piggybackr will amaze you. Here's its manifesto:

We've designed Piggybackr to teach young people how to fundraise by providing tangible actions, resources, encouragement, and the chance to display their hard work, passion, and learning. It's not just about raising the most money. It's about building relationships, rallying supporters, and having the courage to take action and persevere. Piggybackr hopes to support the next generation of entrepreneurs, philanthropists, and innovators who will boldly lead us forward.

There are no setup fees, up-front costs, or monthly fees. You pay 5 percent plus 30 cents per transaction when you get a donation. To get inspired and learn more, visit www.piggybackr.com.

Three Strategies for a Successful Crowdfunding Campaign

1. Passionate videos. Create an awe-inspiring video to convey your message in a powerful way. Keep it under three minutes. How? Write a short script (beginning, middle, and end), practice, and ask for honest feedback from people you trust before posting your video. Be open to their feedback; refine your script; and practice, practice, practice until it feels spot on.

2. Clear goals. Be concise and clear about your business goals. Contributors need to understand precisely what you plan to do with their money.

3. Attractive rewards. Give people something they want or value that you can deliver. Don't overpromise and underdeliver. If your production costs are too high to offer them the product you're raising funds for, offer them a T-shirt with a picture of the product they funded on the front and the names of contributors printed on the back or a major discount or wholesale price on the product if they preorder, and mention their support on your website.

Other Funding Sources

Savings

In most cases, when you start a business, you become your first investor. Often it takes your own financial investment to get things started and to prove to others that you're serious. But not everyone has a savings account, so if you're seeking financial support, you'll have to show your commitment in other ways. A strong business plan, supported by extensive market research and knowledge, often serves the purpose while offering a great way to articulate your intentions and goals. (*The One Page Business Plan for Women in Business* is a helpful tool to get you started.)

Personal Loans from Friends and Family

Friends and family are still among your best and most important resources for the initial funding you need for your business. If you have a good track record with them, if they have the money, and if they believe in your idea, they are much easier to convince than are acquaintances or people who don't know you. And their loan is usually driven by their desire to help you, so it may come with low interest rates—or none at all.

A word of caution: if your business doesn't achieve the success you're seeking and you find that you can't pay back your friends and family, it can be very disappointing for all concerned and may cause persistent tension. If you borrow money from friends and family,

---

SmartyPig (www.smartypig.com) is a fantastic online business that helps you save money in a new way. This site's innovation on the old-fashioned savings account is that it helps people save for specific goals. You provide the date by which you want to achieve a goal, and SmartyPig works backward to come up with the appropriate monthly payment necessary to achieve it. Once you agree on payments that you can afford, SmartyPig automatically withdraws the amount you designate from your checking account and deposits it into your SmartyPig savings account.

If you've determined that you're not in a position to launch your business yet, this is a brilliant tool that can help you save money for start-up costs. For example, if you know that you'll need a new computer, an iPad, and business cards in the next few months, add up the costs and open a free SmartyPig account. The beauty is this: you'll be using money that you've saved rather than high-interest credit cards or loans.

And a little like a crowdfunding approach, SmartyPig also lets you reach out and share your goal publicly with friends and family via your social networks or blog. (See Chapter 8 on how to use social networks to your business advantage.) You can cancel your account any time without incurring fees or charges. And your savings account funds are FDIC-insured through SmartyPig.

make sure that you explain that your venture is high-risk and that you'll do everything you can to pay them back. Some people sign formal agreements with family members; others make informal verbal commitments. However you choose to do this, make sure that everyone involved is comfortable with and clear about the terms of the agreement ahead of time. *Note:* ZimpleMoney (www.zimplemoney. com) is a useful resource that will formally manage your friends and family loans online. It has free loan documents, like sample promissory notes, that you can download whether you use its services or not.

New Online Loans

Traditional bank loans have always seemed promising. In reality, they are often difficult for a start-up or early-stage business to secure. Another new opportunity has emerged in the form of online loans.

For the owner of a small business—especially a product business—one good purchase order for your product can turn your business upside down. Within a few moments, you can experience the exhilaration of seeing the number of units ordered and the dollar amount associated with it. (This happened to me. I once unexpectedly received a $100,000 order, and the customer wanted immediate delivery.). But as soon as the thrill of the moment wears off and reality sets in, you realize that you need money *fast* for a new production run, freight, transportation to warehouses, and delivery to the customer if you're going to fulfill the order, make the customer happy, and stay in business. Not many early-stage entrepreneurs have mountains of cash just sitting in their banks, especially after the costs involved with getting the business launched.

Kabbage (www.kabbage.com) is gaining in popularity right now for delivering immediate, short-term financial loans to support entrepreneurs and small-business owners. Both e-commerce and brick-and-mortar small businesses turn to Kabbage when they need fast cash advances. Companies can get funding from $500 to $50,000 within three days. Since it is not a traditional bank, Kabbage doesn't present the many hurdles of a typical bank loan, but interest rates may be higher. In fact, the application process takes about 10 minutes online, and, interestingly, the company considers how networked you are via social media as one of the determining criteria when granting funding.

SoMoLend (www.somolend.com) has partnered with banks to provide loans and help small-business owners bring their friends and family into the effort. They support people who are investing in people, eliminating the need for a financial institution middleman. Friends and family members, customers, and local supporters can invest in small businesses on SoMoLend. The company says, "We work with banks so entrepreneurs don't have to!" Using SoMoLend, small businesses can get bank loans they couldn't otherwise get. Banks on SoMoLend create a dedicated small-business lending pool of up to $50 million.

Microloans

Microloans are another excellent source of funding. Microloans are small loans for businesses that don't qualify for traditional loans or other investments. These loans are typically offered by nonprofit agencies, although there are exceptions. There is a large demand for microloans, which makes getting them competitive, but if you fit their criteria, it's definitely worthwhile to apply.

One well-known microlender is Kiva (www.kiva.org), which originally focused on microloans in developing countries (outside the United States). Now it is turning its attention to the needs of U.S. entrepreneurs, too. Kiva is creating partnerships with other existing microlenders in the United States. When people want to donate funds on Kiva to a specific entrepreneur, Kiva directs the funds to the appropriate field partner, who makes sure that the entrepreneur receives 100 percent of the loan. Most loans are in increments of $25, funded by regular people who are interested in the entrepreneur's story and inspired to help. In essence, this is a form of crowdfunding; the difference is that these are loans that must be repaid to the lenders. For example, Kiva recently partnered with TMC Working Solutions (www.tmcworkingsolutions.org), an organization that funds start-ups and existing businesses in nine cities in the San Francisco Bay Area, whose mission is to help create jobs and build and strengthen local communities. In fact, I just made the final payment on a $25,000 loan I received from TMC a few years after I launched my business. In addition to offering small-business loans (microloans) called the Kiva Step Ahead Loan Program (which provides loans from $5,000 to $10,000), TMC Working Solutions also offers more substantial loans ($10,000 to $50,000) with fixed interest rates of from 8 to 10 percent. If it funds your business, it wants you to succeed, so it also provides ongoing coaching, support, and referrals to local business resources.

Another microlender of note is Accion USA (http://us.accion.org/), which offers loans from $500 to $50,000 at competitive rates and flexible terms to launch small businesses. While banks typically require three years of financials to qualify, Accion USA offers loans for true start-ups that have been in business only six months.

Another nonprofit loan program to check out is Opportunity Fund (http://www.opportunityfund.org/loans/), which provides small-business loans to low-income entrepreneurs who don't qualify for traditional bank loans. Opportunity Fund's microloans range from $2,600 to $100,000; fixed interest rates are 8.5 to 18 percent (California only).

U.S. Small Business Administration Microlending Programs

The U.S. Small Business Administration (SBA) provides guarantees to specially designated intermediary lenders that are typically nonprofit community-based organizations with experience in lending, management, and technical assistance, like the examples given earlier. These intermediaries administer the Microloan program for eligible borrowers. The Microloan program provides loans of up to $50,000 to help small businesses. The average microloan is about $13,000. Interest rates vary depending on the intermediary lender and costs to the intermediary from the U.S. Treasury. Generally, these rates fall between 8 and 13 percent.

Follow the link given here and scroll to the bottom of the page for an alphabetized, updated state-by-state list of microlenders: http://www .sba.gov/content/microloan-program. This list includes very helpful contact names and e-mail addresses.

Peer-to-Peer Loans

Peer-to-peer loans are increasingly popular as a way to borrow money and are a tangible alternative to traditional bank loans. In essence, you are borrowing money, usually in small amounts, from "peers" who are able to consider your request through a secure online platform. They are motivated by the amount of interest they will earn and how confident they are of your ability to make the payments.

Unlike money raised through crowdfunding, peer-to-peer loans need to be paid back with interest. This works for everyone involved because as you make your monthly loan payments, the lenders (people from the general public who like to invest their money and support entrepreneurs) receive automatic payments into their accounts. You get the money you need, and the lenders get paid back on time with interest.

There are two leading companies in the peer-to-peer loan industry, LendingClub (www.lendingclub.com) and Prosper (www .prosper.com). Although LendingClub was launched after Prosper, to date it has issued a greater number of loans: more than $2 billion in loans to thousands of borrowers. And to strengthen its position in the market, Google just invested $125 million for 7 percent ownership in the company. However, Prosper was first to market and is holding its own. It has issued $550 million in loans so far. Here's how it works:

Borrowers choose a loan amount, state what the loan will be
    used for, and post a loan listing.
Investors review loan listings and invest in listings that meet
    their criteria.

When this process is complete, the borrowers make fixed monthly payments, and the investors receive a portion of those payments directly in their accounts; this is typically facilitated through web-based services created for the purpose. You state publicly on these sites how much money you're seeking and what you plan to use it for; your "peers" (investors) on the site will then fund you if they like what you're creating. You need to have a good credit rating to participate because investors won't know you personally and will look at your credit rating to establish your credibility. One perk of peer-to-peer lending is that you can often get better loan rates than you would from a brick-and-mortar bank.

Bank Loans

A bank loan is exactly what it sounds like—you take out a traditional loan at a given interest rate with the promise to pay it back. As mentioned earlier, traditional bank loans can be difficult for businesses in the early stages of growth to secure because these businesses are considered high risk.

There are literally thousands of banks and credit unions, many of which have special programs to support women, minorities, small businesses, and other groups. It can be worth the time to ask loan agents at local branches about programs they may have that would be good for you to pursue. And if you visit the Office of Small Business Development Centers (part of the U.S. Small Business Administration), it may have information on special programs and lenders in your region. For a list of microloan intermediaries at SBA, visit http://www.sba.gov/loanprograms.

One bank offering SBA-backed loans that caters to small and midsize businesses is Better Bank (https://www.bbcnbank.com/). Scroll to the bottom of the website and click on "SBA Financing." Better Bank offers at least four types of loans: for purchasing inventory and equipment, working capital, financing suppliers, and more, depending on your needs.

Credit Cards

Although they are not the preferred method of funding, credit cards are an often-used source of funding for entrepreneurs—especially in a pinch. While the interest rate is generally comparatively high, this is usually the easiest and fastest way to get financing from a bank or credit union. Many banks have become aggressive in offering credit.

Grants, Contests, and TV Shows

Grants are "free" money—but everyone knows that "free" is hard to find. Finding grants requires lengthy Internet searches, and they are often specific to industries or business niches. But there are a couple of general grant programs I have come across that are worth mentioning here.

StartupNation (www.startupnation.com) offers one of the most popular annual contests called the "Leading Moms in Business" competition. The top 10 mom-run businesses across the United States will be determined by a combination of popular vote and the group's panel of judges. The number one winner is awarded $10,000 by Staples. In addition, StartupNation publicizes the winners using both traditional and social media.

Eileen Fisher grant program. This program seeks applicants from women-owned businesses focused on the principles of "social consciousness, sustainability and innovation to take their established businesses to the next stage of their business plan." Applications are accepted once a year, from early March through May. Five women entrepreneurs receive grants in the amount of $12,500. To learn more, visit www.eileenfisher.com, scroll to the bottom of the home page, and click on the "grants" tab.

The Huggies Mominspired Grant Program. This program awards inspired moms $15,000 in seed money and business resources to further the development of original product ideas and start-up businesses https://www.huggiesmominspired.com/. (*Note:* Huggies does not specifically seek ideas that are diaper- or hygiene-related.)

Amber Grant for Women Business Owners. WomensNet.net (www.womensnet.net) sponsors a grant called the Amber Grant that began in 1998 to honor the memory of a young entrepreneurial woman who died in 1981, at the age of 19. The purpose of the Amber Grant is to help other women achieve their dreams. The primary focus is on assisting women who are trying to start small businesses, home-based or online. The grants are modest, usually $500 to $1,000, and are intended to pay for the small but essential expenses. No repayment is required or expected, although it is hoped that Amber Grant winners will pass on the kindness by mentoring and helping other women along the way. (*Note:* The organization offers free grant tips on its website.)

TV Show Contests

Contests attract a lot of visibility for the TV shows, businesses, and organizations that put them on, but they also create great awareness of and interest in your product business (whether you win or not). While I wouldn't say that this should be your overall strategy for funding your business, it's always a good idea to cast a wide net and try different approaches. The end result may be some cash, but the bigger result may be getting your product on the map (see Chapter 8, "Blowing Your Horn").

Although stories like these are not the norm, they are great examples of what can happen when you take the initiative. What do you have to lose by reaching out? Nothing! By sending an e-mail,

One E-mail Leads to $5,000 Cash Prize

Dawn Firsing-Paris, the inventor of Dripsters (www.dripsters.com), a compressed sponge that absorbs ice pop drips, took the initiative by sending one e-mail message that resulted in a $5,000 cash award for her business. She shares her story with us here.

I love watching Shark Tank! Barbara Corcoran is my favorite. I e-mailed her about my product, asking what she thought of it. I didn't expect a response. But two weeks later I received an e-mail asking if I would be interested in going on her new show called The Revolution. I went on the show and won $5,000 from Barbara.

One YouTube Video Post Leads to $10,000 Cash Prize

Watch Video Message from Allison Brush-Stern

http://www.tamaramonosoff.com/allison-brush-stern/

Allison Brush-Stern, creator of the Collapse-A-Pail (www.collapseapail.com)—a pail that quickly folds up and stores easily in all beach bags—was invited to be a guest on the Anderson Cooper daytime talk show in New York, won a contest for best invention, and was awarded $10,000. All of this happened because of one simple free video post. Read her story:

I posted my YouTube video on a local Connecticut patch news for free, and an executive producer from the Anderson Cooper show saw it. They were doing a show on million-dollar inventions and were looking for some no-name inventors. It was completely amazing. They picked me up the next week in a huge black SUV, did my hair and makeup at the studio, and gave me and two other gals 25 seconds each to pitch our products. They had three successful entrepreneur judges, and I won the $10,000. It was definitely worth calling in sick that day.

Allison got national media coverage and used the prize money to develop and manufacture the Collapse-A-Pail.

submitting your story for a TV segment or contest, or posting your videos in strategic places, new opportunities may arise that otherwise would not.

The famous American reality TV series *Shark Tank* (see sidebar) is another way in which product entrepreneurs are hoping to get funding, but this is "funding with strings attached," unlike the "prizes" mentioned earlier. Although the entrepreneurs who are selected are getting cash to fund their businesses, they are also giving away (equity) a percentage of their business, too. Some *Shark Tank* winners think this is worth it, as there are more advantages other than the money.

Entrepreneurs Pitch Investors for Funding in the TV Spotlight

Shark Tank is produced by Mark Burnett based on the Canadian version of the TV show *Dragons' Den*. The show features a panel of potential angel investors, called "sharks"; each considers offers from aspiring entrepreneurs who are seeking investments for their businesses or products. The entrepreneur can make a deal on the show if a panel member is interested, but if all panel members opt out, the entrepreneur leaves empty-handed. The show is said to portray "the drama of pitch meetings and the interaction between entrepreneurs and tycoons."   Source: Wikipedia and *Shark Tank* website.

To learn how to participate, visit http://abc.go.com/shows/shark-tank/about-the-show.

Other Ways to Get Valuable Support and Services Without Spending Money

Bartering is a system of exchange by which goods or services are directly exchanged for other goods or services without using money. It works best when each partner in a bartering relationship has skills that are of value to the other partner. When suggesting a bartering partnership, make sure that each of your contributions is clearly articulated and that each party involved feels that the tasks are equitable.

As you can see, bartering can be a useful way to save money. However, the risk is that the work you need to have done by your bartering partner will inevitably fall to the bottom of that person's priority list, below full paying customers.

Count Me In—Giving Unprecedented Support to Women Entrepreneurs

My good friend Nell Merlino is the founder of Count Me In for Women's Economic Independence (www.countmein.org), the leading nonprofit provider of "resources, business education and community support for women entrepreneurs seeking to grow

The First Woman Inventor to Win *Shark Tank*

Watch Video Message from Tiffany Krumins
http://www.tamaramonosoff.com/tiffany-krumins/

Tiffany Krumins was the first woman to receive funding on *Shark Tank*. She's the founder of the AVA the Elephant brand (www.avatheelephant.com). AVA the Elephant is a talking children's medicine dispenser that takes the fear and anxiety out of administering medicine to children three months and older. Tiffany's passion for helping sick children has been evident through her years of experience working with kids, including children with cancer and special needs. It was that same passion that brought AVA the Elephant to life!

Tiffany went on the show *Shark Tank* because she didn't see any other way to get the funding she needed to produce her product. Barbara Corcoran invested $50,000 for 55 percent owner- ship in Tiffany's company. Although this is a very large percentage to give away, Tiffany says that it  was well worth it, as it has opened many new doors and opportunities.

micro-businesses into million dollar enterprises." If you apply and are accepted into this nine-month Urban Rebound program, you will receive free coaching and invaluable training. The program is designed to help women entrepreneurs who are currently between $50,000 and $150,000 in annual revenues and help them grow to more than $250,000 in revenues within 18 to 36 months. Urban Rebound programs are supported by a grant from the Sam's Club Giving Program.

Factoring

Factoring is an interesting option for existing businesses with accounts receivable (outstanding invoices or money owed by cus- tomers). This is an option to consider when you receive a "large purchase order." This is how it works: some financial service

The Earbuddy Keeps Ears Warm

....

Watch Video Message from Lauren Meyers
http://www.tamaramonosoff.com/lauren-meyers/

Lauren Meyers, creator of the Earbuddy (www.pedalmore-store.com), a product that keeps your ears cozy while you are riding your bike and compliments most cycling helmets, shares how she used bartering to benefit her business.

Bartering and trading have provided me with key things that would otherwise require hard cash. For example, I helped a dog photographer review a legal contract and offered business strategy advice, and she offered to take my product photos. Additionally, a friend who makes documentary films offered to make a video for YouTube and my website, for no exchange other than a way to say thank you for volunteer work I have done in the past.

companies will offer financing, or "factoring," of your accounts receivable, giving you access right away to money that you're owed at a future date. Say your company ships a containerload of product to a retail store chain. That retailer will pay you 30 to 120 days later, depending on your agreed-upon terms (and the retailer's willingness to pay on time). If the delay between the time you ship to the retailer and the time you're paid will hinder your operations, factoring may be a solution. In this example, the "factor" (financial services company) would pay you 80 percent of the invoice right away, which is probably enough to keep your factory going. Your retailer would now be responsible for paying the factor instead of paying you. In return, the factor earns a percentage of those receivables, anywhere from 1 to 15 percent. The factor then has the burden of collecting the debt. Once the retailer pays the factor, you get back the remaining 20 percent reserve minus the factor's interest and fees. Your local banker can often introduce you to companies that factor receivables. Whether or not factors will work with you, and the terms they offer, will typically depend on the level of confidence they have in getting paid by your customer. Resources include www.factormoney.com, http://newcenturyfinancial.com/, and www.btbcapital.com.

Angel Funding

Angel investors are generally high-net-worth "qualified" professional investors who put money into companies, hoping to earn exceptionally high returns—much greater than they can find with more conservative investment options. Before approaching angel investors, ask yourself whether it's realistic to anticipate the high returns that they expect. Most often, angels invest with the hope of cashing out when you sell your company at a much higher value, or "multiple," then when they invest. Think through your growth potential and be thoughtful in estimating the ultimate return that your investors are likely to earn. This can be a challenge with product companies because, unlike technology companies, they are somewhat difficult to sell at a higher multiple after they are launched. Also know that finding angel investors is a time-consuming process; *this approach makes the most sense if you've tapped into everything else first.*

How Do I Find Angel Investors?

The key to finding angels is to talk to people. Ask others what they think about your business and who might want to offer advice on growing your company. A wise person once said, "The best way to get money is to ask for advice. The best way to get advice is to ask for money." So do whatever you can to expand your circle of advisors. Many times, your advisors will become your investors!

Other potential sources that can help you identify prospective angel investors include local business groups and the local chapter of the trade association under which your business operates. Introduce yourself and establish relationships. Also, ask your advisors—your attorney, accountant, banker, marketing consultant, and even professors—whom they would recommend to you. Your local chamber of commerce and county and state governments may have lists of angel groups and entrepreneur financing programs that they can provide to you. All these people are likely to have an interest in your success; they also have their own networks and generally want to help.

There is a growing population of organized angel "groups." These groups tend to fit one of four different models: region-based (for example, Sacramento Angels), sector-based (for example, Fash-Invest, angel financing for the fashion industry), cause-related (for example, Investors Circle, which funds socially and environmentally conscious businesses), or general (for example, Keiretsu Forum, Band of Angels, and StartUps.co).

The Angel Resource Institute offers a comprehensive list of angel groups by state. Click on the link given here, type your zip code into the search box, and angel groups in your area will show up: http://www.angelresource.org/angels/angel-groups/find-a-group.aspx.

Another great resource that works closely with the Angel Resource Institute is the Angel Capital Association. At the top of its home page is a tab "For Entrepreneurs." It offers links to angel groups in good standing and other resources. It also provides up-to-date news on what's happening in the world of angel funding. If you're interested in getting funded, it's a good idea to educate yourself by reading the latest articles and trends about angel funding.

Even if angel groups elect not to invest in your business, there's still an opportunity to connect with individual members who *are* interested. I have found several angels this way. Because you've had to go through a rigorous screening process to be invited to present to the group, knowing that you've been prescreened by a group they respect can provide comfort to individual angels.

The downside to presenting to angel groups is that there is often a fee associated with being invited to present. For bootstrapping entrepreneurs, these fees can be prohibitive. If your company is a perfect fit for this particular group of investors, then it may be worth the risk; only you can make this determination.

What Is the Difference Between Angels and Venture Capitalists?

While both invest in entrepreneurial firms and take equity (ownership) in those businesses, there are important differences:

Funding source. Angels directly invest their own funds in a business; venture capitalists invest funds from other sources (for example, pension funds, insurance companies, and foundations).

Stage of entrepreneur. In general, angels invest in seed, start-up, and early-stage businesses; venture capitalists invest in later-stage businesses. (There are exceptions.)

Size of investment. Venture capitalists generally invest $2 million and up in a financing round; individual angels make much smaller investments ($5,000 to $100,000). Angel groups can make investments in the midrange between most individual angels and VCs.

How Do I Know that My Business Is Right for an Angel Group Investment?

Angel investment is the right source of funding for only a small percentage of entrepreneurial businesses. When considering investment by an individual angel or angel group, ask yourself the following key questions:

- Am I willing to give up some ownership and control of my company?
- Can I demonstrate that my company is likely to realize significant revenues ("multiple") and earnings in the next three to seven years?
- Can I demonstrate that my company will produce a significant return for investors?
- Am I willing to take advice from investors and accept board of directors' decisions that I may not always agree with?
- Do I have an exit plan for the company that may dictate that I won't be involved in three to seven years?

When Should I Approach an Angel Group?

From my perspective, outside investors, other than friends and family, should be a last resort. Your business should have matured over time to a point where you know exactly what you are doing and you know what is the right amount of capital to accelerate growth.

You may want to consider seeking angel investors when:

◆ Your product is developed or near completion.
◆ You have existing customers or potential customers who will confirm that they will buy from you.
◆ You've invested your own dollars and exhausted other alternatives, including friends and family.
◆ You can demonstrate that the business is likely to grow rapidly and reach at least $10 million in annual revenues in the next three to seven years.
◆ Your business plan is in top shape.

Source: http://www.angelcapitalassociation.org/entrepreneurs/faqs.

Venture Capital Funding

Venture capitalists, or VCs, differ from angel investors in that VCs exist strictly to invest money. VCs are sophisticated organizations (usually limited partnerships) run by professional financial business-people—often entrepreneurs themselves—or MBA types who have pooled investment dollars into a "fund" that can total tens of millions to billions of dollars.

VCs will invest money in several companies each year that fit their investment criteria (for example, industry and stage of growth) and strategic plans with the expectation that maybe one in ten will hit big. It's typically pretty big money—(not less than $1 million per investment and usually more than $5 million). In turn, VCs will often assist in funding the development of new products and services and seek to add value to a company through active participation on the corporation's board of directors and potentially install executives they trust to help you run the company.

Finding a VC

Like angel investors, VCs tend to have market-sector focus areas that can be as general as technology, energy, or consumer goods, or as specific as "business software applications" or "green energy." For example, the venture capital firm Kleiner Perkins Caufield & Byers has recently invested heavily in technology and green energy, while Maveron has shown interest in consumer product brands and retailers. This is important to note so that you focus on firms that specialize in your area. As with the process for finding angels, often the best way to find a VC is to start locally through business contacts and other networks. For instance, I asked my local banker and one of my microlenders for recommendations. Both put me in touch with several potential investors and allowed me to use their names as referrals. In a world where VCs are besieged with unsolicited business plans, a recommendation carries substantial weight.

You can also use the Internet to search for VCs in your specific industry. A number of websites offer centralized directories of VC groups seeking "deal flow" (that is, companies in which to invest). Start with the National Venture Capital Association (www.nvca.org) for a list of venture capital firms investing in your business sector.

Resources to Help You Prepare for Venture Capital Presentations

For start-up and very-early-stage companies, venture capital is generally not appropriate—and historically, women have been at a disadvantage. Women are making progress in getting a larger share of VC funding, but it is still a male-dominated world and heavily focused on investments in technology companies. One phenomenal resource for women entrepreneurs is Springboard Enterprises (www.springboard enterprises.org). Over the past 13 years, it has matched more than 500 solutions-oriented companies founded and/or led by women, in areas including biotech, enterprise software, gaming, robotics, alternative energy, computer and medical devices, consumer products, human resources, education, advertising and marketing, and pharmaceuticals, with more than $6.2 billion in funding.

Another program that supports women entrepreneurs is Astia (www.astia.org). Astia is a unique international, not-for-profit organization that provides innovative programs that ensure that companies can gain access to capital, achieve and sustain high growth, and develop the executive leadership of the founding team.

Speed Dating for Money?

A new funding resource for entrepreneurs created for the fashion industry is FashInvest (www.fashinvest.com). FashInvest is the first community for emerging growth companies within the fashion, fashion technology, retail, and branded goods consumer sectors. It brings together thought leaders, financing strategies, and business experts in the industry. Since its founding in 2009, FashInvest is now regarded as one of the most respected business platforms committed to company growth and formation within these markets.

What's a Multiple?

A "multiple," in this context, refers to the value that the market and investors will place on a company. The value is often determined by the multiples seen within the industry you are in. For example, in software companies, a company with $1 million in revenue may expect to be able to sell for a 5 to 10 times multiple, or $5 million to $10 million, because those multiples are common in that industry. Even though product businesses can be lucrative, they seldom see high multiples like that. Multiples of 1 to 3 times revenue are not unusual. Since high multiples are uncommon in product companies, investors are harder to attract. And, when they do come into a deal, they demand very large amounts of equity or shares in your company.

One of FashInvest's most popular events is its Annual Spring Speed Dating Pitch Event. More than 50 entrepreneurs pitch their company, concepts, lines, and technologies to a roomful of investors and industry executives in a speed-dating-style format. Each "date" lasts three minutes, with participants rotating after each session.

Another funding resource that funds only businesses with social impact is Investors Circle (IC, www.investorscircle.org). IC has a network of investors that includes hundreds of angels, venture capitalists, foundations, and family offices. It has propelled $172 million plus $4 billion in follow-on investment into 271 enterprises dedicated to improving the environment, education, health, and the community.

I've spent hundreds of hours preparing for and making VC presentations, but I have had far more success raising money from angel groups and individual angels, microloans, and friends and family. If crowdfunding had been available when I was raising funds for my business, I would have jumped at the opportunity! An article posted on Forbes.com called "Crowdfunding Will Make 2013 the Year of the Gold Rush" predicts that crowdfunding will take off this year (2014) as corporate America embraces it. Also, President Obama passed the JOBS Act, which will drastically alter the landscape of crowdfunding platforms as well. And the Securities and Exchange Commission (SEC) just lifted the general solicitation ban, making it even easier for entrepreneurs to fund-raise using crowdfunding.

It's thrilling to see the new funding resources that have become available for entrepreneurs since I wrote the first edition of this book. There is simply no "right" way to fund your business. If you are like me, it will probably be an "all of the above" approach, and the options available today are incredible! Getting funding is a journey that requires patience and a thick skin. Learn about the different resources available, then start with the one that seems to be the best fit right now. As with a jigsaw puzzle, begin with the most obvious piece first, then choose another and another until you have creatively funded your business.

Chapter Wrap-Up

Now that you've begun getting a clear picture of the abundance of creative ways to fund your business through crowdfunding, microloans, grants, online loans, bank loans, and contests, it's time to make sure that your business is buttoned up. If your business is organized and properly structured from the outset (discussed in Chapter 10), you can accept funding and hit the ground running. And with efficient systems in place, you'll be well prepared to handle all the sales that are sure to come your way.

Making the Sale

Watch Video: Tamara Monosoff Introduces Chapter 7

http://www.tamaramonosoff.com/tamara-monosoff-introduces-chapter-7/

Getting Your Product on Shelves, Online, and into Customers' Hands

If I must choose a "most important" chapter, it is this one because nothing is more critical to your success than selling your product. The new opportunities and resources that are now available to you since the first edition are incredible.

It's important to note that most people are initially uncomfortable with the idea of selling, so if you feel that way, you're not alone. But, just like ballroom dancing, playing bridge, or typing, with practice, you can learn to do it. You are the most qualified person to sell your product.

The process of selling a product is relatively basic. However, achieving sales of a significant level, especially in a competitive market, is easier if you understand the way a market adopts a product as well as the most effective way to develop a sales plan.

There is so much material to share that I have broken this chapter into four sections.

Part 1 addresses the overarching philosophy of sales and preparation.

Part 2 walks you through the process of selling to online, independent, big-box, and television retailers.

Part 3 teaches sales techniques and covers the ins and outs of trade shows.

Part 4 explains how to leverage the help of independent manufacturers' representatives and distributors and covers setting your wholesale pricing.

PART 1:
Product Sales in Perspective

My goal is to help you achieve extraordinary sales results. There are clear steps and techniques that if learned and implemented, will produce successful results.

If you feel uncomfortable with sales, I will share a few points that will ease your mind. First, I have pretty good reason to believe that anyone who is reading this book has purchased products in literally dozens of different ways: at retail stores, online, from kids raising money for their school or Girl Scout troop, at fairs, from catalogs, at friends' parties, from street vendors, and so on. In other words, you know why you bought certain things, how transactions were handled, and what they cost, which means that you have had some pretty good relevant experience as a buyer yourself.

Second, since you have been a buyer, you know what it is like, and you probably know other buyers as well. This means that you can leverage your personal relationships for your initial sales.

Third, the industry in which your product fits *wants* to buy. Companies have professionals on their staff whose job title is "buyer"! These people have e-mail and LinkedIn accounts, and they are expected to look for and review new products regularly that are relevant to their assigned category. In some cases, the buyers will proactively contact you! I don't mean to make this sound like they will beat down your door—they won't. But there are real differences with product sales—versus other types of sales—that work to your advantage.

So, as you are digesting the techniques for this process, understand that this is not meant to make it more complicated than it really is, but to help you hit it big!

Learn About Pillows Made in Heaven

Watch Video Message from Demetria Phelps
http://www.tamaramonosoff.com/demetria/

Demetria characterizes herself as a "grand mommy with many 'grand' ideas" and as a "63-year-old Senior Entrepreneur." I simply call her "inspiring."

As a single mom, the older of whose two daughters was fighting for her life against an autoimmune disease called lupus, Demetria had a vision of a blanket that would reflect her daughter's personality and that would have healing Bible scriptures on it. Having made a sudden and miraculous recovery, her daughter felt great comfort from this blanket and encouraged her to design and share this gift with others.

Demetria's tough road included a lot of reading and self-education, scraping up capital that did not exist, and seeking support from Small Business Administration mentors through the SCORE program. "I am a shy person. I had to get comfortable with so many people in many different situations. There were times right before a meeting that my hands would sweat and start trembling. I had to work very hard to get over my fear."

Today, her www.PillowsFromHeaven.com line includes more than 100 designs.

Creating Demand for Your Product

Unless you're very lucky or very well connected, you probably won't launch your product directly into mass-market retail stores like Target or Walmart. Instead, there's a product sales life cycle that you should expect to follow that basically takes you from the ground up and allows you to build sales in a smart, methodical fashion. In addition, you'll need to put some thought into defining your market, positioning your product, and creating targeted packaging that reaches the proper audience.

Envisioning Your Sales Life Cycle

This information is intended to be applicable to a broad range of products that will follow a process that is more or less the same.

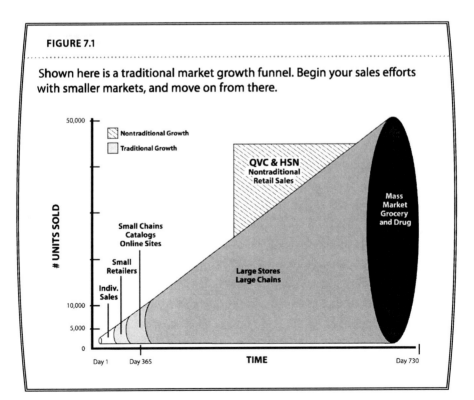

FIGURE 7.1

Shown here is a traditional market growth funnel. Begin your sales efforts with smaller markets, and move on from there.

However, every product is different—its market, target customer, geographical applicability, and so on—so, as you read this chapter, understand that you will need to adapt what is outlined here to the uniqueness of your product.

I start with the presumption that most people who are reading this book will have a product that is new, will need to start small, and will aspire to sell as many units as possible over time.

Now envision pushing enough units of your product through the bottom of this funnel (Figure 7.1) to fill it up as you move from the narrow end to the wide end. The distance from the small end to the large end represents time. You will need more units to fill the expanding funnel the closer you get to the top of the wide end. The narrow tip of the funnel represents the very beginning of your sales effort, and the top of the funnel represents the point in time when you have achieved the peak of your distribution goal. The market growth funnel image visually illustrates how you'll go about creating demand for your product.

Market Positioning

Before you even think of selling your product, it's vital to be armed with the proper information. Market positioning is the discipline that allows you to examine the marketplace, analyze it for opportunity, and discover where your product fits in and how it can benefit this market. This information is critical in helping you decide whom to sell to and how to position your product as unique and worthy of a buyer's attention. While market positioning is a huge and complex discipline, here are a few basic elements that will serve you as you begin.

Your first step in positioning your product should be to clarify and define your target market, as outlined in Chapters 1 and 3. This effort will dramatically improve your chances of success when you hit the road (phone or e-mail) selling. It's important to clearly understand whether your product fits a narrow niche market or whether it has more of a mass-market appeal. For instance, a scrapbook designed for brides fits a niche market—women who are planning their weddings. To define your own target market, identify who sells similar products and familiarize yourself with any competing products. Then, once you've defined your largest potential market (see Figure 7.2), you'll need to determine your customer profile in order to properly position your product.

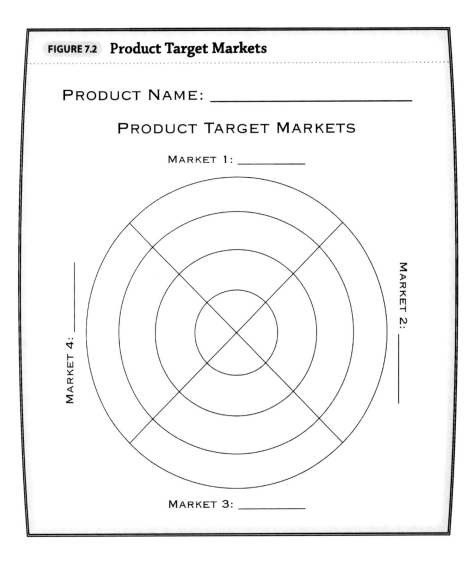

FIGURE 7.2 **Product Target Markets**

PRODUCT NAME: _____

PRODUCT TARGET MARKETS

MARKET 1: _____

MARKET 2: _____

MARKET 4: _____

MARKET 3: _____

Positioning Your Product

You know exactly how your product can help people. But your potential customers don't. If you are to sell your product effectively, your customers must feel that your product provides them with a benefit that is worth the money you are asking for it. *Product positioning* is the process of describing these benefits and features verbally and in writing. Depending on the market, your positioning may also illustrate how your product differs from others in the marketplace.

Your product's *benefits* explain how, in the long run, the product will enhance consumers' lives. For example, a specialized cleaning product may cut down the time it takes to clean the kitchen. Your product's *features* are the specific characteristics that describe your product. In the cleaning solution example, features might be "organic," "environmentally safe," "antibacterial formula," "easy to apply," and "fresh, clean scent."

Truly knowing your customers and the benefits that they value is essential because a great product that is positioned incorrectly will not sell.

Meredith LaMirande, creator of the Dropper Stopper (www.dropperstopper.com), a product that prevents dropped baby items from ever hitting the dirty floor, helps illustrate this point.

I have learned that my niche market is boutiques and specialty stores. I have more of a high-end customer. They are looking for something unique, creative, and well-packaged, and they are willing to pay for good quality. I would have liked to have been a "Target-type" product, but my items have a higher price point that just won't work with most big-box stores.

Product Packaging

There are a number of other issues that need to be addressed before you launch your sales campaign. Packaging design was discussed in Chapter 5, but equally as important is the type of packaging and its size. Also important is the size of the outer and inner cartons in which your products are packed and shipped. If your target retailer is accustomed to receiving shipments in cartons of 12 units, it will be important for you to have your product shipped to your warehouse in this configuration so that it can be easily reshipped without the cost of repacking. Some retailers will also expect you to keep a certain number of units available in your warehouse so that they can replenish their own inventory quickly.

What Do Top Retailers Think About Your Product?

This is a good time to mention a cool new website called Buyerly (www.buyerly.com). This site was created by Vanessa Ting, a former Target buyer, and her tech partner, David Liu, to help new product companies get feedback on their product from the nation's top retailers.

Smart Sales Planning

A sales plan should not be perceived as a complex hurdle. Instead, view it as a written road map that helps you think through and organize your approach to sales. Unless you are crafting your plan for another audience, such as investors, only you will see it, so design it in a way that works best for you. Typical elements of a sales plan are your sales goals, sales activities, target accounts, tools required, and timelines.

Setting Realistic Goals

Goals should be specific and measurable. You should base these goals on the specific nature of your product, and they should consist of realistic, attainable steps. For instance, when you first begin, "selling a million units" is more a dream than an attainable goal. Goals must be both volume- and time-based and broken down into manageable parts—for example, sell 5 units to end customers within 60 days and sell 100 units to independent retailers in my state within 6 months.

Sales activity is what drives results, so a rule of thumb is that if you wish to increase sales results, you must increase sales activity. While this is nearly always true, keep in mind that some types of activity will be more effective than other types, and that you should evaluate the effectiveness of different activities on a regular basis. You will also want to be prepared and willing to seize shortcut opportunities that present themselves.

For example, you may find that visiting local retailers personally is much more effective than calling them on the phone. Remember that often, small local retailers are entrepreneurs too and are likely to want to help you. Your tactics and activities will also change as your targeted customers change. In other words, showing up in person at Target isn't going to work. In this case, researching online to find the e-mail of the appropriate category buyer will be much more effective.

For most brand-new companies, the initial target customers are actual end users rather than retailers. So, an activity associated with this sale that you can write in your sales plan might be, "Set up a website with a shopping cart," or, "Rent a booth at a local event." Similarly, activities associated with targeting independent retailers would be likely to involve goals like, "Mail introductory letters with follow-up calls," or, "Attend an industry trade show."

The benefits of this kind of plan are especially pronounced for brand-new companies because the challenge is bandwidth. Planning will help you get clear on the prioritization and order in which you will do things. Oddly, this kind of organization is what also enables you to respond to new opportunities, which always come up, because you will see what you are sacrificing in order to do so.

Develop a Timeline

An essential element of a useful plan is a timeline. By basing your activity and results on a realistic timeline, you give yourself clear steps to take within defined periods of time. In addition, you are able to measure your own progress on a regular basis.

Your plan, however, should also be fluid. If you are underachieving your goals, you will need to take corrective steps: increase your activity, change your activity, recruit (or pay for) help, or adjust your goals. The most important point is to be kind to yourself without being critical—simply make adjustments and move forward.

Follow a Proven Process

In most sectors, your plan should follow a process for creating a market. Create "referenceable customers," customers that you can contact and get positive stories to share when you are selling to others later on. This gives you an opportunity to get feedback on your product and packaging that can improve your chances as you expand to retailers.

Once you've achieved some success and worked out some wrinkles, you want to start thinking about increasing the leverage in your sales efforts. By *leverage*, I mean the ability to increase the volume and dollar value of your sales without increasing the amount of effort you put out. For instance, to sell one unit for $10 to an end consumer at a local craft show, you had to do a lot of hard work; you had to be there and pay for participating in the show, speak directly to that person, and handle the transaction for the sale—all to sell one $10 unit. An alternative way to increase your leverage is to meet with the buyer for a local craft store, make one sales presentation—describing the value your craft show customer saw in the item—and have her buy 24 units (at a 50 percent discount), which she will then sell to 24 customers that visit her store. In this case, you have only one sales presentation, but you have earned $120, and you don't have the cost of attending the craft show. And, if your product is successful, your retailer will buy it again without another meeting!

So, following your initial direct-to-consumer sales, your next target customer group would be local independent specialty stores and online stores. For instance, if you've designed a line of greeting cards, approach your local gift shops. Note that retail buyers are risk-averse. They have to be because they have little influence on their customers' preferences. Proving sales of your product in smaller local stores will give larger regional chains and catalogs the kind of justification they need to feel comfortable with trying your product. Such local sales are a good way to build a case study with little or no risk to either the retailer or you. I have commonly offered new products to local retailers on the basis that they pay me *nothing* unless they sell. The caveat is that they agree to share customer feedback and to place a regular order if the product moves; either way, you gain knowledge.

Success locally and online will then give you leverage to get placement of your product with larger regional independent stores and with catalogs. As you generate success with this group and continue

Toaster Tops

Watch Video Message from Julie Condy
http://www.tamaramonosoff.com/julie-condy-3/

Julie Condy, creator of Toaster Tops (www.toastertops.com), launched her busi-

ness at a church event. "After showing it to family and friends and receiving positive feedback, we decided to have a booth at our church craft fair. Since we received so much excitement and sold most of them, we did a larger run. We began selling online three months later."

to expand your roster of independent and online retailers, you have begun to "create demand for your product."

Generally, it is at this point, which could take months or years, that the opportunity and decision to enter sales channels considered to be "mass market" begin to open up. For traditional retail, these include national stores like Sears, Target, Walmart, Kmart, and Bed, Bath & Beyond.

Knowing Your Niche

Some products will find tremendous success in niche areas that you may not have initially considered. In the children's industry, for instance, there is an entire market for products sold for school or extracurricular fund-raisers (for example, Girl Scout Cookies). Talk to people who are in your target market to discover more about where they shop and then cast a wide net to see what works.

While specialty stores usually won't reach as large an audience as a big-box store, there are still benefits. One of these is that the profit margin is usually stronger. Customers who shop in these stores generally aren't seeking the lowest price, but are looking for high-quality products and better service. The challenge is to generate enough volume to be lucrative. Try specialty chains, buying groups, and trade shows (covered later in this chapter) to reach these stores more efficiently, rather than trying to sell to each small store directly.

Basic Tools to Approach Buyers

Tools Required
- Product sheets
- Website
- Price list
- Business phone line
- Voice mail
- Testimonial letters

Create a Sales Plan

Sales Goals

	Monthly	Quarterly	Yearly
Number of units 1st year			

Date	Activity	Results
1st month	Establish website; create product sheets	Sell 2 units to end users
2nd month	Attend 1 event; e-mail friends and family a coupon and ask for referrals	Sell 4 units to end users
3rd month	Make appointments with 3 local retailers and contact 10 online stores	Sell 24 units to retailers
2nd quarter	Contact 20 retailers within region and 1 catalog Sell 24 units to online retailers	Sell 24 units to end users Sell 36 units to retailers
2nd half of year	Contact more regional and national independent retailers Contact 5 catalogs Contact buying groups Contact small chain-store buyers	Sell 24 units to end users Sell 48 units to online retailers Sell 192 units to independents Sell 48 units to catalogs

PART 2:
Putting Your Plan into Action: Sales 101

Once you've thought out your plan and put it on paper, there's nothing left to do but sell, sell, sell!

Step 1: Sell Directly to Customers

When you sell directly to end-user customers, there is no middleman. You inform potential customers about the product, and they decide to purchase it from you. The advantage is that you don't need to convince a retailer to take a risk by buying your product, and you don't have to share the profit. Plus, it's the simplest way to start selling. The disadvantages are that you're not utilizing an established channel to reach a larger number of consumers, such as a storefront or catalog would provide. Nonetheless, direct selling is likely to be your first line of attack in creating your market.

Big New Opportunities

When I wrote the first edition of this book, there was a major shift toward shopping at large big-box retailers and major department stores such as Walmart, Target, Costco, and Sam's Club. At the same time, e-tailers such as Amazon.com and eBay were growing rapidly as well. Many small independent retailers had vanished, as they could not compete. In the last few years, a proliferation of new e-tailers with proven platforms have launched many new products.

Watch Video Message from Francene Dudziec

http://www.tamaramonosoff.com/francene-dudziec/

Francene Dudziec is the creator of Hello Beach (www.hello-beach. com), a beach tote that allows beachcombers to collect shells but leave the sand at the beach. Francene is also the owner of a boutique retail store. She was able to demonstrate this approach perfectly. She started by making enough units to stock in her store. When she found that she consistently sold out, she came up with a way to produce a larger amount of inventory. What I like most about her story, is how she managed to avoid financial risk. She says, "Luckily I was able to secure a few pre-wholesale orders for my first shipment, so I did not have to use any of my own money to launch. We have been reinvesting our profits ever since."

There are a number of ways to get in front of your customer, and I recommend utilizing as many as possible.

One way smaller e-retailers use to compete with larger chains is by carrying unique or new items and building online traffic, often using their own unique sales angle, to generate meaningful sales.

First, you should list your product for retail sale on your own website. There are numerous options for creating your own website, including e-commerce capabilities. Most web-hosting companies

---

Marketplace Sites Help Build Product Awareness and Sales

Women Inventorz Network (www.WomenInventorzNetwork.com) is a website run by Melinda Knight and Dhana Cohen that is specifically designed for women inventors. It's a non-e-commerce-based store where female inventors can showcase and promote their product(s) for free, using multiple marketing tools and generating media buzz.

Those listed here are far from the only unique models, but I offer them to help spur ideas for you to expand your options.

Social coupon marketplace sites allow you to offer discount deals to customers by using a quasi-advertising and marketing platform where there is revenue sharing involved. These sites also help you promote your product geographically. In other words, you can target your local community or reach nationally, depending on your product and goals.

These are sites like:

> Groupon (www.Groupon.com)
> Living Social (www.LivingSocial.com)
> Life Booker (www.LifeBooker.com)

A favorite of mine is www.TheGrommet.com, whose mission is: "We launch undiscovered products and help them succeed." It cleverly refers to the site as "the birthplace of Citizen Commerce."

Other sales channels that offer a nice way to generate some revenue and get your product out to the market include some of the new online sites that offer deep discounts through sales "events" or "steals":

> Unbeatable Sale (www.unbeatablesale.com)
> KidSTEALS (www.KidSteals.com)

offer website templates. You can then create a shopping cart and set up a merchant account or use PayPal to accept payments.

I love some of the new systems available that have addressed the old problem of having to piece together the website, the shopping cart (for example, Zencart.com, and 1ShoppingCart.com), the payment gateway (for example, authorize.net), and the merchant account (your bank). Three companies that provide complete e-commerce solutions that make it easy to set up a website with e-commerce are www.shopify.com, www.prestashop.com, and www.bigcommerce.com.

An option that reduces your development effort and costs, and can potentially leverage their existing traffic, is to list your product on a third-party website such as www.Amazon.com, www.ebay.com, or community-based sites that have ways to connect to their larger community or audience, such as www.storenvy.com, www.Etsy.com, and www.OpenSky.com.

Watch Video Message from Ally Arnold

http://www.tamaramonosoff.com/ally-arnold/

Ally Arnold, creator of the Kiddie Catch-All (www.kiddiecatchall .com), a wonderful car accessory that gives kids access to their toys, has aggressively promoted her product by testing some innovative channels. One of her most successful runs was with Skymall (the inflight airline catalog, www.skymall.com). She also had tremendous success with kidSTEALS.com. Three sales on kidSTEALS.com this year have resulted in selling thousands of units through special sales, including "BOGO" (oth-erwise known as "Buy One Get One"), while getting great exposure for future growth.

To submit to kidSTEALS (as of this writing), send your sample to:

StealNetwork—Attn: Buyer Sample
1385 Swaner Road
Salt Lake City, UT 84104

Roberta Wagner, creator of the Carry-Her Doll Carrier (www.carry-her.com), is on track to sell 85,000 units this year through major retailers, including Toys"R"Us. When asked how she first reached them, she said,

I connected with a bunch of Toys"R"Us buyers through LinkedIn. I e-mailed a few asking if they could connect me with the doll buyer. I was fortunate to get connected with the most amazing lady. She requested samples... her niece loved it. Now I am looking forward to my first holiday season in this and other retailers.

Some websites make it simple to submit a product for review. Zulily (www.Zulily.com), another "deal" website, conveniently offers a "vendor" link in its "About" section, whereas I was unable to find a way to contact a buyer at Gilt (www.Gilt.com). This is a situation in which using channels such as LinkedIn to find buyer contacts can be effective. I typed "Gilt Buyer" in the LinkedIn search window and a number of contacts immediately popped up.

There are literally thousands of online retailers with a more standard sales model that serve both general consumers and virtually every niche you can think of, from baby gear to outdoor gear, cooking and housewares, crafts, kites, optics, and medical. Here's a list of websites to explore to help you get started:

www.Amazon.com
www.Drugstore.com
www.greatbabyproducts.com
www.diapers.com
www.backcountry.com
www.highlinekites.com
www.musiciansfriend.com
www.allmodern.com
www.save-on-crafts.com
www.elderstore.com

Nearly every major retailer also has its own online store, often operated by a different business unit with its own buying department, as with Walmart.com, Bed Bath & Beyond, Target.com, Macys, and so on.

Catalogs

Catalogs are similar to e-tailers in that most of them also have an online store. Some catalogs offer a tremendous way to get products to new consumers and help build publicity as well. One Step Ahead (www.onestepahead.com) was one of my first retail accounts. And, my first order for more than $100,000 came from LTD Commodities (www.ltdcommodities.com). To find the right catalogs for your item, visit www.catalogs.com and www.catalogmonster.com. *Note*: For retail catalog contact lists and other valuable sales resources visit www.TamaraMonosoff.com under the Books & Tools tab.

Step 2: Selling Wholesale

You are now well prepared for approaching your next market: wholesale outlets, the small, independently owned retailers, "mom-and-pop" shops, in your town and other locations. At this point, you can also use customer references and testimonials that you've received from selling directly to consumers to help you secure your first wholesale sale accounts.

There are several reasons to start with these smaller retailers rather than chain stores. First, since they lack the volume or financial muscle to compete with the major chains in their area, they often need to differentiate themselves by offering new and unique, hard-to-find items. Second, the owner is often working in the store, so you can speak directly to the decision maker. Finally, these people are typically local and will be inclined to help another local entrepreneur.

To sell to independent retailers, you will need a minimum of five basic tools:

1. **A business card.** It should have your company name, contact information, and a QR code that links to your website URL, to a video of you introducing your business, or to a video demonstrating your product. (More on how to create QR codes in Chapter 8.)

2. **A product "sell sheet."** This is a simple document with pictures or illustrations of your product, a list of features and benefits, pricing and shipping requirements, and your contact information. (You can download a sample sell sheet at www.TamaraMonosoff.com/Guides.)

3. **High-quality product photos.** These should be available in high-resolution format for print catalogs and media opportunities (300 dpi), and low-resolution for websites and online stores (72 dpi).

4. **A succinct introductory letter or e-mail.** Write it with your customer in mind. For example, retailers are not particularly interested in why you came up with your idea or how many kids you have. However, they are interested in specific product features and benefits, real customer testimonials, other retailers' experiences with your product, minimum order size, discount options (for example, prepay, free shipping, and the like), and their potential profit margin. Most important, keep it brief. While you will undoubtedly modify it for different people and purposes, a template to start with can be useful (see the example cover letter later in this chapter).

5. **Product samples.** These will illustrate firsthand the quality, features, and benefits of your product.

When approaching store owners and managers to make your sale (techniques are covered further along in the chapter), always be professional, no matter how they act toward you. Keep in mind that this retailer knows others in the community and that they speak to each other. Once you've created a good relationship, ask for their help—and offer yours in return. For example, after including my first retailer in a press release I wrote, she offered to show my TP Saver to all her peers at the upcoming industry trade show.

Cheryl Hajjar and Amy Perreault shared the story of selling their book *The Paci Pixie* (www.indigopixies.com) to the retail chain Learning Express.

We just went into the stores ourselves, pitched our book, and told them why we thought it would be a good fit for their stores. There is no magic way to do it, just a direct pitch. It is definitely an advantage to use the "home court" advantage pitch.... We didn't have any specific contacts; rather we just walked in and asked for the store owner or the person responsible for buying the products to carry in the stores.

You've Got to Lose Some to Win Some

Many new companies expect to make good profits from their first sales. But sometimes it's more beneficial to think of these initial sales as a marketing investment rather than as profit-making sales. Though these strategies may cut into your initial profits, over the long term, you'll more than make up for it.

For example, offer the retailer a few free units as a trial. Also, consider offering low minimum-unit introductory purchase quantities; instead of requiring the retailer to buy a minimum of 20 pieces, make it 10. Also, refer your direct customers to this retailer instead of selling the products yourself. It will pay off in the long run.

Step 3: Selling to the Big Guns, the Mass-Market Outlets

It's common for new inventors (myself included!) to think that if they could just get their product into Walmart, they'd make millions. While this surely has been the case for many companies, it's not a realistic goal for most products. That's why you should approach the mass retailers only after you've created a proven market through the sales channels described previously. This is not just because of the difficulty of getting the mass retailers to buy your product, but also to allow you to get yourself set up well enough to support this type of sale. When dealing with these major accounts, the sale is just the beginning of the deal. Handling fulfillment, returns, rollbacks (forced price concessions), slotting fees, advertising, electronic data interchange systems, (EDI, discussed later in this chapter), and other mass-market-specific issues will require infrastructure and proper resources to handle the process successfully.

Dealing with Fear

Selling your product for the first time may not just feel intimidating—it may even feel like what you are saying is false. I remember the first time I called a buyer at a big-box retail chain. I was terrified. I couldn't help but think, "I made up this company; it doesn't really exist. And, how is she going to believe me when I say I am the company president?" I also worried that she might ask me questions I didn't have answers to, or use terms I didn't yet understand. Worst of all, what if she didn't like my product?

I now recognize that most of my fear had to do with my potentially revealing my inexperience and my fear of the unknown. As

Kids Get Dressed All by Themselves with Myself Belts

Watch Video Message from Talia Goldfarb
http://www.tamaramonosoff.com/talia-goldfarb/

Talia Goldfarb, creator of Myself Belts (www.Myselfbelts.com), has sold more than $2 million since launching about 10 years ago. She says, "Not having experience can often be an asset. I didn't know to be intimidated when calling a store buyer. I just picked up the phone and called."

She obviously managed to sell to a lot of them!

it turned out, this buyer didn't want the TP Saver until there were proven sales elsewhere. Therefore, I ended the conversation with, "Once I have a proven track record, may I call you back?" She agreed. Once I got over my initial fear of calling, I was able to end with a question that left me with an open invitation to call back. I subsequently built my sales by "creating demand for my product," and I did eventually sell to her. The point is, don't be afraid of what you don't know.

Once you are ready to approach mass-market retailers, it's necessary to be prepared. While there's no magic formula for knowing the perfect time in your product's life cycle to approach a mass retailer, there are some practical things to keep in mind when you do decide to do so.

1. Get to the correct buyer. Finding the proper person in a large organization can be one of your biggest challenges. Be sure to do your homework, or if you find it's too daunting, hire a distributor or a manufacturers' representative (these options are covered later in the chapter). Often these third parties have established relationships with buyers, which makes it easier to open doors. Plus, mass retailers are often wary of working with unproven companies that could potentially disappoint them.

2. Take advantage of special programs. In response to a new "buy local" trend, mass retailers are increasingly offering local sales programs that give the store manager and the district manager some authority to try a local item. If they take a chance on you and your product sells well locally, it might encourage the store to take on your product regionally or nationally. This is a powerful backdoor method of launching your product into the stores as opposed to calling the corporate office yourself. Other options worth looking into include special programs, like minority business offices.

3. No matter how you plan to approach a mass-market outlet, realize that the timeline is going to be long; it could be a year or two or more before you get a decision or see your product on store

Watch Video Message from Stephanie and Nancy Tomovska

http://www.tamaramonosoff.com/stephanie-nancy-tomovska/

Stephanie and Nancy Tomovska, the creators of Unmarx (www.unmarx.com), a reusable cleaning pad that easily erases a variety of unexpected clothing marks, have found several regional programs of large retailers to be effective.

They attended fairs organized by Whole Foods and Ace Hardware that were geared to finding local products. And they tell their story about landing their first major retailer, Walgreens:

We got into our first major retailer, Walgreens, by walking into our local Walgreens store and speaking with the community manager. He liked our product and agreed to test it in six stores in his region. We asked our family and friends to buy our product at Walgreens and were able to generate successful sales results. As demand grew, we were able to expand to more regions and many more Walgreens stores.

shelves. And, you could still hear the answer no. But, the answer is definitely no if you don't even try, and I can tell you from firsthand experience that it can be well worth the wait. It took me two years to get into an account with a distributor who served grocery stores nationwide. It took me gently nudging about every three months. When the time finally came and the distributor said yes, we began receiving *weekly* orders for 25,000 units at a time! *Note*: For retail store contact lists and other valuable sales resources visit www.TamaraMonosoff.com.

Walmart's New Program for Women Vendors

In addition to its local purchase program, Walmart is encouraging women-owned businesses to submit products. Visit http://corporate.walmart.com/suppliers/. Click on "Apply to be a supplier" and then "National Product Suppliers (US Only)." Follow the submission

Watch Video Message from Lisa Hoskins-Holmes and Karen Wildman

http://www.tamaramonosoff.com/karen-wildman-lisa-holmes/

Lisa Hoskins-Holmes and her sister, Karen Wildman, are the creators of the www.bheestie.com, a line of products that remove moisture from personal electronics devices such as mobile phones and iPads. Karen tells how Lisa got them into the REI retail chain.

Lisa called REI (corporate office) and explained who she was and what our product was, and she was given the buyer's name and where to send a sample to. She wrote a letter of introduction about us and sent a sample of Bheestie. The buyer e-mailed us and said he wanted it for REI. He then set us up with someone from the company that does distribution for REI. We were so excited to be in REI, such a great company, and we really appreciated the company's giving us our first chance at retail. When Lisa did this, we thought it was such a long shot, but you never know who might be your next yes.

process, and in step 2, select "women-owned business" and enter "Empowering Women Together" in the buyer name field. Save your application ID number, as you will need it for future reference.

Seeking Out Shortcuts

While a steady, progressive approach to creating demand for your product, as described in this chapter up until now, should be the rule for burgeoning entrepreneurs, there are certainly exceptions that can help you get big sales in a much shorter timeline. One such outlet is TV shopping networks like QVC, HSN, and TSC (www.theshoppingchannel.com in Canada). These programs have large, loyal audiences.

It is important to consider the unique aspects of this sales model before pursuing it. First, read the networks' sites for the specific audience demographic breakdown, but know that viewers are predominantly female. Additional considerations should be made based on this specific model.

- ◆ Does your product demonstrate well?
- ◆ Does it solve a problem or make life easier?
- ◆ Does it have unique features and benefits?
- ◆ Does it appeal to a mass audience?
- ◆ Does it appeal to women?
- ◆ Is it topical or timely?
- ◆ Does it meet similar price points of other items you see?

Watch for special programs in which your product would fit, and jump at any opportunities that come up. There are some manufacturers' reps who base their business on selling to QVC. This may provide another avenue for success.

Note that although the process may be relatively simple, it is still very competitive to get a product accepted. And, be prepared for the networks' "guaranteed purchase" clause. This means that even though a purchase order is placed and the network holds inventory, it doesn't pay you until your product is sold. And if your products don't sell, the network returns them. Not only is it costly to produce and deliver the inventory required in case of a tremendous success, but there are costs associated with taking back unsold merchandise. The other challenge is that these networks may require that your product be packaged specifically to meet its shipping process requirements. If you get a return, it can be difficult to resell merchandise to another retailer that was previously packaged for QVC, HSN, or TSC.

QVC

QVC is the market leader in this space, reaching into more than 250 million homes globally with over $8.5 billion in sales revenue in 2012. When you sell through these television sales systems, you or your designee speaks directly to the customer on camera. This is a great way to reach a mass customer audience. There is a clear process for submitting your product for consideration, with tips and a clear description of the types of products that QVC accepts and those that it does not sell. QVC also has an innovative program called "QVC Sprouts" (www.qvc.com/QVCSprouts), which gives small vendors a chance to post a product on the QVC.com website to gauge consumer interest and sales potential. If it's voted a winner, then the product has an opportunity to be featured on-air on QVC.

Home Shopping Network (HSN)

HSN.com is another option, reaching 90 million homes with $3.3 billion in sales; it ranks among the top global retailers as well. Similarly, its vendor submission process can be found on the "partner" link on its website.

The Shopping Channel (TSC)

TSC (www.TheShoppingChannel.com) is a great option for people to get started. TSC is based in Ontario, Canada, and reaches about

Watch Video Message from Angel Ruelas

http://www.tamaramonosoff.com/angel-ruelas/

Angel Ruelas, creator of the Bra Tree, www.bra tree.com (a fabulous way to organize your bras), sold her product through the Sprouts program. QVC.com purchased 500 units of her product. Think about how long it would have taken to sell 500 units (one at a time) on your website. And, QVC handles the shipments to its customers. Clearly the opportunity that QVC offers can be incredible in terms of sales and publicity. In my book *Secrets of Millionaire Moms*, I included interviews of several women who have made millions of dollars on QVC. I will never forget the rush of experiencing a QVC sellout myself. But it should be considered carefully, as it does not work out for everyone and there is some risk that if your merchandise does not sell out, it will be returned to you in QVC packaging, which makes it difficult to resell later to other retailers, which I have also experienced.

Watch Video Message from Jenny Moore

http://www.tamaramonosoff.com/jenny-moore/

Jenny Moore, creator of BlingGuard (www.blingGuard.com), products that make your jewelry look and feel fabulous by resizing your ring size in seconds with BlingWraps so that your beautiful rings don't twist around on your finger and BlingDots for supporting and stabilizing earrings.

Her products are a great example of what online shopping channels seek. When asked about her experience, she said, "Exhilarating. Gratifying. Fulfilling. I first had the idea for Bling-Wraps nine years ago, when I got engaged, and then it took almost two years from when we first started working on the product to the time we went on-air."

She sold out on HSN her first three times on air!

7 million Canadian homes. In addition to television shopping and e-commerce sales, TSC also offers other distribution and warehousing services to product companies. Like QVC and HSN, TSC lists the vendor process on their site, which currently includes an open house for product reviews every month.

Direct Sales Television

Direct response marketing, which is sometimes referred to as "infomercials," a label that people in the industry seem to detest, is the process of creating a short television program or commercial that shows your product and offers a way to purchase it immediately online or by calling a toll-free number. The ads are then run on cable television channels, often late at night, to generate sales.

To be clear, these are television production services that you pay for, in addition to the airtime when your direct sales program runs.

There are two ways in which this can be approached. Practically every new inventor with a website and a phone number will at some point get a call that goes something like this:

"Hi, this is the producer for XYZ television show.... I am looking to discuss featuring 'your product' on our show.... Can you direct me to the person who makes these decisions?"

Because this sounds—intentionally—just like a call from a *real* television show, although you will not have heard of the show, most inventors will get very excited and start the discussion. Eventually, often 30 minutes or more into the conversation, you will find out about the "production and media cost." I have been offered these "deals" for $25,000. It seems that an offer of $8,000 to $10,000 is now more common.

After having spent way too much time with a couple of these calls myself, I learned how to differentiate a true media opportunity from a situation in which someone is selling me an "opportunity." First, don't let the caller gloss over the name of the TV program, and look it up immediately. Next, if it does not appear to be a regular television program, ask whether the caller is selling a service. I got to where I was able to detect these situations very quickly; I would simply say, "How much do you pay me for my appearance?" Being salespeople, these callers do not want to waste time with you if they see that you are on to them.

That said, as illustrated by the success of QVC, HSN, and TSC, television can be a powerful sales channel. And, not all of these firms are "below-board." Those that I would be most comfortable using are not actually media sales companies, but more along the lines of branding agencies that can offer production and media-buying services as part of their other services. Proceed in this area with caution. The best way to check for any negative experiences with these companies is to type their name with the word "complaint" into your search browser.

You can also search their name to see if there are any complaints posted at the Federal Trade Commission website, www.FTC.gov.

You can also contact the Electronic Retailers Association (http://www.retailing.org) and the professional association for design, AIGA (www.AIGA.org), to see if they are members in good standing.

If you do elect to try this route, read the contracts carefully. I would also have a business lawyer review the contract before you sign anything. It may contain future commitments regarding your product that you do not wish to make.

PART 3:
Doing It Yourself—
Sales Techniques and Tips

When it comes to reaching your customers, you have options: selling to customers and retailers yourself or hiring someone to sell your product for you. Obviously, the advantage of doing it yourself is more profits for you: you won't have to give a salesperson or distributor (covered later in the chapter) a cut of the sales. In addition, because you're creating demand for your product, it makes sense for you to make the initial sales yourself. When you do, it's important that you follow a few strategies and understand some key tactics for closing the sale, all of which are covered in this section.

Warming Up the Cold Call

Once you have a target list of retailers that you want to contact, you'll need to prepare before picking up that phone. A proven strategy is to draft a letter introducing yourself and send it to the retailer before contacting him or her. With your letter, include your product sheet and if possible a referral from a customer. While this can and should be done online if possible, don't underestimate the value of using old-fashioned mail. And if you send it in a USPS priority envelope, it is likely to land on the desk of and be opened by the intended recipient. The goal of this letter is not to sell the person product but to open the retailer up to your call. This is known as "warming a cold call." (*Note:* Depending on the size and cost of your product, it may make sense to also send a product sample.)

Once you've sent your letter, give it one week, and be sure to make the call. Making calls, even when they have been "warmed," can be difficult and nerve-racking. Some tried-and-true sales strategies include the following:

1. **Get the decision maker on the telephone.** Knowing this person by name is critical. When possible, get that information prior to this call, rather than asking for the "buyer" or the "owner." The latter is a sure way to have your call filtered. Instead, look up the company on the Internet and find out who the owner is, or call another

---

Sample Introductory Letter

Dear _____ :

I recently learned about your store from _____ . From what I have learned, I would be honored to sell my Unique Thing in your store.

My Unique Thing is the only product ever made that does _____ . Stores such as _____ have found it to be a solid addition to their offerings.

This product retails for _____ and garners 50 to 60 percent gross margin with minimum orders as low as _____ units. To first-time buyers, I am offering the following added bonus (free shipping, extra unit, free display, extra discount, or whatever).

I have enclosed a product sheet with our website and contact information. I will follow up by phone next _____ . In the meantime, please feel free to contact me with questions.

Yours truly,

Your name

Phone number

E-mail

Website

QR code: video demonstrating your product in less than 2 minutes (covered in Chapter 8)

---

time and say, "I want to send some free product information to the owner; can you give me the correct spelling of his or her name?" *Warning:* Also be prepared for the owner to answer the phone. If this happens, be ready to jump in with your pitch.

2. Plan your call. Your script should be brief, informative, and rehearsed. It should close with a question or a call to action (see "Telephone Sales Calling Tips" for suggestions). During business hours, store owners are juggling everything from landlords to personnel to advertising to customers. They seldom have time for phone discussions. That said, mornings are typically better than afternoons for cold calls. And often the best time to reach the owners is before or after hours and even on holidays—they often answer because they don't want to miss a customer.

3. Understand that rejection is an essential part of sales. Sales is a numbers game. The more prospects you have in your sales pipeline, the more chances you have for a yes. Having more prospects also means that you will receive more noes. So make a mental shift and see a no answer as being one step closer to your next yes. You have a clear decision; don't waste additional time on that prospect, and you are now one step closer to your next yes. And never take it personally. The worst thing you can do is respond to a retailer in an unprofessional manner. Use a rejection, instead, as an opportunity to start a relationship with this buyer. I've even had buyers who didn't buy my product, but who referred me to stores that did.

4. Remind yourself that no may just mean "no, for now." Always graciously ask a buyer why she didn't like the product. You will be amazed by what you learn. She might like the product, but it's bad timing—for example, the big-box stores (Target, Walmart, Babies"R"Us, and the like) may have already set their planograms for the quarter or the year (a planogram is a map of the product selection for the entire store). Or the buyer may not like one aspect of the product, which can be easily changed. No matter what, it's important to listen and to understand that your product just may not be a good fit for the store. Being disrespectful and annoying to a buyer is the kiss of death! Later, you may call the buyer with a different product, so keep your communications warm and cordial.

Telephone Sales Calling Tips

- Use a familiar tone, like you would use when you are calling a friend. Also, smile... it can be heard.
- Speak slowly. If you rush, your voice goes up and you don't sound confident.
- Be important. Without sounding arrogant, you must come off as someone of substance. Speaking slowly helps.
- Understand the challenges and be prepared for them.
  ▷ The challenge is to control the conversation discreetly, yet effectively. Whenever you come up against a difficult gatekeeper or buyer, phrasing your request as a question enables you to remain discreetly in control of the conversation (for example, "This is Jane Doe for John; is he in? Okay, would it be better to call him in the morning or afternoon?").
- Hang up. Once you get a sale, don't continue to chat. Say thank you and hang up.

After the Order

Now that you have the sale, you need to deliver.

Here's something to keep in mind: the graceful art (and value) of a simple thank you note has somehow been lost in our culture. Think about how many thank you notes you have received this year. You will realize two things: there have been very few, and, most important, you remember who sent them. Use the fact that nobody does this anymore to your advantage. If you send a simple thank you note, you will dramatically stand out with your new customer. Even when someone has said no, thank him for his time. *E-mail does* not *suffice*. It must be handwritten, on a simple piece of stationery or card simply saying "thank you," and don't use preprinted "thank you" stationery. Resist the urge to mix messages and incorporate follow-up sales information. That can be done in a separate letter. Delivery can have other complications as well. If you have just gotten into a mass retailer, there can be additional steps that you must take.

In some cases, you will need to make special arrangements just to land the deal! Then you need to meet those expectations.

Break the Rules

Don't forget that no matter what you are trying to achieve with your product, no matter how big the company, *you are dealing with people*. So, don't be afraid to break some rules and get creative. Use common sense, but if you need to make an impression or get a breakthrough

Watch Video Message from Pazit Ben-Ezri

http://www.tamaramonosoff.com/pazit-benezri/]

Pazit Ben-Ezri, creator of the Lulyboo (www.Lulyboo.com) tells this story:

The buyer of a major retailer was happy with the test results of my product and asked if we had enough inventory to fulfill an order for another 300 stores within seven weeks (at this point I almost fainted!). On the one hand, this was a dream and I understood that it was a one-time opportunity, but... on the other hand, I didn't have enough inventory to fulfill her need. My turnaround time for a new production run was 10 weeks. So, we got to work. I had my factory rush to produce just the covers of the Lulyboo and ship by air freight—at double the cost. We purchased the foam fill locally. The shipment arrived from China three days before the deadline, so we then hired a local team to assemble the product 24/7 at our California warehouse. We closed the final box as the freight truck arrived for the pickup. Of course we lost money on that order, but we earned a place on this major retailer's shelves, which also led to placement in other stores that want to carry the same items that it carries.

with a particular person, do something different. Make him laugh or find a way to get your message across in a positive way. During baseball season, we once sent a giant plastic baseball bat to a potential buyer with the line, "Hit a home run!" Not only did he see our samples, but he called us back. One time we had an inventor ask us to review her invention. When I clicked on the link, she had created a personalized message and greeted me by name!

Leveraging Prior Sales

As you sell more and your customer base expands, it will make sense for you to leverage prior customers to penetrate larger groups. Some independent retailers are part of larger buying groups. These are

Annette Giacomazzi, creator and CEO of CastCoverZ! (www.castcoverz.com), a business that provides cast covers and orthopedic products, illustrates creativity, follow-through, maximizing every opportunity, and a bit of serendipity:

As children are often our best teachers, customers can be our best mentors! I was involved with one of Tamara's mentoring programs when her seven-year-old daughter broke her ankle. After her daughter unexpectedly got the inside of her cast wet from a pool incident, Tamara was eager to resolve the problem. I was happy to introduce her to the CastCooler. Two hours later her cast was dry, but the doctor was skeptical. So Tamara and her daughter went back to the clinic. As the cast was being taken off two days later, Tamara was raving about CastCoverZ! and our products. Their doctor, Scott Hoffinger, M.D., became a believer when the dry cast was removed. He had never seen a soggy cast dried out so effectively. In a few short days, our products were displayed at his orthopedic clinic for new patients to use, and case goods were purchased by the clinic. Even better, just a few months later, Dr. Scott Hoffinger, now associate chief of pediatric orthopedics at Stanford University, became CCZ!'s medical advisor.

From that experience, we learned that whenever we speak with our delighted customers, we ask for the doctor's name and follow this "spread-the-CCZ!-love" process:

1. Ask for the doctor's name from a delighted customer.

2. Research contact information (learn about the doctor's background before you call).

CASTCoverZ!™

3. Call and stop in if that is geographically possible to demonstrate products. *Note:* If this is not feasible, then shoot a one- to two-minute video demonstrating how your product works and e-mail it to the doctor (covered in Chapter 8, "Blowing Your Horn").

4. Contact the doctor with a short *handwritten* note, "Your patient, Jenny Jones, loved our XYZ and ABC products. We thought you and your other patients would, too."

5. Follow up within a week or two with a cool die-cut or dimensional item mailing (something that relates to your business that is memorable and unique). Die-cut source: www.ThinkShapesMail.com; contact: Jim O'Brien

6. Follow up with another mailing, this time giving free samples.

7. Follow up with a phone call. The goal: the purchase of case goods and/ or display of our brochures. We have also secured many guest posts from doctors for our "Feel Better, Heal Better" blog this way, too!

8. Offer a die-cut display to physicians' offices to display your products.

What Is EDI?

EDI is an acronym that stands for electronic data interchange. Most major retailers will require you to use EDI to electronically manage the interface with their ordering and delivery systems. There are many EDI providers that provide both the technology and the consulting support needed. (*Note:* A quick search on Google uncovered many different providers.)

central committees or actual distribution centers that work to lever-age larger group purchasing power to garner better pricing and other marketing advantages. Once you have some of the members of these groups as your customers, it may make sense to approach the buying group directly. (Ask your customers for the names of their buying groups and ask if they would be willing to make an introduc-tion for you or at least provide a point of contact.)

More Ways to Make the Sale: Trade Shows

In addition to contacting consumers, retailers, buying groups, or other sales channels by phone or via individual meetings, there are other options for reaching a large volume of potential buyers in a very efficient way. Trade shows provide another way to do it yourself by meeting with potential consumers or retailers that are interested in your product, showing them the product, and making the sale firsthand.

Virtually every industry in this country has a member-based trade association. These organizations serve two main functions. First, they represent the industry to government policy makers as a united front, and second, they help facilitate business for their members. To support the second function, they often organize and host trade shows, creating a venue for their members to display products to industry buyers. These trade shows can provide a great opportunity for you to promote your products to interested buyers. One of the main reasons retail buyers attend these events is to see the newest products on the market.

To help you decide which trade shows are worth your time and investment, ask some of your best customers which trade shows they attend. They can give you insights into which shows their peers attend and the perception in the industry of various shows. Another deciding factor will be cost. Space at smaller, regional shows will cost less to rent than space at the larger national shows. Finally, be sure to consider the nature of the attendees closely. While some

Watch Video Message from Felicia Barrow

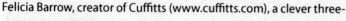

http://www.tamaramonosoff.com/felicia-barrow/

Felicia Barrow, creator of Cuffitts (www.cuffitts.com), a clever three-

in-one pot holder, learned this lesson the hard way. She tells the story—not that uncommon—of spending $1,500 to attend her first trade show: "When I got to the show, I realized that it was a jewelry and gift show, not a home and housewares trade show."

Felicia Barrow pictured here with husband Shadrach H. Barrow, III

shows will cater to independent retailers, others will be dominated by buyers from mass merchants. Still others will be oriented toward grocery and drug outlets. And finally, others are direct-to-consumer trade shows selling directly to customers (also called "end users") at full retail price rather than selling wholesale to retail stores.

The cost of exhibiting at trade shows can vary widely based on the industry, the size of the show, and its popularity.

1. Be sure that the show you plan to attend is right for your product. It is worth phone calls and online research to make sure that you are using your limited marketing funds in the best possible way. Find out about these at www.tsnn.com and www.eventsinamerica.com.

While trade shows are a good way to make sales, be sure to set realistic expectations. And, find out if the show is known as an "order-writing" show or more of a brand-building and networking show. If you can't tell, call the show organizer and ask directly. If you have a high-quality product that fits the industry, you should expect some sales, but keep it in perspective. A trade show should be just one component of your sales plan. If you expect to make your entire investment back immediately at your first show, you are not being realistic. It took me three consecutive years, attending the same show, where I met the same buyer of one large retailer each year. Finally, after the third year, and seeing our growth and success, she placed her first order for 100 stores. Also, sales should not be your only goal for the show. Use your attendance there as an opportunity to gain industry knowledge, make contacts, get feedback on your product, and build your product and brand awareness.

Make the Best of Your Booth

Booth space. Your booth space at the trade show doesn't need to be elaborate. As long as your booth is clean and conveys your product to the buyer, it is adequate. Today, you can search online and literally find hundreds of exhibit design companies that make and sell compact, easy-to-carry, and impactful booth display features that are much better than those available just a few years ago. To add to your booth without spending thousands on high-end panel displays, be creative. Find stands or shelves at a discount store. Bring pretty tablecloths to cover inexpensive tables. Create a sign or banner to communicate the name of your company. (*Note:* Do a quick Google search to find a banner company. I've used www.vistaprint.com.)

Booth location. Location is the most critical element of securing your trade show booth. Get a map of the show layout to determine your preferred locations. Most vendors jockey to be as much in the line of the main entry way as possible. Keep in mind that people tend to veer right after entering rooms. The corners of rows benefit from traffic in multiple directions, so they are preferred. Some shows also permit you to indicate whom you'd prefer to be placed near. Avoid being next to any vendors who will clearly dwarf you by their booth size. Also, avoid being placed next to any direct competitors. A good location is near food vendors and bathrooms, since everyone who attends the show will use these facilities at some point in the day.

Get some preshow attention. Before the show, send an e-mail, letter, or postcard to key customers with an overview of your product,

Watch Video Message from Kimberly Nimsgern

http://www.tamaramonosoff.com/kim-nimsgern/

Kimberly Nimsgern, creator of the Click-n-Curl (www.click-n-curl .com)—a brush that lets you dry, style, and set in one step—was attending the America's Mart show in Atlanta. Her experience is a perfect example as to the unexpected that can occur:

This was an order-writing show, which I have come to learn are attended by more than just buyers. An older gentleman was walking past my table. He glanced in my direction, which was all the encouragement I needed to ask if he was interested in hearing about Click-n-Curl.

He paused and said, "Sure." [I thought]... he... probably just wanted a piece of chocolate from my candy bowl, but I launched into my pitch anyway. He listened politely to my 60-second spiel and then asked to see the brush.... He then said, "I really want to work with you. This is the best new product I have seen at the show so far." He gave me his card. It turns out he was a sales rep that specializes in direct marketing or mail-related sales. Within a few weeks, he secured the Click-n-Curl placement in the Time for Me catalog. Click-n-Curl went on to be a top seller and was eventually featured on the back cover of the catalog—a coveted placement reserved for the best-selling products.

your booth number, and an invitation to visit your booth. Also mention any promotions, such as free gifts or prize drawings, to convince them to visit you. (If you can, choose a prize that will entice people to visit you, such as an iPhone, Kindle, or Nook.) While you don't have to break the bank on your mailer, an unusually designed direct-mail piece (www.thinkshapesmail.com) can serve to really get people's attention before they've even met you.

To further reach media, as well as target customers, another pre-show strategy is to draft and send out a press release prior to a show.

Even if the media don't write about it, send the release to your target customers. They may come by to see what is going on with your company.

Work it, work it! While you are at the show, be sure to welcome buyers into your space. As they pass, engage with them. They have come to the show to buy product, so give them a quick product demonstration, then tell them about your great "show specials." You may wish to offer free shipping or additional discounts for placing orders at the show.

Things You Will Need at a Trade Show

There are two main categories to consider:

1. Your booth:
    a. TV monitor displays; rolling video demonstrating the product (plays on a TV monitor); media samples (magazines and news clips featuring the product); and products (samples of your product).
    b. Good candy, gift for giveaway drawing, bowl for business cards (or, better yet, download a free app that scans business cards and badges right into your smartphone [https://bloodhound.com/lead-retrieval]), manual sweeper, packing tape, pens, a dolly (ask ahead if a dolly is allowed; some shows restrict using your own tools), scissors, paper towels, all-purpose cleaner.

2. Sales presentation tools:
    a. Think of things like handouts, whether hard copies, thumb drives, postcards with QR codes, testimonials, product samples, business cards, and so on.
    b. If it is an order-writing show, things to facilitate your transaction, such as an electronic payment system like Square (for a free Square Reader, visit https://squareup.com/), which allows you to take orders and accept payment on the spot via

your iPad or iPhone. Bring receipt books and order forms if you plan to take orders manually.

Trade Show Tips

- Wear comfortable shoes (not heels!). You will be on your feet a lot.
- Don't leave your booth unattended.
- Don't eat in your booth.
- While this is tempting, try not to chat with your booth neighbors, when prospects are around and when they are speaking with potential buyers.
- Have at least two people work the booth. Every so often, take turns leaving the booth to keep your energy up.

Tony Deitch, Founder of Sasquatch! Pet Beds Shares a Surprising Lesson

Tony Deitch, creator of the Sasquatch! Pet Beds (www.Sasquatchpetbeds.com), shares his success and the lesson he learned from a trade show he attended:

At our inaugural trade show, SuperZoo (http://superzoo.org) 2008, and winning Best New Product, we were selling to every independent pet store that walked by when a very small retailer with just two very small stores based in the Detroit airport came into the booth. We were busy, and, because our product is large, I was concerned that she would not be likely to have space to carry our large beds. I must have worked with that buyer for two hours, questioning this investment of time during the entire conversation. I finally persuaded her to put one Sasquatch! Pet Bed in each of the show windows. It turned out that they were the most important two beds we ever sold. This is because the exposure to people who were flying from around the world landed us many orders, including a distributor for Mexico. So, our biggest lesson is that, "every customer, no matter how big or small, is an important one."

Look for Deals to Save Money on Trade Shows

Look into preset rates, negotiated by the trade show, for hotels, car rentals, and airlines. Then investigate on your own for better rates.

Use the chance to meet others in your industry and learn all you can from them.

Amy Bonini (left) and Lisa Anne Kleine, Founders of Uber Mom and Creators of the Wipebox

Watch Video Message from Lisa Anne Kleine and Amy Bonini

http://www.tamaramonosoff.com/lisa-anne-kleine-amy-bonini/

Lisa Anne Kleine and Amy Bonini, creators of the Wipebox (www.ubermom.co)—a reusable designer wipe container for use on the go—share their experience. "We were at the ABC Kids Show; we were so eager and anxious that we pitched our Wipebox to everyone who walked by, even the janitorial crews! It paid off. The last day, we pitched the owner of a huge publicity firm. He told us we couldn't afford him, but he offered to help us out anyway because of our enthusiasm."

Jill Boehler, creator of the www.chillyjilly.com (a warming shoulder wrap in a compact silk bag to be kept in a women's purse) illustrates this last point perfectly. After spending six years building her business, with the arrival of her four grandchildren, she decided it was time to sell the business. After spending time with acquisition brokers, she ended up selling her company to someone she already knew. "They brought several buyers to the table, but I ultimately sold Chilly Jilly to a company, TotalStockRoom.com, whose owner,... Adam Slater, I had met at several trade shows and whom I had developed a relationship with."

PART 4:
Duplicate Yourself:
Growing to the Next Level

Sales Representatives

Hiring salespeople is one way to increase sales efforts by duplicating yourself. However, unless you have a large cash reserve, hiring direct staff is typically difficult. Independent manufacturers' representatives represent a solution to this challenge.

Manufacturers' representatives are professional sales individuals who have struck out on their own, "repping" various manufacturers' products. These manufacturers' representatives, often called "sales reps," will normally carry a handful of products from different manufacturers within the same industry. They generally have exclusive rights to present and sell each manufacturer's line to the customers in their territory and are paid predominantly on commission from the sales they generate. Territories can be defined in a number of ways, including geographic region (for example, the Pacific Northwest), account type (for example, all drug and grocery stores), or even specific account name (for example, Walmart and Kmart). A manufacturers' representative carries samples of your product but does not take ownership of your product. When a rep gets an order for you, he will send you the purchase order, and you will ship to the customer and invoice the customer directly.

While developing a network of manufacturers' representatives sounds like the ideal solution, it is not without challenges. First, it is difficult for a new, unproven company to attract reputable sales reps. Because these people live on the commissions from their product sales, they cannot afford to spend much time "pioneering" new products or taking on too much risk. Therefore, they prefer products that have a strong likelihood of substantial revenues, such as products from well-established brands or new versions of high-volume items. When they do "try" your item, they tend not to push a buyer beyond some initial resistance, as they want to move quickly to the next product, which might make for an easier sale.

Second, manufacturers' reps are difficult to find. Since they are independent entrepreneurs specializing in particular industries, who often base their business relationships on their personal network, they can be tough to identify. One place to look for them is through your industry trade association, which may have a database of registered representatives who attend its trade shows. Probably the best place to find them is through your retailers in various territories. Ask them about the reps who call on them, who their favorites are, and who they think might be the best fit for your product. While you're at it, ask for a referral. A call from a retailer who says that she is about to order your product is a great way to convince a rep to take on your product. Prior to our first trade show, I sent letters to 300 registered manufacturers' reps inviting them to visit our booth, in hopes that we would be able to quickly establish a national network of sales pros selling our product. We had exactly *zero* reps visit our booth. However, by the time we went to our third show, we had developed some accounts in their territories, and they began to seek us out. This is the most effective strategy I know to lure them in. If you can, tell prospective reps that if they rep you and bring in new accounts, you'll give them your already existing accounts in their region. This can provide a good incentive for them to join your team. Don't worry about the commission you'll give up; in the long run, this is a small cost for a high-quality rep. In addition, they will assume the burden of supporting the accounts you pass along to them.

The last challenge is monitoring the rep's performance. It is common to hear manufacturers complain about their reps' productivity. But, if you have an unproven product, it's difficult to motivate them with your limited leverage. To counteract this problem, continue to push for accounts yourself, even in their territory. Eventually they'll realize that you may stop passing accounts to them if they can't prove their worth.

Sales representative compensation varies widely, depending on your individual agreement. Commissions are often commensurate with the accounts that reps secure. For mass stores, including grocery and retail, an average commission is about 5 percent. For specialty and niche retailers, which may take more legwork and are more about "pioneering" than about simple "order taking," commissions average 10 to 15 percent. Different reps will have different expectations, but I prefer to pay them on collections rather than on orders. This way, they have a vested interest in making sales to customers who will be likely to pay.

There are associations that have rep lists that you can buy or "join," but since reps tend to be industry-specific, this may be a less direct way to find them.

> United Association of Manufacturers' Representatives: http://
> www.uamr.com/rep_info.html
> Association of Independent Manufacturers' Representatives:
> http://www.aimr.net/

And there are other "connecting" services, such as: http://www
.manufacturers-representatives.com/

Distributors

Another option for duplicating yourself, and thus your sales efforts, is to work with a distributor. A distributor buys product from you (the manufacturer) and resells it to its retailer customers. Dealing with a distributor is more like dealing directly with a large retailer. The distributor takes ownership of inventory and assumes responsibility for selling, shipping, invoicing, and supporting its accounts. In many cases, a distributor will have its own network of sales reps and staff.

A distributor is often necessary if your goal is to sell to major mass-type distribution channels, such as drug and grocery stores and big-box discount stores. While it is not impossible to sell to these mass-oriented retailers directly, it is a challenge. Large retailers tend to avoid working with small companies that have just one or two products. A distributor, on the other hand, will combine your item with his list of multiple products and assume the handling issues associated with dealing with small companies.

Unfortunately, recruiting a distributor is even more difficult than recruiting a sales rep. Since distributors are going to be dealing with you, the small, "risky" company, as well as taking on responsibility for inventory management, merchandising, and collecting payment from the retailer, they are highly selective as to whose products they'll represent. One strategy for securing a relationship with a distributor is to get your target retailer to say that he wants your item, and to have him refer you to one of his distributors. Even though you will have to give up a large amount of your profit margin to deal with a distributor, it will be more than worth it. In addition to shipping and warehousing services, the distributor is responsible for ensuring that the mass retailer has your product displayed properly and keeps inventory on the shelves—an impossibility for a small company.

For example, when Roberta Wagner, creator of Carry-Her (www. Carry-Her.com), the easy-to-use doll carrier, had piqued the interest of Toys"R"Us to carry her item, the company actually offered to connect her with a distributor who worked with it. While not true in every case, this can be very beneficial, as many times, distributors sell to multiple large retailers, meaning that they can quickly introduce your item to others.

When we first started out, we had often felt that some of our items would be perfect for the clip strips that we saw hanging in the grocery store. After a couple of years of approaching supermarket buyers, we learned that these items are often handled separately by distributors who specialize in clip-strip programs. While this is not right for many items, if it is a fit, you can sell a lot of units this way. Some of these distributors sell into thousands of retail stores. We sold thousands of units each week, through some 9,000 stores, this way. The three largest clip-strip distributors of this kind, also known as "impulse merchandisers," that I am aware of are:

ATA Retail (www.ataretail.com)
Lami Products, Inc. (www.lamiretail.com)
Imperial Distributors (www.imperialdist.com)

Other Distribution Paths to Consider

Are there direct sales companies that would like to sell your products? According to the World Federation of Direct Selling Associations, "Direct selling is a dynamic, vibrant, rapidly expanding channel of distribution for the marketing of products and services directly to consumers." Examples of direct sales companies include www.Silpada.com, www.Nuskin.com, www.Initials-Inc.com, www.StellaandDot.com, www.petlane.com, and www.Discoverytoys.com.

Promotional Products

Companies spend millions of dollars on promotional items with their logo printed on them. Is your product well suited for this? Note that these companies are not likely to be interested in products that do not have a patent. Here are some examples of promotional product companies: www.Norwood.com, www.Branders.com, and www.halo.com.

Dollars and Sense

Of course, before you sell anything, you'll need to know how to price it. While initially this may seem overwhelming and difficult to figure out, fortunately, there's a formula that can help ensure that you're recouping your investment, making enough profit to stay in business, and making some money in the process. The key to pricing your product is to understand the concepts of gross margins and markups, and how to use these concepts to work out a winning formula.

Understanding Profit Margins

The entire process of bringing a product to market is driven by profit margins. If the gap between what customers are willing to pay for a product and what you can earn distributing it to them (that is, the profit margin) is not large enough to justify producing the product, the product should not be produced. In earlier chapters, we covered the costs associated with planning and producing (manufacturing) the product. Here we will cover some basics about margins as they apply to distribution of your product.

I will begin by defining four terms that are often confused. First, *retail sales* are the sales of a product to an end user. For example, when you buy cookies at the grocery store, it's a retail sale. Second, *wholesale sales* are the sales by a manufacturer or distributor to a retailer, who will in turn sell to end users. Using the same example, this would be Nabisco selling its cookies to your grocery store chain. The third term to understand is markup. *Markup* is the difference, in both dollars and percent, between what a retailer will pay you for a product wholesale and its retail price (that is, what the end user will pay). So, if Nabisco sells a bag of cookies to the grocery store for $2, and the store sells it to you for $5, the markup is $3. The fourth is *gross margin*. The gross margin, which is often confused with markup, is the percentage of profit derived on the transaction. The best way to convey these meanings is through more examples (discussed later).

Demystifying Markup

If I, the manufacturer, make a product that we'll call Unique Thing for $1.00, and I sell it wholesale (to a retailer) for $3.00, my markup was $2.00 ($3.00 − $1.00 = $2.00), or 200 percent (2 divided by 1 = 2.00). If that retailer, in turn, sells Unique Thing for $8.00, her markup is $5.00 ($8.00 − $3.00 = $5.00), or 166 percent (5 divided by 3 = 1.66). Remember the math trick: when converting a decimal to a percentage, you just multiply the decimal by 100. For example, 1.66 × 100 = 166 percent, or skip the multiplication step and just move the decimal point two places to the right and add the percent sign.

Getting to Know Your Gross Margins

Gross margin is calculated by dividing the markup by the cost at which you sell it. Again, my Unique Thing markup is $2.00 ($3.00

– 1.00 = \$2.00). To figure out the gross margin, simply divide the amount of this markup (\$2.00) by the amount I sold it to the retailer for (\$3.00). The manufacturer's (my) gross margin in this example is \$2.00 divided by \$3.00 = 0.67, or 67 percent gross margin. So in this case, a 200 percent markup resulted in a gross margin of 67 percent.

The retailer's gross margin for Unique Thing would be calculated the same way, just using her markup and costs: \$5.00 divided by \$8.00 = 0.625, or 62.5 percent. The retailer's 166 percent markup resulted in a 62.5 percent gross margin.

There are great free tools available on the web that can be used to calculate these numbers automatically. If you log onto www.tamara monosoff.com/Guides and register, you can watch our free margin calculator tutorial. This calculator can help you determine the selling price for your products to achieve a desired profit margin. By entering the wholesale cost and either the markup or the gross margin percentage, we calculate the required selling price and gross margin. To know what your pricing should be, it is important to ask your prospective retailers what their margin requirements are. This will vary widely, especially between specialty/catalog/online retailers and distributors and mass-market retailers.

It is not uncommon for retailers to request a minimum gross margin of 50 percent, often referred to as a *keystone markup*. An easy way to figure out this number is to double your wholesale price to the retailer. (For example, if you sell your product wholesale to a retailer for \$5.00, a keystone markup means that the retailer will sell that product at retail for \$10.00, which equals a 50 percent gross margin for the retailer.) When you need to work backward to come up with a price that gives your retailer his desired margin, it is helpful to use this as a starting point. High-end specialty retailers will often require an even higher gross margin.

In case the retailer doesn't mention how much margin she expects or "needs" to make on your product, do not be shy about asking her. You may feel that you are asking her to reveal her private financial information, but this is not true. This is how retailers think and how business works!

Distributor margins vary by industry and segment, but a margin of 25 to 40 percent is not uncommon. Keep in mind that a distributor will be selling to a mass retailer who will also want a 25 to 50 percent gross margin above what it will pay the distributor for the product.

For example, the margins and markups for a product sold through a distributor might look something like the following (assume a $10.00 retail price, a 50 percent retailer gross margin, and a 30 percent distributor gross margin).

$10.00   retail price
 $5.00   wholesale price (to retailer from distributor)
 $3.50   distribution price (from manufacturer to distributor)

If the manufacturer's cost is $2.00, her gross margin is 43 percent ($3.50 − $2.00 = $1.50 and $1.50 ÷ $3.50 = 0.43. Therefore, 0.43 × 100 = 43%)

Make sure that there is something left for you! You may have to get your production costs down in order to make money and still meet the margin requirements of both your distributors and your retailers. This is possible to achieve because going through a distributor normally means that sales volume will be higher and the distributor incurs much of the cost of delivery.

What's an Adequate Gross Margin?

Unfortunately, there is no simple answer to this question. Gross margins vary dramatically by industry and product type. And even within an industry, they will vary. A large company with substantial scale may be satisfied with a 20 percent gross margin. Of course, its massive volume enables it to be profitable at this rate. On the other hand, many small-business people I know have a 50 to 70 percent margin. Keep reading for tips on how to figure out where you should fall.

Temper Your Early Profits

When you first begin selling, it's natural for you to be eager to recapture your initial investment. If you can do this, great! But keep in mind that this is a long-term venture, especially when it comes to pricing.

While you want to make an adequate gross margin, you don't want to price yourself out of the market, thus forfeiting valuable relationships with retail accounts. Because early manufacturing runs are often small, your costs are often high, and you may be tempted to pass on the higher price to the retailer. But remember that you need to create demand for your product, and it's often difficult to create substantial sales traction early on.

It may be necessary to forgo large profits in the beginning to get some sense of what the sales and profits could be at a "customer-friendly" price point. Ideally, you'll conduct market tests (see Chapter 3) to arrive at an approximate price point to start with.

On the high end, your gross margin should be "as much as you can get." As illustrated earlier, the factors affecting this outcome are your production costs, your retailer's margin expectations, and the market price at which your product will sell, with the last one being the most important. If your production cost is so low and your product is in such demand that you can sell enough of them at a 1,000 percent gross margin, go for it!

That takes me to the low end. When is the gross margin too low? Obviously, you can't have margins so small that they won't sustain your cost of doing business. The answer to this is based on knowing your goals and your expenses. If simply creating some part-time income satisfies you, and your labor is your only major expense, then you can tolerate a rather small gross margin. For instance, if you're making jewelry to sell locally, and your main "cost" is the time you take to produce each piece, you can get away with a low gross margin percentage. On the other hand, if your expenses are high and growing, and you are trying to generate a substantial return for yourself and other shareholders (investors, if you have them), you need a larger return. Remember that all of your company's costs, such as your salary, phone, staff wages, marketing, rent, and other operating costs, must be covered by the gross margin earned on your sales. In fact, there's a term for the percentage of money that's left after paying for all these expenses—it's called your *net profit margin*. And only you can decide what net profit margin is acceptable—unless, of course, you have investors who have a specific expectation for their return.

Of course, your own gross margin target should be specific to your product and goals and enough to cover your operating costs. For me, a gross margin below 35 percent would raise the question of whether the product should be pursued (unless I was doing millions of dollars a year out of the gate). I would tend to target 40 to 60 percent as a reasonable gross margin, and again, on the high end, get as much as possible. You will know that your gross margins are too low if you find that you are unable to meet the costs you regularly incur to operate your business.

Chapter Wrap-Up

Creating demand for your product is a methodical process that helps you build your sales from the ground up. As you find success in each phase of the process, you should then move on to the next bigger sales outlet or find a method to expand your distribution. Once you understand your customer and have positioned your product, create a sales plan. Start by selling direct to consumers, then to small independent stores, and finally to larger mass retailers (if this is appropriate for your product). Remember, consumers are not going to rush out to buy a product that they do not know exists. Also note that while understanding theory and process is important, there's no substitute for sweat equity—making the calls and doing the selling! "Sales" is a skill that anyone can learn, and you are your product's best salesperson! Lastly, be patient. For most people, this process takes longer than they originally envisioned.

Jill Boehler of Chilly Jilly (www.chillyjilly.com) voiced a common comment from those who shared their full stories with me. "What most surprised me about running the business is how difficult it is to get the product out there. If you are not a known entity, or you do not know a movie star, it is difficult to get past the first-level contact. It takes many rejections to get one positive response, but *it can be done.*"

In the next chapter, I will cover approaches to leveraging traditional advertising, public relations, social media, and some of the newest tools and techniques, including video marketing, for making a big impression.

Blowing Your Horn

Watch Video Message: Tamara Monosoff introduces Chapter 8

http://www.tamaramonosoff.com/
tamara-monosoff-introduces-chapter-8/

Marketing That Works!

Marketing and public relations are the *golden tickets* to your business success. If no one knows that your great product exists, or where to find it, your business (and your product) will go nowhere. While getting your product onto store shelves is a major achievement, if the public does not go and buy your product, there are many other products vying for that space. So, you need to help create awareness so customers seek and buy your products off those shelves. The great thing is that it is easier now than ever before to broadcast news about your product in creative ways without breaking the bank. In this chapter, you will learn about a variety of the hottest new tools to make a lasting impression on your customers, retailers, buyers, and the general public, including video marketing tools, iPhone and iPad apps, and QR codes (like the ones featured in this book). The goal of marketing is to get people talking about your brand, product, and business, while your job is to continue rewarding their loyalty and enthusiasm.

First Things First: What's Your Story?

Before I show you the exciting marketing tools that are available to you today, you need to craft your brand story and think about the message and feeling about your business that you wish to convey. Inventors often get so wrapped up in developing their product and are so eager to move forward that they rush through, or ignore completely, this important part of the product development process.

Learning the Lingo

When I first began this adventure, I didn't understand the differences among public relations, marketing, advertising, and branding. In fact, I often used the terms interchangeably. Before you adopt specific tactics to increase awareness of your product and your business, you should understand the lingo as it applies to marketing, public relations, advertising, and branding. There are entire books dedicated to these topics, but I just wanted to take a brief moment to define them here.

Marketing. Marketing is a broad term, often used loosely, that includes branding, public relations, publicity, advertising, product pricing and positioning. The term can also be stretched to include everything from market research to website promotion to direct sales. "Marketing" firms across the country offer a broad array of services, most of which work toward a common goal: making the public aware of your product. So, marketing, in its broadest terms, is simply the practice of researching your market, positioning your product to fit, and letting people know that it's available.

Marketing plan. A written marketing plan helps you identify your customers and the strategies you plan to implement to reach them. It details the necessary actions that you plan to take to achieve the marketing goals for your product (or product line), service, or brand. It is often part of a larger overall business plan for your business.

Branding. Your brand is a distinctive name or symbol that communicates a message and position directly to your target customers. More than a simple logo, a brand identity conveys a specific feeling, attitude, and personality that defines the brand and creates an impression that lasts. Designing your brand is one of the most critical business steps that you will take. Your brand will be the core of your business, regardless of the products that you sell.

Public relations. Public relations is the process of communicating your message, usually through the unpaid media, to your target customers. Your public relations efforts should promote a positive image of your business, so that customers will have a good feeling about purchasing goods or services from you. Your public relations strategy can involve everything from getting "free" editorial coverage in media like TV, newspapers, and magazines, to sponsoring seminars that support your product, to backing social causes that will help generate goodwill for your company.

Social media. Think of regular advertising media as a one-way street, where you can read a newspaper or listen to a report on television, but you have very limited ability to give your thoughts on the matter. Social media, on the other hand, is a two-way street that gives you the ability to communicate too via social media platforms (Facebook, Twitter, Google+, Pinterest, and so on) on the Internet. (Source: About.com.)

Advertising. Advertising differs from public relations in that it is a paid form of messaging. You see or hear hundreds or thousands of ad messages a day through TV and radio commercials, newspaper and magazine ads, Facebook and YouTube ads, and the list goes on. The advantage of advertising is that you control the message completely, as opposed to public relations opportunities, in which you are reliant on reporters to craft the message.

"Apps." Apps stands for applications that run on a mobile phone or tablet; hence "mobile apps." There are two main types: "native" apps, which actually reside on your phone once they are downloaded from the App Store, and HTML5 apps, which are really designed to simply view websites by using the web browser of a mobile phone. No App Store download is necessary.

We tend to relate to other people's stories, so the goal here is to engage customers, retail buyers, the media, and investors in your own story and your mission. A mission is a short, powerful statement about the "heart" of your business. (Your mission is also part of your business plan. More on business planning in Chapter 10.) Before you market your business, you need to have clear, well-crafted stories that you are going to communicate to the public.

In his book *Start Something That Matters*, Blake Mycoskie, the founder of TOMS Shoes, talks about the power of stories.

> When you have a memorable story about who you are and what your mission is, your success no longer depends on how experienced you are or how many degrees you have or who you know. A good story transcends boundaries, breaks barriers, and opens doors. It is a key not only to starting a business but also to clarifying your own personal identity and choices.

Building Your Story

You will need different stories for specific purposes and varied audiences: a "personal story," a "brand story," a "product story," a "media story," an "investor story," and so on. While these messages may vary, they should not contradict your mission. Whether it's video marketing or TV show appearances, it's all about your story. In fact, the *first* question that is most commonly asked by TV hosts and reporters is, "Why did you start this business?" or, "Tell us about your business." And often, this is where the inexperienced entrepreneur stumbles. If you have your well-crafted story fleshed out, you'll be ready to go on the spot! One thing to keep in mind: your stories need to be *short*, engaging, and authentic.

To get started, answer the following questions.

1. What's your personal story? How did you think of your product or business? How has the decision to go into business changed your life? In what way? For example, when I became a mother after my high-powered career at the White House, I suddenly was at home with my new babies, and I felt disconnected and isolated from the outside world. I didn't feel that moms were being valued or recognized for their intelligence and creativity. I wanted to change that, which is what inspired me to create the Mom Invented brand.

2. **What's your brand story?** What is the "meaning" of your brand? What is special or different about your business? Give a lot of thought to your brand and its meaning. For example, the Mom Invented brand does offer simple solution-oriented items to solve common, everyday problems. But, most important, what I love about the Mom Invented brand is that it's not about me. It's about both celebrating the intelligence and creativity of mom inventors who create our products (every inventor is pictured on our Mom Invented packaging to give her credit for her great idea), and inspiring other moms to be inventors themselves.

3. **What do you want your customers to think and feel when they see your brand logo?**

  ▷ Write down words to describe your company. For example, do you want your brand to convey *cutting-edge*, *family-friendly*, *exclusive*, *upscale*, or *community-oriented*?

  ▷ Write down associated images that fit with the descriptive words you listed (for me, it was a circular motion image that illustrated community and fit the words *mom invented*). Is your company high tech, homey, or fun?

  ▷ Write down who your customers are. What images do you think would encourage your customers to buy from you? Why?

  ▷ Think of names for your brand that your customers can relate to. Should it be abstract (Google), or should it be descriptive (Mom Invented)?

  ▷ Test your name and initial brand messaging either through informal focus groups or via an e-mail blast (see Chapter 3 to learn how to do this).

  ▷ Make sure to listen to this critical feedback. It is easy to get attached to your brand in the same way you get attached to your product idea, but remember that you will ultimately benefit from hearing people's honest reactions.

▷ Listen also to what your heart is saying. After you have listened carefully and incorporated the useful feedback from others, it is important to also consider what you are feeling.

4. What's your product(s) story? This is often referred to as your "creation story." Why did you create your product? What benefit will your product have? For me, it was all about toilet paper! My daughter started pulling toilet paper into the toilet, which was cute until she clogged it. I went to the store to purchase a gadget to prevent kids from doing this, and it didn't exist. So, I decided to invent it. The media loves this story and look: I said it in three short sentences.

5. What's your story for the media? You may use bits and pieces of your personal, product, or brand story when you speak to the media, depending on context. Some TV segments that I do are simply "show and tell," demonstrating a table full of products. Other

What to Do When You Receive *the* Call

When reporters, producers, or editors call you, because of their time constraints, they will quickly ascertain whether you're a fit as a guest or a feature story. They don't want to waste any time, and they will usually immediately launch into asking you a series of questions. First, try to determine the angle of their news story and what they want to convey about you and your business or product. Once you have determined that, be short and concise with your answers (these are called "sound bites" in the media world). They are testing you on the call to see if your answers are too long-winded (and it is likely that the TV host, for example, will be asking you the same questions, because the producers usually write them for the hosts). Speak to them as if you're already on TV: be engaging and concise.

times, I am an expert guest and offer tips about the product development process or speak about trends.

Be True to Yourself

There are times when a TV segment is simply not a fit. Once, I was asked to go on a major TV network during prime time to discuss something that was really off topic for me. The media exposure would have been huge; however, at times like this, it's important that you trust yourself. I graciously declined and told them that I hoped they would consider me in the future when they covered topics that were related to my expertise. Sure enough, I was invited back shortly after.

6. Investor story. At some point, you may decide to seek investors (see Chapter 6, "Get Funded!," to see other options and opportunities). This story is very different from the others just mentioned. If you go this route your story needs to be about money. Investors want to know how they are going to make money from your business. Therefore, your story needs to cover the gap in the market, how you (your business) are filling that gap, the sales that you are already achieving or are projecting to earn, and what you are offering them (equity, aka "ownership" in your business).

Be authentic! People can detect inauthenticity a mile away, so be true to who you are.

Building Your Brand Takes Time

Your brand is an extension of your mission as well. The most successful brands—think Apple, Nike, Target, and TOMS shoes—elicit reactions and feelings before a word is even spoken or communicated. Simply put, strong brands are easier to sell. And strong brands engender long-term loyalty, translating into repeat sales.

Creating your "brand" is all about instilling the impression that you want your target customers to have of you and your product or service, in addition to connecting with your customers through ideals that they care about. It generally takes more than a single communication for the meaning of your brand to settle in, even with the people you do reach. We will discuss some strategies for creating and strengthening your brand, which in turn supports your success at selling.

While your message will initially come from you in some form, your success will ultimately be determined more by what other people say about you, your product, or your service than by what you say yourself. This is the highly valuable "word of mouth" marketing that you ultimately want to inspire in others. (Be sure to sign up for the www.wordofmouth.org newsletter, which offers some of the best weekly marketing tips I have found to date).

Create a Strong Brand Logo

Along with your brand's message, you will want a brand logo that represents your business. One of the best options is to use one of the following websites to get a variety of sample designs from different designers. When I started out, I hired an expensive marketing firm to create the Mom Invented logo, and I was given only three options from one designer. Now there are inexpensive and fun ways to get a great logo (and website graphics) designed with hundreds of freelance designers at your fingertips. Check out 99designs (www.99designs.com), which is a crowdsourcing platform of graphic designers. You can create a contest for your logo design where designers compete for your business. Fiverr (www .Fiverr.com) is a marketplace for services starting at $5 for the initial design. And crowdSPRING (www.crowdspring.com) gets rave reviews as well.

Your Business in the Spotlight: Get Press!

Although there are advantages to hiring a marketing company, I believe there's a lot you can do first on your own when it comes to getting your message out (especially if you're working on a shoestring budget). These efforts are focused on helping you get editorial coverage rather than advertising coverage. Editorial coverage ranges from being asked to provide expert insight for an article on your industry to seeing your product featured in a newspaper or magazine article. The one thing all these results have in common is the ability to create awareness about your product with potential end users without having to pay for the exposure.

Crafting Your Press Release

Your first step in garnering editorial coverage for yourself or your product is to write a press release. This is usually a one- or two-page document that tells a story about your product. Most important, this story needs to be compelling and exciting—it needs to have a fresh or relevant angle so that reporters will feel that they are drawn deeper into your story. For example, did your product make life a little easier for harried mothers? Is there any element of drama that can be added? If not, create one!

Everyone Loves a Little Drama

Realize that reporters are constantly looking for interesting new stories, so give them one and add a little drama. If you are an expert in a particular area, you could write "The Five Tips for [your industry]." Get creative, but, of course, don't get carried away—and never lie. This isn't just a matter of personal integrity; you also risk getting caught when the media does its fact-checking. If you need help spicing up your story, ask others to offer their perspective and listen to what they say. Your friends, family members, customers, and colleagues may surprise you and view you in a way that you never even imagined.

Putting Pen to Paper (or Fingers to Keyboard)

Once you've really thought through your story, you'll be prepared to begin the actual writing process. Keep in mind that you can write multiple press releases; in fact, it's advisable to do so. Whenever you have a new angle on your product to offer the media, consider drafting a press release to let them know about it. Just be sure that the angle is fresh and interesting enough to warrant a press release. Other goals might be to establish credibility or show company growth.

Create a Catchy Title

Need help generating an appealing headline? Look no more! For years I have racked my brain trying to come up with compelling headlines, and this headline creator helps you generate multiple headlines for free! Visit www.InternetMarketingCourse.com, then click on the button called "Free Headline Generator" on the left side of the screen. You can use this for your blog posts, too, and it's fun!

If you need tips on drafting and formatting a press release and sample templates, sign up for Bill Stoller's *Publicity Insider* newsletter (http://www.publicityinsider.com/release.asp). Many other resources are available if you Google "press release templates."

Embed Video!

If you want a big open rate with your press release, include video! Embed a YouTube video (or at least a link to your YouTube video) of you demonstrating your product or talking about your company into your press release. It should be under two minutes to keep viewers' attention. And, make sure to include your website address (URL) in the description underneath the video to make it easy for viewers to click from the YouTube video to your website to learn more.

Announcing the News

Once you draft a release, getting it out there is key. Use powerful resources like PR Web (www.prweb.com) and PR Newswire (www

.prnewswire.com), which are Internet-based wire services. They, and others, give you the option of sending your press release "over the wire," where the media have access to it. You also have the option of paying more to get higher placement in the news feeds. I was extremely lucky in that the *Today Show* picked up one of my stories from PR Web. Though I've since discovered that this kind of pickup is extremely rare, it still can happen. Keep in mind that you will be using the press release mostly for yourself as a tool to share new information with others.

You could also be proactive and use e-mail. Identify specific reporters, editors, and producers who you would like to target, and e-mail the press release directly to them.

If this Savvy Grandma Can Do It, then So Can You

Watch Video Message from Trish Cooper
http://www.tamaramonosoff.com/trish-cooper/

Trish Cooper, inventor of Zatswho (www.zatswho. com), a soft photo game for little ones to learn to recognize loved ones, is a savvy grandmother who pitched her story to *Fox & Friends* in New York, and she and her daughter were invited to be guests on the show. Here's how she did it:

I look at different show websites to see what types of stories they do, whom they recently had on (so as not to be redundant), and who the various segment producers are for these morning shows by searching on Google. Once I find their names, I begin the search for their e-mail addresses, which are usually not available. I look to find the common way the shows use e-mail. Sometimes you can find the pattern of the e-mail by going to the bottom of the website and clicking on the "Advertise with Us" or "Corporate info" button. Companies almost always include a contact person with an e-mail address on these pages. Then I take the producer's name (which I found on Google) and configure it in the same format.

Continued

I also pitch my story differently for different shows. Sometimes it's the mother-daughter angle, or the mom entrepreneur's angle, but for Fox and Friends, I pitched the military angle. I know that Fox does segments supporting our military. My daughter Carrie's husband is an Army sergeant who served in both wars: Iraq and Afghanistan, and one of the organizations that we donate Zatswho sets to is called Operation Shower, which gives baby showers to the moms-to-be of deployed members of the military. This angle not only gave us an opportunity to pay it forward and plug Operation Shower, but gave us a chance to meet actress Melissa Joan Hart (Sabrina, the Teenage Witch), which resulted in publicity pictures of Zatswho and additional media coverage.

Sweet Success!

So, you've crafted a great release, sent it out on the wire or e-mail, and voilà! You've received interest from some of your target media. Great job! Once you get past the initial excitement, the news will begin settling in, and you'll realize that you'll soon be under the hot lights. And whether it's the literal hot lights (you've been asked to be on TV) or the figurative type (a magazine reporter wants to interview you), it's natural to feel some nervousness or apprehension about what you'll say, how you'll look, and how you can best get your message out.

Relax. You'll do fine! If you've gotten this far, you've already demonstrated your publicity savvy. Now for the fun part—getting the word out about your awesome new product to hundreds or even thousands of people.

Stay on Point

Your reason for courting the media is to sell your product and grow your business. It is fun to be interviewed but be sure to think about the message(s) you want to convey. I usually think of some succinct main points (not more than three) that I want to convey and rehearse them out loud.

During your own interview, look for opportunities to get your message out. One mom inventor I know got a "big break" to feature her product on television. She demonstrated her product beautifully on TV, but she was so excited that she forgot to say where people could buy it. It was a fun segment, but it ended up having little business value.

Targeting Celebrity TV Hosts

Watch Video Message from Melanie Cruz
http://www.tamaramonosoff.com/melanie-cruz/

This strategy is a long shot, but sometimes it works! If you have a product that could resonate with a TV host who is experiencing something (for example, she just had a baby, and you have a great newborn product) or something that you think will fit with the host's personality, give it a try.

Melanie Cruz, creator of Bebe Doos Perfect Ponies (www.bebedoos.com), sent her fun product to Ellen DeGeneres, and tapping into Ellen's good humor paid off... big time! Melanie shared her strategy here:

I needed more exposure for my product, so, I sent in samples and a letter to the Ellen DeGeneres Show. She is hilarious and seemed personable, so I figured, "What could I lose?" In her package, I also made her a giant adult-size Bebe Doos Perfect Ponies headband. Well, she ended up putting on the one for a baby on her head like Rambo, and one of the men who is on her crew came out with the giant headband. She said it was made for her bald aunt on the show; she definitely "half" made fun of my product, but shortly after that episode aired, my sales went crazy... especially in Australia!

As Seen on TV

This section focuses on TV appearances because, by far, they're the most demanding and stressful of all your media appearances—if only because you'll be seen and heard, often on a live broadcast.

Since launching my business, I have been fortunate enough to appear on dozens of local and national television programs, including all the traditional broadcast networks (NBC, ABC, CBS, FOX, and CNN) as well as cable networks such as Warner Brothers. Programs I've appeared on have included NBC's *Today* show, *CNN Live*, and ABC's *Good Morning America*. In addition, I have been interviewed by reporters from a number of international, national, and local magazines, newspapers, and radio stations, including the *New Yorker*, the *London Times*, and CNN radio. Each experience has been entirely different, and it would have been great to know what to expect in advance. To help reduce some of your own pre-show jitters, here are some good strategies:

You are what you wear. Though this doesn't mean that you need to spend a lot of money on your wardrobe, you do need to think carefully about what you'll wear. I've worn my own clothes, borrowed outfits from family members, and even bought one jacket for $18 that I wore on KTLA *Los Angeles Morning News*. What they all had in common, though, is they conveyed the right look, with the right colors. Colors that work well on TV include red, blue, and black; white is never a good idea. In addition, learn about the viewing audience in advance, and be sure to look the part in order to best "connect" with it. For example, dress like an executive to appear on a business news show, and tone it down for a "sophisticated mom" look to appear on a soft news show targeting women. When I appeared on *CNN Financial News*, for instance, I wore a bright red, yet conservative suit. The viewers of this program are primarily men, and I wanted to make sure that I was taken seriously. You also never know when prospective investors may be observing you and may approach your company. Therefore, it is important to look and speak like a professional.

Also be mindful of the region you are in. Fashion dos in southern California may be fashion don'ts in Indiana. And, when in doubt, look professional. If you want to be taken seriously as a business-woman, wear something conservative that will drive attention to your face, which will focus attention on what you're saying, not what you're wearing, especially on TV.

Makeup matters. You may be a makeup expert dating back to your teenage years, but everyday makeup is vastly different from TV interview makeup—something I learned the hard way after watching myself on my first television appearance.

I knew I needed help, so I visited one of the makeup counters at my local mall. I asked specifically for a makeup artist who was knowledgeable in makeup for television. Two hours later, one of the firm's top artists had taught me how to apply shocking amounts of makeup without scaring my kids!

Jen Fleece of Fleece Baby had a makeup experience of another kind. For her first TV appearance on ABC's *News Now*, Jen had a half-hour drive to the studio in Atlanta. She left two hours early so that she could dress and do her makeup when she arrived. She couldn't have anticipated a rainstorm and traffic jam that brought her to the doorstep of ABC one minute before show time. As she ran in, she was told that she needed to be on air now. Jen had to go on national television for the first time with wet hair and no makeup! Lesson learned: never leave your house for a television broadcast without being fully prepared to walk on the set, even if it means that you have to wake up at 4:00 a.m.!

Expect the unexpected. It's also important to note that each time you make a media appearance, your experience can differ wildly. That's because different shows have different formats. I wish I had understood this before going on camera for the first (or second, or third) time.

My first experience was with Katie Couric on the *Today Show*. Katie is lovely, and although I felt nervous, she put me at ease. I found that if I focused on her completely and listened and responded to her questions, I was just fine. After reviewing the tape, I also learned that there were times when I was on camera and didn't realize it. Lesson learned: smile and look focused, even if you think the camera is not on you.

In one of my appearances on *CNN Live*, not only was it 4:00 a.m., but I was seated in a room with an automated camera. The only human contact I had was with the anchorman, across the country, through my earpiece. There was not even a monitor on which to see him. It was pretty surreal. With my earpiece in my ear, looking into the void of a camera, I did my best to listen carefully and respond with an animated face. It wasn't easy, but it worked.

Tips from the Hot Seat!

Over the past decade, I have become a regular media contributor on a variety of topics. However, it didn't start out that way. I was a mom, starting a business, and trying to navigate my way with little knowledge or direction. Here are a few things I've learned from the "hot" seat.

Five Tips to Ace Your TV Segment

1. **Prepare questions for the TV host even if she doesn't ask for them.** I have found that if I send questions ahead of the TV segment to the producer, they will be used about 99 percent of the time. They may change the wording a bit, but for the most part they are the same. This will help you relax because you already know the answers to the questions you've created. And, your preparation greatly helps the overworked producer save time. Bring an extra copy with you. More than once, I have handed a frazzled reporter my questions (bullet point format and large 16-point font) just minutes before going *live*.

2. **One private minute with the TV host that counts!** In most live interview settings, even when done by remote split screen, you will have at least a brief moment with the host prior to going live. While most guests respond

to the host with a smile and some chit chat, you should make sure the host remembers why you are there. Make these seconds count!

For example, for my last book tour for *Your Million Dollar Dream*, I met every TV host with a smile and said, "I wrote this book because so many people are at a crossroads trying to figure out what to do next for work. I'd like to talk about the three approaches to entrepreneurship. I have three quick, great examples. My book hit number one on Amazon in all three business categories." Then I took a breath and smiled again. Nearly every time, the TV host directed the conversation based on that 60-second summary (my own message) that I had just shared.

3. Avoid darting eyes. If you are being interviewed by a host, look directly at the host and not at the camera (unless you are instructed otherwise). If you are feeling nervous, imagine that you are sitting in your living room speaking to a friend. If you are being interviewed remotely, you will be looking into the void of a dark camera lens, and you won't be able to see the person you are speaking to. This can be a challenge your first time. Focus your eyes at the center of the camera, and force yourself to be expressive and engaged. As long as your eyes are on the camera and not darting around, you will convey confidence and comfort, which is what you want viewers to feel.

4. Make the host look good. The main concern of most hosts is how *they* look and sound, not how *you* do. Answering a question by beginning with a brief, "That is such an insightful question," makes the host feel good, builds rapport, and leads you into your answer. Do this only once or twice during the segment (not for every answer), or it will feel contrived.

5. Show your appreciation on social media. After each TV segment (or radio show), jump on to Twitter and Facebook. Tell your followers and fans how great the segment was, and express your gratitude to the TV show and host for having you as a guest. Often TV shows are posting the video segments on their websites within 24 hours of your segment. If so, grab the link and share that on your social media networks, too! Not only will this create a good rapport with the TV show, but it further extends the reach of your appearance.

Me with Daughter Kiara (six months) and Katie Couric of the *Today Show* in May 2004. I brought Kiara with me to New York City and nursed her minutes before my national television debut. Multitasking at its best!

On some shows, I have been instructed to speak directly to the on-air host, while on others, I have been told to speak directly to the viewers through the camera. For example, Gayle Anderson, morning news reporter for *KTLA Los Angeles Morning News*, warned me to expect a nonconventional "Jerry Springer–style show, but with clothes and no fighting," which I definitely now understand. She expects her guests to connect directly with their viewers by looking straight into the camera. It is important to ask the producer of the show about the format beforehand, so that you can be prepared. Also, make sure to put the earpiece in the ear that feels most comfortable and the least distracting. Even though I am right-handed, I like to have my earpiece in my left ear. One last point about earpieces: you may hear a voice other than the anchor speaking in your ear. This is the producer. While you should listen and respond to the anchors, you must *not* respond to the producer while the segment is in progress.

Tough Questions

Business reporters often feel obliged, as part of the nature of their job, to ask you financial questions about your company. Be prepared! You don't want to skirt around this or look skittish, because it calls your credibility and legitimacy into question. Here are three suggestions for how to handle financial questions: (1) Share the information if you are comfortable doing so. The producer may or may not use it, and your financials, good or bad, may be what makes the station want to write about you. (2) Avoid sharing by saying,

Roberta Wagner's (inventor of the Carry-Her Doll Carriers (www.carry-her. com) disappointing TV experience fueled her internal fire, which turned out to be a blessing in disguise.

Never give up on your dream. If you can dream it, you can do it! I was cut from a major TV show last summer. After working with the producers for three months, they cut me a week before my scheduled flight. I was beyond devastated. I wanted to give up. I was so tired of the roller-coaster ride. My closest mompreneur friends were aware of my situation, and they all told me the same thing; "I didn't need the show. I could do this on my own." This knockdown made me push harder for my goal to get my product into FAO Schwarz. I succeeded six months later, and I don't have to share my sales with anyone."

"My company is private, and we do not disclose our financial information." (3) Skirt the issue by using future projections rather than historical figures. For example, "Our projections for next year are $500,000." If you feel uncomfortable talking about financials, practice your preferred answer until you can say it without a pause.

Since you are dealing with live television and relying on others, go into it knowing that things don't always go as planned. When this happens, just roll with it.

The Power of Public Relations

Small businesses often have big ambitions and slim marketing budgets. In comparison to paid advertising, press coverage can be much more cost-efficient. Also, media coverage—when positive—has tremendous credibility. Unlike paid advertising, which may state claims about your product or service, an article about your business in the news media comes across as unbiased and can be far more persuasive.

As with any business strategy, it takes time and finesse to make PR work. Media professionals that you seek out, like a PR firm, can

It's All in the Pitch

....

Watch Video Message from Ann Noder
http://www.tamaramonosoff.com/ann-noder/

Ann Noder, CEO and president of Pitch Public Relations
(www.pitchpublicrelations.com), and I have worked
together for nearly a decade. During that time, I have
received unprecedented media coverage for both my
business books for entrepreneurs and the Mom Invented
family of products.

I interviewed Ann for this book and asked her to share her best insider tips
that you can use right now to secure media coverage.

**Tamara: When you are pitching a client, how do you determine the best
media angle?**

Ann: The trick to successful media placement is to pitch the right story to
the right outlet. Do some research on your target publications and outlets to
determine what kinds of stories they cover. Also, make sure your angles have
a "timely" element to them. In other words, what makes this a news story *now*
rather than six months from now or a year ago?

**Tamara: Should you pitch your story to all media outlets in the same way?
If not, how do you change it to be a better fit?**

Ann: A business writer at the *New York Times* is not going to respond to the
same angle as the parenting editor at *Working Mother* magazine. Tailor your
messaging accordingly, depending not only on the outlet that you are targeting, but, more specifically, on the individual contact! If you're doing the
PR yourself and you're not sure who the best contacts are, don't be afraid
to reach out to the outlet and ask for a recommendation on the appropriate contact. Magazines typically have a full list of their editorial staff right in
front of the issue. That will help you pinpoint contacts there. Many reporters,
producers, and editors are on LinkedIn, Twitter, and other social media channels. Many of them encourage pitching via these methods. Do a little online
research to find the right contacts in your space.

Tamara: How do you know if your story is best suited for TV (national or local), magazines, newspapers, or blogs?

Ann: Don't overlook the value of local and regional opportunities in pursuit of national coverage. Often, those outlets can provide more extensive and thorough coverage—giving you more value! And in some cases, an article in a local paper can get syndicated and run in dozens of others. Or a local TV segment could catch the attention of a national producer. For your specific market, focus heavily on your local story. Offer to do a show-and-tell type segment on your local station's morning newscast (offering five tips for viewers is a great hook). For print, is there a milestone or major achievement that you can point to? Blogs can be a very effective way to create a viral buzz about your business. Look for bloggers who have a loyal following and an active online presence. These writers are considered "influencers" in their space and can go a long way toward raising a company's national profile.

Tamara: What should you prepare ahead of time?

Ann: Get all your marketing and PR collateral in place, including a strong website and professional product or company photos. It's difficult to succeed without laying the proper groundwork. Magazine editors can easily be turned off by unprofessional packaging. A strong website can help you get national exposure.

Tamara: What are some of the biggest mistakes people make when they are in the media spotlight?

Ann: Landing the media opportunity is only part of the battle. Taking advantage of that moment in the spotlight is equally important. Make sure you have nailed down your messaging beforehand. Can you explain your product or service or business in 20 seconds to someone who knows nothing about it? You should! Don't leave it up to a reporter or anchor to ask you "just the right questions." What do you want the readers or viewers to know? Getting the critical information into a story is key, including saying the name of your business and its website (leave off the "www") several times.

One of my clients landed a coveted interview segment on *Good Morning America*. She looked great, and her product was beautifully displayed! *But* she never once said the name of her product or her company. Instead, she kept

Continued

saying, "I created this" and pointing to it. Throughout the whole segment, she kept saying "this" and "that" instead of the actual name.

Lesson: always get the name of your product or business into your answer! In fact, you should say it multiple times. And be prepared for the very open-ended question that **many** TV anchors start with: "Tell us about your business." It was that question that got her off track.

Also, once you land that great coverage, make sure to leverage it! For manufacturers of products, that means getting the media coverage in front of pending retail buyers. Share it with potential investors. Use the news!

Tamara: Any secret tips?

Ann: A "pitch" to a media contact shouldn't be more than two or three short paragraphs! Get right to the point of your story in the first sentence. Don't include a long backstory. And here's a nugget that many people don't know: be very clear in your pitch on why you are sending to that contact (do you want him to interview you, do a story, run a bylined article, or try out the product?). Don't expect your contact to read between the lines. Ask for what you want!

Tamara: Do you have any other advice you'd like to share?

Ann: Yes! Be realistic. If you've never done PR before, it's going to take some time to get the results you want. Don't be afraid to start off small and grow from there. You're not likely to land the *Today Show* right out of the gate. Also, identify your goals right away, so that they coincide with your PR strategy. Want more local awareness? Focus on news outlets in your market. Need to drive national consumer sales? Target mainstream press outlets across the country. Want to gain retail and distribution channels? Identify industry and trade publications that suit your business. You can't hit the ground running until you know where the finish line is.

Pitch Public Relations is a leading boutique PR agency based in Phoenix, Arizona. The firm focuses on consumer PR in many industries, including healthcare, family and parenting, business, nonprofits, and technology, among others. Pitch PR offers an array of services, including PR strategy and story development, media outreach, press release and pitch writing and distribution, media training, and social media, among others. CEO and president Ann Noder is frequently featured as a top public relations expert on Yahoo!, CNN, CNBC, and *Entrepreneur*.

become what I like to think of as extensions of yourself. They help you share your story and have established relationships with traditional media outlets.

Using Editorial Calendars

Kim Nimsgern, creator of the Click-n-Curl (http://www.click-n-curl. com/) mentioned earlier in the Chapter 7, shared how she landed media stories using editorial calendars, which are a publication's schedule of upcoming articles and special sections on a particular topic or focus. You can use editorial calendars to your advantage when you are promoting yourself and your product. If your story is compelling, a publication is likely to pick it up. Like sales, garnering publicity is a numbers game.

"Prior to hiring Pitch PR, I was working at it on my own, using free resources such as HARO (www.HARO.org), editorial calendars, and LinkedIn.

Editorial calendars are typically found in the Media Kit, which is often found in a link in the tiny print at the very bottom of the magazine's website. Editorial calendars are actually for folks who want to advertise (which is why, on Oprah's site, it's in the Ad Sales link). Sometimes magazines are managed by media companies, and it's on their site that you will find the calendar, so at times, a little research is required. Here is an ehow article on how to find editorial calendars: http://www.ehow.com/how_4479860_get-magazines-editorial-calendar.html.

Once you find the Editorial Calendar, you will see that it is chock full of great information for people like us who want to pitch a product for editorial consideration or inclusion. The Media Kit and the Editorial Calendar include the planned theme for each issue and each month, the deadline dates for ads (and I would also assume content) for each issue and sometimes the names of the editors. This information helps you target the right editors at the right time with the right information for the right issue.

Award and Recognition Programs

Nominating yourself for award programs is another way to generate press! There is no shame in doing this, and it is a great promotion tool that you can add to your websites or social media.

To find out if there are any award programs in your area, contact your local chamber of commerce and search Google.

Here are a few national recognition programs to get you started. Many of these are focused on children; however, type "innovation awards" into Google, and you will find a large variety of opportunities.

- **Stevie Awards** (www.stevieawards.com/women). For women entrepreneurs.
- **The Edison Awards** (http://www.edisonawards.com/) recognize and honor innovation and excellence in the development, marketing, and launch of new products and services.
- **Moms Choice Awards** (www.momschoiceawards.com). Product swards.
- **Cribsie Awards** (http://cribsieawards.com/). Product awards for tots and toddlers.
- **Parent Tested Parent Approved** *(PTPA)* (www.ptpamedia.com). Seal of approval.
- **Dr. Toy's Best Children's Products Awards** (www.drtoy.com/toy-awards/). Awards are given for the most useful, outstanding new toys and products to promote activity, creativity, learning, and fun.

Video Marketing

One of the most important and effective ways to entice both the media and consumers is by creating captivating videos. This tactic can attract many more visitors to your website and can result in more sales.

So What Exactly Is Video Marketing?

Video marketing is simply incorporating videos into your overall marketing strategy. The reality is that people watch videos more than they read. Why? Because most of us are visual learners. Here are some interesting facts:

- Approximately 65 percent of the population are visual learners. (Source: Mind Tools.)
- The brain processes visual information 60,000 times faster than it processes text. (Source: 3M Corporation.)
- The online video audience reaches 84.5 percent of the United States. (Source: comScore.)
- A web page that has a video is 50 times more likely to appear on the first page of Google. (Source: Forrester Research.)
- E-mail subject lines with the word "video" included get higher open rates, from 7 percent in the past to 13 percent. And there is a 24 percent higher average order value (think about people ordering your products!) when compared to e-mails that relied on static images. (Source: Liveclicker.)
- Video is on pace to account for about half of all web traffic by 2014. (Source: Experian.)

Video is no longer an option. It is a necessity, and it needs to be an essential part of your marketing plan. When I launched my last book *How Hot is Your Product?*, I spent a month writing my video script. Then I uploaded it to the teleprompter (iPad with Teleprompt App) and read it out loud over and over again before I began recording. You might make mistakes during recording, but you can edit your video by using editing programs such as Camtasia by TechSmith (for PC and Mac) or iMovie on the Mac, or hire a professional on Elance. com or Odesk.com. It takes a combination of preparation, practice, ups and downs, and a bit of courage. I know that if I can do it, then you can too!

There are a variety of both on-camera and off-camera options to improve your brand visibility, and you can see the many options here.

On-Camera and Off-Camera Video Options

Video marketing is fun! As I mentioned earlier, whether you plan to do on-camera or off-camera videos will depend on your business and your branding goals. If there is a resource that I mention here that just fits for you, start there. After that, earmark this page and come back for more ideas to test out what works best for you and your business.

On-Camera Tools

You can use your camera, smartphone, or webcam to create "direct to camera," sometimes called "talking head," videos. In other words, it's you speaking directly to the camera to communicate with your

Lights. Camera. Action! How to Build a Home Video Studio

Once you start churning out videos, you may want to invest in a home studio. I built a studio for under $1,500, but you may be able to create it for less.

Camera. Most cameras have a built-in video function. There is no need to invest in an expensive video camera unless the videos are your business. Make sure that you buy a camera with an external microphone jack. You will need a tripod.

Lighting. It is important that you have good lighting. You can find professional lighting tools on Amazon, and it's usually more cost-effective to buy a kit with three lights rather than buy them individually. Search "Softbox Lighting Kit," which includes special fluorescent bulbs.

When recording on my webcam, I use two lamps on either side of my computer that have a flexible head so that I can aim the lights directly at my face. For a warmer appearance, purchase "full spectrum" lightbulbs (hardware stores often carry them, or purchase them online).

Light diffusers are also useful, and the ones I use came with the Softbox Lighting Kit that I mentioned. These diffusers soften your appearance; the ones I use on my small lamps look like shower caps. These do two things: (1) make it easier for me to see rather than having bright lights blind me, and (2) soften the light on my face.

Background/backdrop. For your in-home studio, you can buy backdrops of any color in cloth or paper in a roll (you will need a backdrop stand to hold it, too, which can be found on Amazon). If you use a white background, you will need extra lighting on the backdrop itself to prevent shadows. You can also use a "green screen," which will give you a lot of flexibility by allowing you to change your background electronically. iMovie has this feature built-in for the Mac. This feature is available on most video editing software. *Note:* Pay close attention to your background. I recently watched a video of someone selling graphic design services, but I was distracted by the messy room in the background.

Backdrops purchased online can range in price. I bought my 6 × 10-foot Black Muslin Photo Video Backdrop for under $20 on Amazon.

Microphone. Sound quality is essential. Make sure that you test your sound before you film. I purchased a Lavalier Omnidirectional Condenser Microphone that clips to my shirt. It has an especially long cord (30 feet), so that I can be far away from the camera and it won't affect the sound quality. If you're using a camera, make sure that it has an external jack for a microphone.

Teleprompter. Need a little help staying on track with your message? One of the coolest Apps ever is Teleprompt (you can download it from the App Store onto your iPad for under $20). You can easily adjust the speed and font size. *Tip:* When you're reading a teleprompter, keep your eyes at the top line. Don't read ahead and look down at the lines below, because then it will look like you're reading. You may need to increase the speed of your teleprompter so that your eyes can stay at the top. *Another tip:* Know your script. I find that just having the teleprompter is comforting so that I don't have the pressure of memorizing everything that I want to say.

customers, fans, and followers. If it's a video for your home page, you may tell the story about your business, what inspired you to start your business, and how others can get involved. You can also use programs like Google Hangouts, ooVoo, iMovie (Mac only), iPad, or Skype, all of which use your built-in webcam cameras from your computer, phone, or tablet. These videos can then be posted to You-Tube and your other social networks, as well as being embedded on your website or blog (learn more about blogs and social media later in this chapter).

Google Hangouts (www.google.com/hangouts)

Google Hangouts brings conversations to life with group video calls for free. At the end of the recording, you get a link that can be shared and posted directly to YouTube and Google+. *Note:* You can have up to 10 people on camera at a time on Google Hangouts.

ooVoo (www.ooVoo.com)

Similar to Google Hangouts, ooVoo is a great video tool. I like this program because it allows you to have a split screen as you converse with someone else. You can add your name and title under your screen when you are speaking, just as when you see people being interviewed on television. The videos are then saved as an mp4 that can be edited (Camtasia, iMovie, or FinalCutPro for advanced editors). Once edited, it can be uploaded to websites like Screencast, which will not only host your videos but also provide links that make it easy for you to post and share them everywhere.

iMovie

iMovie uses your webcam on the Mac to create videos where you are speaking directly to the built-in camera. You can then edit your iMovie to switch between you and a Keynote presentation (Power-Point on a PC). Either way, the presentation can be recorded and saved as a link to share on all of your social media networks.

Skype

Skype is a great way to make video calls over the Internet instead of using the telephone. Callers can see each other through their own webcams (similar to Face Time on the iPhone) and, as with Google Hangouts and ooVoo, the screen can be recorded and shared via social media.

VideoStir

Another innovative video option is called VideoStir.com. With Video Stir, you film a quick direct-to-camera video and add your website address (URL), and your video (of you) will appear on your website.

Things You Can Do with Video

Watch Video Message from Lou Bortone
http://www.tamaramonosoff.com/lou-bortone/

My good friend and video mentor, Lou Bortone, is an expert when it comes to video marketing! Here he has offered some great ideas to help you get started. For more tips, visit Lou's "wicked cool video marketing" website: www.loubortone.com.

Keep in mind that, with video marketing, as with any endeavor, your goals should drive your direction. Different kinds of videos are more effective for different kinds of objectives.

Consider using some of these video styles based on your specific business objectives:

1. Talking head. This is what most people think of when they think video: basic "head and shoulders," direct to the camera, standard shot. The talking head video is popular because it works. It's perfect for most personal promotional videos, whether it's a direct appeal, an "about me" video, or a "first impression."

Continued

2. Live demo (on-camera). On-camera product demonstrations can be one of the most effective videos you can produce.

3. Photo montage. One of the easiest types of video to create is a photo/video montage. Websites such as Animoto.com, OneTrueMedia.com, and Stupeflix.com make it "drag and drop" easy to turn your text and photos into a video. Add some text and music, and you've got a professional video!

4. Sales video. You could argue that any video is a sales video, but here we're referring to video sales pages, where often the sales page is nothing more than a video and a "buy" button.

5. Video testimonials. Testimonial videos are a powerful, yet underutilized tool for providing social proof. These can be used on your website or on a sales page promoting a specific product or services. I usually bring my iPhone to conventions or events, and grab quick testimonials while networking with colleagues and clients.

6. Video e-mail. Saving what may be the best (or easiest) for last, video e-mail is a great way to connect and engage with your customers (retail buyers), colleagues, or prospects. It's incredibly simple to record and send a video e-mail, using just your webcam and a free website such as MailVu.com. Just click, record, and send. Video e-mail provides a powerful, personal touch that makes you stand out and not get lost in the flood of traditional e-mail.

With so many video formats to choose from, you could create dozens of videos and never run out of ideas or different ways to produce your video. What video style appeals to you most? Which one will you choose for your next video?"

Lou Bortone is an online branding specialist and video pro who helps entrepreneurs and service professionals build breakthrough brands on the Internet so that they can have more visibility, credibility, and profitability. Drawing on his work as a former television executive for E! Entertainment Television and Fox in Los Angeles, Lou delivers innovative online branding strategies, including video production and editing, social media marketing, and online video consulting.

Take a look at www.videostir.com. You can also hire actors to deliver your message on your website for about $250 for a 30-second message. Check out www.websiteactorlive.com.

Off-Camera Video Tools

You can use the following programs to create videos without recording them yourself.

- **Animoto** (www.Animoto.com). Its online video maker turns your photos, video clips, text, and music into video in minutes.
- **VideoScribe** (VideoScribe.com) helps illustrate your ideas in an engaging way. Make sure to watch the tutorials before you get started.
- **Video Blocks** (www.VideoBlocks.com) allows you to purchase blocks of professionally shot "royalty-free" videos for you to use.
- **Intro Designer App** (www.IntroDesigner.com) is a quick way to create a dramatic introduction to your product or business.

Blogging Matters

A blog (short for "web log") is your own personal website that allows you to connect to others. Blogs can also be a smart business tool. For instance, professional and amateur journalists use blogs to publish breaking news, and some blogs even command thousands of hits per day. Websites are one-directional, in that you are speaking to your audience and not receiving feedback, but blogging is two-directional in that it is interactive and engaging.

I encourage you to set up a blog of your own and use it as a marketing tool to seek information from consumers and elicit feedback from prospective consumers about your products and services. A great way to encourage people to connect with you is to end your blog posts with questions asking for their thoughts and feedback.

Does Your Business Need to Be Active on Social Media?

The answer is a resounding yes! Social media provides an online platform for people with common interests to connect with one another. There are social networks organized around virtually every subject imaginable, from geography (local businesses or events happening in your community) to meeting people with common interests.

What surprised me the most about joining Facebook and Twitter several years ago was that many of my customers, community members, and competitors were already there. There are also other networks that are growing fast, like Google+, Pinterest, and Instagram. And these are only a few of all the social networks available. There are literally hundreds of other online social networks that you can use to your benefit. In many cases, they will be moret effective for your specific business than the major ones discussed here. There's a great map that you can download for free at http://www.ovrdrv.com/social-media-map/; it will give you a visual picture and the names of hundreds of social media platforms organized by category.

Regardless of which social media platforms you choose to participate in there are some overall perks:

They're mutually beneficial. The old model of communication was based on the idea that the loudest, funniest, most elaborate ad gets customers—to the benefit of the advertiser. Social networks are different. There is a mutual sharing of information and connection for each other's benefit.

They're free. One of the most powerful aspects of social networks is that for the most part, they are free. This levels the playing field when you are competing against larger companies that carry similar products and services.

Their reach is unlimited. Social networks have tremendous reach. With mobile phones and wireless technology, you can download social network apps directly onto your iPhone or Android and stay connected with people around the world 24 hours a day, if you wish. As a business mom, this is a relief, because I can take my kids to lacrosse practice and still get "business" done.

Their power is undeniable. The ability to reach so many people at one time is mind-boggling. Check out the following statistics:

Facebook	665 million active users / 751 million mobile users
Twitter	500 million users / 200 million active
YouTube	1 billion users / 4 billion views per day
Google+	343 million users
LinkedIn	225 million users / 2.7 million business pages / 1.5 million groups
Pinterest	48 million users
Instagram	100 million users

Source: http://bit.ly/SocialMediaStatsApril2013.

Facebook

Facebook is one of the largest social networks in the world. Many people create a personal profile page, but there is also an option to highlight businesses, products, and brands with Facebook pages that are similar to your personal profile page, but focused specifically on your business. Go to www.facebook.com, and underneath the sign-up section, in smaller print, there is a link titled "Create a Page for a celebrity, brand, or business." It's a great visual way to engage with your customers. By building a Facebook page for your business, product, or brand, you are giving customers a great way to find you, become a fan, and promote your product through word of mouth by sharing your information with their friends. You can also promote your page with Facebook Ads, which Facebook pushes out to thousands of people based on the criteria you select. Learn more about Facebook Ads here: www.Facebook.com/Ads.

Twitter

Initially, Twitter can look intimidating. If you don't understand Twitter right away, don't despair. This is a common reaction for people in the beginning. Because of the 140-character limit for each "tweet" (which is similar to a Facebook status update) various methods are used to squeeze as much information as possible into that small space. For instance, because of the condensed format, people tend to use shortened links that don't resemble the URLs that we're used to. You can get shortened links at www.tinyurl.com and www.bitly.com. Most important, be sure to write a bio to give people a sense of who you are and what you do.

Twitter hosts a lively community of business owners, marketers, and news media people, but the real power of Twitter is the real-life connections it can help you make. TV hosts, reporters, producers, and editors are all there and you can reach out to them directly.

YouTube

Arguably, YouTube has become the most powerful social platform today. This video-sharing platform is being used by 1 billion people worldwide! It's simple to upload your videos to YouTube and share them on all your other social media platforms as well as your website. Here are some quick ideas to extend your reach on YouTube:

- Create a product demonstration video.
- Leave helpful and nice comments on other YouTube videos. If you really want to get attention, create a video response. This can help drive traffic back to your page and can help you form connections with other YouTube posters.
- Create a video from an event that you've hosted, and be sure to feature some of your guests. If they're savvy about their online presence, they'll post the video on their sites, too.
- Make sure to include a call to action at the end of every video. In other words, tell people what you would like them to do: visit your website, purchase the product you are demonstrating,

or vote for your product on a contest website like Walmart's "Get it on the Shelf" Contest.

When posting your video on YouTube, make sure to include keywords in the title of the video and in your description, and remember to include your website URL.

Google+

Google+ is a social networking service from Google (plus.google.com). The idea is pretty similar to other social networking services, but Google attempts to differentiate Google+ by allowing more transparency in whom you share with and how you interact. It also integrates all Google services and displays a new Google+ menu bar on other Google services when you're logged into a Google account.

Google owns YouTube, which means that it's easier than ever to post your events. For example, if I were to host and record an event on Google Hangouts, in one click I can post it to my YouTube channel and share my recording on Google+.

LinkedIn

LinkedIn is the leading online professional directory of individuals and companies. Here are some strategies for using LinkedIn to further your business goals.

- Access key contacts you have identified via your own connections.

What Is a Keyword?

Search engines use keywords when they include your website, blog, or YouTube video in their search results. Use keywords because it can improve the ranking of your post, which, in turn, means that more people will view it.

- Use it as a professional, public résumé so people can see your credentials and what you do.
- Answer questions and establish yourself as an expert.
- Search and contact buyers at retail stores or catalogs to sell your products.
- Promote your sites and your blog.
- Connect with old colleagues, coworkers, and friends in a professional capacity—you never know when they can help.
- Send private messages to connect with people in your industry or other people you're interested in meeting (buyers, suppliers, or media).

Creating a powerful presence on these networks can strongly reinforce your brand—or, in fact, create it.

Advertising

You probably have gathered that I have placed an emphasis on using PR and social media for my own marketing. However, there is a place for paid advertising; especially when it is integrated with, or includes, social and online components.

This might be an overstatement, but not by much: there are almost an infinite number of places you can buy advertising. Most people think of newspapers, television, radio, Internet, and magazines as advertising venues because these are the major media outlets that we see every day. However, if you stop to think of the number of ways marketers reach us every day, it's dizzying: direct mail, coupons, e-mail, telemarketers, bus signs, website ads, and on and on. That ubiquity is also one of the principal problems with advertising from the advertisers' perspective. The sheer number of messages creates clutter and makes it difficult for any one message to get through.

However, there are also advantages to paid advertising. First, with paid advertising, you have 100 percent control over your message. You write the content, design the ad, and choose the music, message, and visuals.

Second, because there are so many possible places to buy advertising, it is often possible to get your message in front of a very specific or niche target audience. If you sell a product for scrapbooking, for example, there are magazines, websites, and catalogs that serve scrapbooking enthusiasts. And you could probably even narrow your ads to scrapbooking enthusiasts within a specific geographic region.

Getting your own carefully crafted message in front of your target customer is helpful in the process of creating the designer perception of you, your product, or your service. However, because advertising is well understood to have been bought by the company that's promoting its own wares, it seldom will create, by itself, the kind of buzz and confidence that other methods can generate. If the impression of your brand is already solid and well established, advertising can be useful to communicate changes or special offers such as discounts, or to reinforce your brand and maintain top-of-mind awareness.

What Is a QR Code and Why Should It Be a Part of Your Marketing Plan?

A QR code is a shortened term for "Quick Response Code." Today, virtually everyone has a smartphone which is becoming a preferred way to get information. QR codes help make that process easy. You are seeing QR codes featured throughout this book as an example of what is possible. A QR code is an unobtrusive, two-dimensional bar code that, when scanned with your smartphone camera, brings your message, products, and brand to life. You can attach a video, a website (URL), or a coupon directly to the QR code, depending on its purpose. QR codes were originally developed in Japan in 1994 by a division of Toyota to track inventory in the automobile manufacturing industry. Since then, QR codes have been used around the world and are becoming more and more popular.

Here are some fun ideas for weaving QR codes into your marketing plan. QR codes can be printed or scanned from your computer screen. All you need to do to read them is to download a free QR reader. I used Kaywa for the QR codes in this book. Here's how to do it:

Step 1. Download a free QR code reader onto your smartphone by searching the App Store. I selected the Kaywa Reader because it was free of advertisements.

Step 2. Go to the QRcode.kaywa.com website to get started making QR codes. You'll be able to make dynamic QR codes within minutes, and you get your first five free. I also picked Kaywa because it allows you to turn your logo into a QR code (discussed earlier), which is an incredible branding opportunity.

Scan the following QR code to see how you can start creating your own QR codes with Kaywa.

Watch Video Message: Tamara Monosoff Talks About the Power of QR Codes

http://www.tamaramonosoff.com/
tamara-monosoff-talks-power-qr-codes/

Fun Ideas to Engage Your Customers with QR Codes

Spice Up Your Boring Business Cards

I've seen QR codes on business cards that take you directly to the person's LinkedIn page, but why not take it a step further and introduce yourself on video, what you offer, and something special for the viewer, like a free 30-minute consultation or a coupon for your online store?

T-shirts Are Walking Billboards for Your Business

Every day we see people sporting billboards with company logos (aka T-shirts). This is a great way to advertise your business in a

Watch Video Tutorial from Kaywa—How Do I Create a QR Code?

http://faq.kaywa.com/about-qr-codes/how-do-i-create-a-qr-code/

fun and engaging way—if you don't mind getting scanned! This may not be right for every business, but it can get people talking about your brand or your product.

Dazzle the Media

Add a QR code to your press release with a video demonstrating your product, sharing something intriguing about your business, or telling an inspiring story about why you started your business. You could also add a QR code to your bio. This will set you apart from the crowd.

The Skinny About Mobile Apps

The term *app* comes from *application software* and implies that an app is designed to help the user perform a specific task.

Apps are wildly popular both as stand-alone products and as powerful marketing tools for your business. They extend your reach and create interaction between users (your customers) and your business.

Still Not a Believer?

Marketing expert Heidi Cohen (www.HeidiCohen.com) shares some fascinating comScore data with us, and these numbers are continually growing.

- 78 percent of smartphone users access a retail site via a mobile app.

- ◆ 56 percent of tablet users access a retail site via a mobile browser.
- ◆ 63 percent of mobile commerce (aka m-commerce) happens on a smartphone, underscoring the need to provide a mobile app.

As you can see, there is no question that you have an opportunity here. By designing an engaging app that fills a need and offers key information that your audience is seeking, you have just discovered a new way to market your business.

What Elements Make an App a Winner?

A great app has to fulfill a few simple criteria.

1. Design. The user interface (UI) needs to look great.
2. Relevance. Know your audience. Make sure that the app is relevant for the intended users.
3. Sticky. Hook your users into wanting to return to your app. You can offer tips or coupons, or make new information easily accessible. And, you can update the information regularly to keep your audience engaged.

An excellent example of a successful app that includes all of these key elements is EmbraceHer Health (www.embraceher.co), the leading medical app for pregnancy, designed by board-certified doctors, that empowers women with mobile access to expert health guidance from OB-GYN doctors. Read the following sidebar to learn more.

Building Your App

In the story about the Pregnancy Companion app, the creators worked with a firm called EmpiricalDevelopment.com to design and launch a native app. This is essentially an app that is custom-built from scratch with your design specifications.

However, there are now free web app tools available that you can use to create an app to add to your arsenal of marketing tools! These are sometimes referred to as HTML apps (or web apps) because

Learn More About the Pregnancy App

Watch Video Message from Denise Terry

http://www.tamaramonosoff.com/denise-terry/

Denise Terry, CEO of EmbraceHer Health (www.embrace her.co), and her cofounders, Dr. Jan Rydfors and Dr. Aron Schuftan, board-certified OB-GYNs in Silicon Valley who specialize in high-risk pregnancy and infertility, have helped deliver thousands of babies and know that pregnant mothers have hundreds of questions throughout their pregnancy. Terry explains, "We wanted to support women with trusted information, emotional guidance, and support to help them give birth to healthy babies, so we decided to build an app that would provide any pregnant mom with a smartphone with the guidance of an 'OB in her pocket' to help her in between prenatal visits."

With more than 250,000 downloads and 60,000 monthly active pregnant users, Pregnancy Companion (http://www.pregnancycompanionapp.com/) is the most comprehensive pregnancy app on the market and the only one providing information directly from board-certified OB-GYNs. The app features an "Ask the Docs" feature, so users can message directly with doctors anytime, anywhere. Pregnancy Companion provides women with daily pregnancy tips and tools to track the baby's growth and due date and to check drug safety.

I asked Denise a few questions about the app development process.

Tamara: What steps did you take to have your app designed?
Denise: We did extensive interviews with pregnant moms who visit our OB offices throughout their pregnancy and asked them what they would find most useful that other apps were not providing. We also interviewed other OB-GYNs to determine the top questions and issues that pregnant women ask and struggle with at various stages of gestation. Using that customer development research, we partnered with a designer to create wireframes (a visual guide that represents the framework) of the app with the goal of driving active usage and engagement with the app. We used our own doctors'

Continued

knowledge built from more than 20 years as obstetricians to design an experience that would engage pregnant moms on a daily and weekly basis.

Tamara: What surprised you the most about bringing an app to market?

Denise: We were surprised by how quickly pregnant mothers found the app with little or no initial marketing effort or spending on our part. We knew that "mom-to-mom word of mouth" was extremely powerful, and in addition, other obstetricians and doctors started to download the app and recommend it to their own pregnant patients as a result of moms telling their own doctors they are using the app, which has contributed to significant growth of our user base.

Tamara: What has been your biggest challenge so far?

Denise: One challenge was underestimating the interest from pregnant women in having access to an OB-GYN through the app using the "Ask the OB-GYN" doctor feature. We are expanding our team of OB physicians available to answer support questions through the app, since we receive several hundred questions from pregnant users each day, and our OB-GYNs are all practicing doctors who still deliver babies on a daily basis in addition to supporting our users of the app!

Tamara: Where did you find an app developer?

Denise: Through existing relationships with patients, we received several referrals. We have been working with an app design and development partner called Empirical Development (www.empiricaldevelopment.com).

they run inside the web browser on your mobile device. The beauty is that they can link to any page or pages that you designate: your website, social media pages, promotional materials, or photos.

One fantastic tool is called TheAppBuilder (www.theappbuilder.com); it helped me build my first web app with no technical know-how in about 90 minutes.

Watch Video Message from Lauri Chertok

http://www.tamaramonosoff.com/lauri-chertok/

Lauri Chertok developed an app called Measuring Up (www.measur ingupapp.com) that is an ideal tool to help moms, dads, and grandparents successfully buy clothing for their children by getting the right "fit" the first time.

The idea originally started as a book with a measuring tape, but I started to wonder if my little Measuring Up book could be made into this new and highly popular phenomenon called an app. I began to notice more and more people carrying iPhones to have tons of information at their fingertips. We have become an "on-demand generation." With the Measuring Up app, moms could have their kids' clothing sizes and measurements in their hands whenever they were shopping, with or without their kids in tow. I experienced this problem myself when my kids were young. My own children are grown up now, and this idea continued to fester in the back of my mind as I worked in a retail store helping moms buy clothes for their kids.

Believe me, I knew nothing about computers, coding, or even how to download an app when I started. I worked with a friend who knew how to build iPhone apps. When we met, I showed him the original pocket-sized book, and he felt that he could translate that into an app. Developing the prototype was a challenge, since I had no previous experience, but once I began to wrap my head around what it looks like on the screen, and how it works and doesn't work, I had to rethink what the content would be and how to whittle it down.

Getting the Measuring Up app into the iTunes store was probably the easiest part of the story. iTunes has an application and a set of guidelines. Once you qualify and pay, you are in. It can take some time and patience, but it's worth it.

I was surprised when I realized that if you build it and launch it, people do not necessarily just come. Building Measuring Up has been a huge learning curve for me regarding social media. That is where my audience lives, and I had to learn and continue to learn about how to navigate that always-changing space. As an artist, not a "techie," my biggest surprise was my tenacity in embracing this new knowledge and not giving up.

How Can I Use an App as a Marketing Tool?

◆ You can essentially use many of the marketing ideas that have been mentioned in this chapter to market your app. Only native apps can be sold in the App Store. However, marketing apps can be shared on every marketing outlet you can imagine.

Make a QR code that links directly to your app that can be printed and used in all of the instances mentioned earlier.

Print your app as a link on:
  ▷ Product packaging
  ▷ Receipts
  ▷ Clothing tags
  ▷ Packing slips
  ▷ In-store displays
  ▷ Stickers
  ▷ Postcards
  ▷ Brochures
  ▷ Business cards

◆ Prominently feature your app on your website and social media networks. Have an ad made for your app (again using resources like Fiverr.com and 99designs). You can offer something special if people download your app. Don't forget to capture their names for your opt-in e-mail list in order to get the ad or the special offer.

◆ Create videos on YouTube that
  ▷ Walk people through what your app does and how it works.
  ▷ Describe features and benefits of your app.

At the end of the videos, make sure to invite people to download the app for free to enjoy (blank).

Source: www.TheAppBuilder.com.

E-mail Marketing

E-mail is still one of the most important vehicles for *getting the word out* about your products, brand, and business, and the tools that are now available to help you are worth mentioning.

The Power of the Inbox

E-mail is still one of the most important, effective, and inexpensive Internet tools for reaching out and communicating with people. When messages are well constructed, e-mail campaigns can lead to dramatic results. Depending on your business type, your e-mails should include:

- Insightful information
- Discounts
- Press releases
- Engaging videos
- Virtual coupons (ones that can be forwarded and used over and over by friends of friends)
- Invitations to special events and/or a monthly newsletter

The intention of these special offers and invitations is to encourage your readers to click through to your website and ultimately purchase your products and services. And remember, adding the word *video* in your subject heading will get many more people to open your e-mail. But, don't disappoint! Make sure that you do indeed have a good video that's worth watching, or people will quickly remove their name from your list. Here are a few great e-mail marketing tools: Mad Mimi (www.madmimi.com), Mail Chimp (www.mailchimp.com), Feedblitz (www.feedblitz.com), Constant Contact (www.constantcontact.com), and InfusionSoft (www.InfusionSoft.com).

Chapter Wrap-Up

Marketing is essential to the success of your product. Without it, no one will know about your product, much less where they can find it! Hopefully, you can adopt some of the useful tools shared in this chapter to support your marketing and sales strategies, including defining your branding story, creating effective press releases, making engaging videos, and experimenting with QR codes and apps—all for the purpose of connecting with your customers and the media in a powerful way. When you first begin, try to generate media coverage for yourself. And if you're not having luck or you're overwhelmed with other business tasks, consider hiring a public relations firm or video marketing expert. Such a person's expertise can often mean the difference between success and failure.

Finding a Partner

Watch Video Message: Tamara Monosoff Introduces Chapter 9

http://www.tamaramonosoff.com/tamara-monosoff-introduces-chapter-9/

Licensing 101

You've learned in the previous chapters that developing your invention and setting up your own business is a doable undertaking, but certainly not a minor one. Taking a product from concept to market requires an enormous commitment of time, energy, and money. Of course, if it is successful, the financial rewards and personal gratification can be well worth the effort.

However, perhaps you don't have the time or the inclination to set up a full-fledged business that addresses everything from manufacturing to marketing. Maybe you love the process of developing your idea, but not necessarily the prospect of running your own business. Or maybe you just don't have the financial resources to get a business off the ground. Or you've come to the conclusion that you can achieve more success by passing the item on to another company that has the resources to extend your success and compete on a larger scale. If this is the case, there is another option for launching your idea into the marketplace: licensing your invention or product.

So what is licensing, anyway? A *licensing agreement* is a contract between the inventor of a product (you) and another person or company, usually a manufacturer that already produces and distributes products in the same category as your item, that assumes the responsibility for developing and selling your product in the marketplace. In this agreement, the inventor (licensor) licenses the rights to her idea, patents, copyrights, and trademarks to a manufacturer (licensee). Typically, in return for the idea, the inventor/licensor will get a percentage of the "net" sales revenue.

In an ideal licensing relationship, your manufacturing partner will work collaboratively with you in getting the product rolled out and swiftly placed in major retail channels, and you will enjoy cashing your quarterly royalty checks.

If you are already familiar with this concept, it may be from having read some of the inventing literature—and invention promotion ads—I have seen that portrays licensing as a "no-brainer," "easy for anyone," "hundreds of companies eager for your invention," "you can earn thousands of dollars," "no investment," "just file your patent and you can make millions," and the like.

While success is entirely possible, I want to bring some perspective to this notion. Licensing is not simple. Period. I want you to be successful. And, if you understand why it is not as easy as some people make it sound, the challenges you encounter won't be a surprise, and you can create a plan so that *you* can join those who do succeed at licensing.

Why Should You License?

You may wonder, "If I'll end up with only a small percentage of the profits, why should I license my product in the first place?" Well, there are definitely benefits to being a licensor, especially if running your own long-term business isn't something that interests you. Some of the benefits are as follows:

1. If you license your product to a manufacturer with established distribution channels, it can quickly be integrated into the product mix and get rapid market penetration. This will probably achieve a much broader distribution faster than a new, sole inventor with a single product and no existing retail relationships could achieve.
2. The licensee assumes all the costs of producing, marketing, and distributing the product; thus taking the financial burden off you.
3. The licensee assumes most of the risk associated with the product. This applies to a number of areas, including possible market rejection of the product, product liability issues, and other unforeseen market conditions.
4. The licensee is the majority stakeholder and therefore has a vested interest in pursuing legal or costly patent enforcement issues in the face of competitive knock-off threats.
5. You, as the licensor, receive a royalty payment, usually based on a percentage of product net sales, as compensation for assigning rights to the licensee.
6. Your time and financial commitment to the product are diminished significantly. A successful licensing agreement that generates sales, even on a modest scale, is a nice way to generate supplementary income while you pursue your next idea or other interests.

What Do You Give Up?

While all of these benefits are very compelling, there are definite trade-offs when you go down this path.

1. **Control.** Manufacturers have in-house product and marketing teams with their own ideas. Even if they "love" your product, they will probably want to incorporate their own ideas into the design, packaging, and marketing of the item. While you can address some of these issues through the required approvals you incorporate into

your licensing agreements, you may find that, in practice, these teams don't relish hearing your opinions or appreciate the need to gain your "input" and "approval."

2. Prioritization. This is a "biggie." When you are developing, launching, and selling your item, it is your top, and perhaps only, priority. Every aspect of your business day is focused on one thing: the success of your one item.

If you have partnered with a high-quality manufacturer, it is probably in the process of developing and launching numerous new products, in addition to changes that it is always making to its current product lines. Since your product is one of several items, and the only one that requires the approval and consent of an inventor, it can easily find itself on the back burner. Minimum sales and performance measures can also be incorporated into the licensing agreement, depending on the strength of your negotiating position (how badly the manufacturer feels it needs your item), but again, in practice, this can be a challenge to enforce.

When a product is licensed after proving successful in the market, you have already overcome one of your partner's biggest concerns. And, because you are giving your partner a new product that is already selling, the terms you can negotiate are often more advantageous. And personally, you will have also had the life experience of actually developing and launching your product, which can be extremely satisfying.

3. Running a business. Some people like the challenge and rewards of building a business. Once your product is licensed, unless you retain versions of the product that you still sell, you will in essence become a cheering spectator.

Why Do Manufacturers Want to License?

There are three main reasons that manufacturers license products from inventors: innovation, innovation, and innovation! OK, so there is one reason. But, there are actually several components to "innovation" that are important to understand from the perspective of the manufacturer/licensee.

First, large companies are beholden to standard processes for product development. They have good people with creative ideas and many resources, for example, focus groups, marketing experts, and so on. However, with a standard corporate approach, the truly innovative ideas will often be dismissed. Independent inventors are bound only by their own creativity and ability to convert their idea to reality.

Second, licensing new items can help an established manufacturer get a speed-to-market advantage when it wishes to open new lines of business or categories. While the in-house product team can remain focused on the company's core product lines, an outside inventor can provide a virtual outsourced product development expertise.

The third reason is related to the first, but slightly different. Even when large companies recognize innovative ideas, they still may be constrained by what they perceive as inadequate market potential and decide against taking the risk of pursuing something that is unproven. For example, the idea of creating small trinkets to decorate a sandal would probably not be thought to have meaningful market potential. However, one inventor decided to create exactly that.

Sheri Schmelzer decided to design small decorative charms that can be attached to Croc shoes. This is clearly something that the manufacturer of Crocs could have undertaken itself. However, without hard evidence that this could be a viable pursuit, there is little incentive for a manufacturer such as Crocs to shift its focus from its successful core product: Croc shoes. As it turned out, Schmelzer, from Boulder, Colorado, told her local newspaper that within a year, she sold $2 million worth of her Croc accessories, called Jibbitz. While licensing would have been a clear option for her, she and her husband sold the company to Crocs in 2006 for $10 million.

Step into the Manufacturer's Shoes

It is not uncommon for first-time inventors to express frustration when they start the process of courting manufacturing licensees. Assuming that you are approaching firms of some size, ideally mid-sized companies with existing similar products on the market, there are six things to consider.

First and foremost, understand that these businesses' primary interest is in growing their revenue and profits. If a product business does not sell products successfully, it will fail. Unless the manufacturer sees clear sales opportunities, your product will not pique its interest.

How can you make your prospective partner confident that your product will generate new sales? Rather than you expecting your partner to sell, the onus is on you to show your prospective partner that your item will generate new revenue and profit for it. Do your homework, and go beyond what someone would expect. When you are in a position to educate your prospective partner on the subject with facts and figures about the market your product addresses, you will see a major shift in how you and your invention are perceived. Having personally experienced this difference, I cannot emphasize enough the impact that this has. Rather than trying to persuade someone why he should take a risk and getting frustrated if he doesn't "get" your product, instead, you are so knowledgeable that he becomes totally sold on you and your product with no further persuasion.

Second, these people are extremely busy. Every business and department, including the product teams, has more to do than can be accomplished in a workweek. They are in a constant state of prioritization and stress. Think about how you can minimize the added workload to your partner as much as possible.

Third, prospective partners have internal tensions that they are probably dealing with. Even if you find one person who seems to be an advocate, she undoubtedly must navigate internal politics and possibly rivalries herself. You cannot do much about a company's internal conflicts, but you can do a lot to demonstrate that your product is not a risk. You do this through the work you do to prove the market for your item or ideally generate sales. Businesses will embrace you quickly if you hand them active sales accounts.

Fourth, manufacturers are approached by inventors (usually unprepared) with a "breakthrough invention" weekly—often with items that they have seen several times before. Be a different kind of inventor. Show them the concrete evidence of how unique and useful your item is. Take it a step further and show them the direct competition (snipped photos are fine) and why your product is better.

Fifth, some manufacturers have had negative experiences working with inventors. Not every product and every relationship works out. Inventors with unreasonable expectations or demanding personalities may have soured the well for future inventors. Convey to them your understanding of the challenges of dealing with inventors. You can negotiate a fair deal, but also show that you really understand their experience and that your expectations of success are realistic.

Sixth, there can be intimidation and/or incompetence by in-house product teams. Some companies have product teams that feel threatened by innovations from the outside. They may see outside developers as a threat to their job security. Or, they may simply see the introduction of new items as an added workload. Establish an open line of communication. From the beginning, request a go-to-market strategy. Listen to what they propose and offer additional ideas and contacts if you have them. If they embrace this open communication and you find that they are easy to brainstorm with, then this is potentially the "right" partner. However, if you sense resistance, insecurity, or incompetence, then trust your instincts and graciously move on to identify a better partner.

Get the Deal!

Now that you understand both the reasons a licensing deal is beneficial and the challenges of pursuing one, you are in a position to decide whether this is the direction you want to pursue.

The Squirrel-Proof Bird Feeder

I share this story because it is the best I have seen to illustrate the advantage an individual inventor has over a large product team.

A store advertised a new product called a squirrel-proof bird feeder. After having wrestled with vandal squirrels for months with his own bird feeder, "Joe" went to the store, eagerly grabbed one of the new bird feeders, bought it, took it home, and set it up. Over the next few days, he noted with excitement that the squirrels circled it, yet were apparently stumped, and the birds enjoyed the full benefits. But one morning, about a week later, he was shocked when he found his bird feeder empty of seed when it had been full the day before! He refilled the feeder and spent the rest of the day observing the squirrels as they made repeated visits to the bird feeder, helping themselves to his bird seed.

Outraged, he went back to the hardware store and began to protest to the storekeeper.

"How can you advertise this as a squirrel-proof bird feeder?" he asked.

The storekeeper said that it was the manufacturer making that claim, not he. But he added, "I will be happy to give you back your money. We shouldn't even sell a product making such a claim, because anybody knows there's no such thing as a squirrel-proof bird feeder."

Joe asked how the storekeeper knew.

The storekeeper answered with two questions: "How many minutes do you spend each week thinking about how to keep squirrels out of the bird feeder?"

"At least 30 minutes *every* day," Joe responded.

To that, the storekeeper asked, "How many minutes a week do you think your squirrel thinks about how to get into that bird feeder?"

Independent inventors who are seeking out a solution to their own challenges—rather than someone else's—can offer creative and inspired insights born of personal experience. The product teams of larger companies, with dozens of products in process, don't often have the luxury of being able to focus on one product.

Now it is time to outline the strategies you should follow to get a deal.

This is going to be a three-step process, with a lot of small steps in between. If you look carefully, you will notice that it is quite similar to the sales process outlined in Chapter 7.

First, get clear on your strategies for licensing your product. These might include:

- Complete a thorough market analysis of the viability of your product (see Chapters 1 and 3).
- File a patent or get a provisional patent application on file (see Chapter 4).
- Develop a working prototype and/or a presentation prototype that illustrates your product (see Chapter 2).

Optional steps:

- Get your product to market and prove market acceptance and adoption.
- Find customers and retail buyers who will attest to their demand for your product.

Second, identify the most probable companies that would be good licensing partners.

- Companies with product categories within which your product could fit.
- Companies that manufacture products using similar materials (for example, a textile manufacturer would probably not want to take on a plastic gadget).
- Midsized or small companies that are well funded and growing. Often very large companies are more difficult to deal with unless you are participating in a formal product search program that they have created (discussed later).
- Companies that you can meet in person. This can occur in a number of ways, such as attending trade shows. Often geography actually comes into play. If you have a chance to get to

know a person in a company because his kid goes to school with yours, or you know someone else who works there and can actually meet a person, you can more easily achieve success.

Third, take into consideration the challenges your prospective partner is facing and address them as well as possible, as outlined in the previous section: sales, workload, political dynamics and risk, seeing similar products before, don't be difficult, and communication.

Be Prepared

Here are some of the things that you will need to begin the process.

You will need to prepare information that you can encapsulate into a brief e-mail, a single-page "sell sheet," a website, and/or a PowerPoint presentation. Make sure that you communicate this information in a concise, brief, and intriguing way. Remember to think about why the manufacturer "needs" to add your product to its existing product line.

The points should include:

1. Introduction of yourself (one or two sentences only).
2. Introduction of your product (three or four sentences only—what's the *wow* factor?)
3. Your goal—for example, license the rights to the XY Widget to a manufacturer in the widget industry (one sentence).
4. Summary story (see Chapter 1) (three to five sentences only).
5. The problem that your product solves (one or two sentences only).
6. How the XY Widget solves this problem (one or two sentences only).
7. Specific data showing the market size (two to four sentences only).
8. Customer validation and expert endorsements (for example, a doctor approves of your product; three to five good testimonials).

9. Intellectual property assets summary (one sentence; for example, utility patent number).
10. Include other key elements, such as manufacturability, existing accounts, buyer testimonials, sales data, and so on.

So Many Fish in the Sea

Once you've prepared your prototype or sales materials, your next big question is, "To whom do I offer this great business opportunity?" I recommend that you identify an initial list of 20 to 50 prospective targets. If you pinpoint the manufacturers that would be the most likely to produce your product, you will have a better chance of making a deal. From the steps in Chapters 1 and 3, you probably have a good set of competitors and prospective licensees already. But if necessary, expand on that number.

To start this process relatively easily, spend time in stores where you might expect to see your product sold. Look at the product packages and jot down the names of manufacturers that produce and sell similar products.

The trade press can also be a resource for finding prospective licensing partners. Look in publications that relate to your industry, and scour the editorial content and advertising for leads.

As discussed in Chapter 1, the Internet is an obvious place to find these companies. Thirty minutes on a website like Amazon.com will yield any number of products related to yours. Look at who makes them, and then use database sites like www.zoominfo.com to learn about those companies. Once you've generated your list of possible target companies, you should "qualify" each lead to determine which companies it makes the most sense to approach. There are a number of factors to consider when developing this list:

◆ **Size.** As mentioned earlier, while very large companies may be easier to find, and generally have tremendous distributions, they aren't necessarily the best prospects. Instead, smaller companies might stand to benefit the most from the labor and intelligence of an outside inventor. Also, smaller companies are typically less burdened with bureaucracy such as multiple layers of decision makers across departments. Another plus is that there are more medium-sized manufacturers to choose among. Therefore, I recommend fast-growing midsized companies—$10 million to $50 million in revenue—as your best licensing prospects (zoominfo.com shares this information on the company's profile page).

◆ **Geography.** If there are companies that are geographically near you, they might be good prospects, especially if it is possible to leverage local contacts to meet the decision makers.

◆ **Similar product line.** As mentioned earlier, a manufacturer with a line in which your product is a natural fit is a good prospect.

◆ **Competition.** Your product could potentially help a company face a competitive challenge. For example, if you see one company launch a product that is similar to yours, think about that company's competitors. In all likelihood, these competitors have also witnessed this new launch and may be trying to figure out how to meet this competitive threat quickly. What a great time to show up with your product! Also note that competition could work against you. For example, if one of your target companies has recently launched a product that is similar to yours or that might make your product seem like yesterday's news, it probably isn't such a good prospect.

◆ **Ability to reach the decision maker.** If you can, find out who ultimately decides which products to license, how many different people need to weigh in, and what steps the company typically puts a new invention through. The less complicated the process, the better and faster it will be for you.

◆ **Company policy.** Find out a company's policy for accepting submissions. Also find out if it will sign your nondisclosure agreement (NDA; see tamaramonosoff.com\guides for a sample), or if it has one for you to sign. What if the company doesn't have an established policy? That can be either good or bad. It can be good if it means that there won't be an abundance of submissions with which you are competing for attention. However, it could be bad if the company has a policy, stated or unstated, of carrying only products "invented in-house."

◆ **Manufacturer's reputation.** If possible, find out if this company has licensed other products, and then try to contact the inventors to ask them about their experience. *Note:* Regardless of who licenses and sells the product, the original inventor's name remains on the patent listed publicly at the U.S. Patent and Trademark website (www .uspto.gov).

Making the Sale

With one exception that I will outline, I am not a proponent of randomly sending your sell sheet and licensing pitch to prospective partners. Based partly on my own experience, I believe that manufacturers will not look at anything sent to them that they have not first discussed with an inventor. Before you start soliciting, I believe you need to first find a way to communicate directly with a person at the company you are targeting.

Several techniques to help you include:

◆ Read the website and product release announcements on the press page of each target company website. Look for an "inventor" or "product submission" link to see if there is an established process for reviewing submissions. (*Note:* We have found that just because a company has a tab like this, you cannot assume that this means it will be responsive in reviewing your submission.)
◆ Call the company directly and ask who handles product submissions for licensing.
◆ Approach prospective companies at relevant trade shows.
◆ Ask a retailer you know for an introduction (depending on the size, stores buy from dozens to hundreds of manufacturers every month).

- Reach out via social media (Twitter, LinkedIn, and the like).
- Leverage personal network connections.
- Use professional organization contacts such as membership in industry associations.
- Get creative. Find a way to get in the door and make your product relevant to the needs of the target company.

Once you have had a chance to speak with a relevant contact, you will want to send the summary information that you have already prepared and seek to either set up an in-person meeting or schedule a phone or Skype appointment.

As with your sales process, in every communication you have with a prospect, make sure the next steps are concrete. What I mean by this is, if you speak to someone who indicates that he is interested and would like to "review the material and get back to you," it is tempting to say, "OK, great." I suggest that you say instead, "OK, that is great; let's set up a follow-up call in two weeks—is this time on Tuesday or Wednesday of that week open?" Even if he has not had time to review your item, you will be on his calendar.

Exceptions

There are likely to be hundreds or even thousands of companies in the industry where your product fits. Since you probably know where your item would fit best, you are the best person to find and approach those companies. That said, the idea of "outside innovation" has really evolved since the first edition of this book. Many companies that historically had clear "in-house only" development policies have opened up to more outside ideas. Now some well-established companies have a clearly outlined process and requirements for contacting them and submitting your product. Examples include the following:

Telebrands (the As Seen On TV brand) is most famous for selling products using infomercials. Visit www.telebrands.com and click on the <inventor> link.

Procter and Gamble (P&G) has a program called Connect and Develop at www.pgconnectdevelop.com.

Housewares is a large (more than $300 billion industry) that covers many categories that are often relevant to inventors. Seek out the companies that are most relevant for your product and check their websites for an "inventor" tab. For example, companies that sell hundreds of household products through clip-strip and inline sales programs at housewares stores, grocery stores, and drugstores often seek outside inventions; such companies include:

EvriHolder (http://www.evriholder.com/)
Jokari (http://www.jokari.com/)

In addition to going directly through corporate submission channels, there is a small number of legitimate invention licensing companies that will review your submissions for their corporate clients. The emergence of these legitimate firms and the exposure of scam invention promoters (see sidebar) is another very positive

The use of the term *royalty-basis* in the previous discussion is meant to make sure that you carefully distinguish between firms that review and represent inventors' products for a portion of the royalties and those that offer invention promotion services for a large fee. This latter group is referred to as *invention promotion firms*. Initially it is difficult to tell the two apart. But the invention promotion companies tend to offer an initial "market feasibility study" for a fee, say $500 or $1,000. They then come back with "great news," and they just need another $10,000 or $20,000 to get your product to the market or to find licensing partners for you. Their ads are often seen on late-night television. This is not to say that every firm that helps inventors is bad. But there are definitely bad apples that we hear about often. The USPTO has information about what to look for as well as published complaints about companies: http://www.uspto.gov/inventors/scam_prevention/index.jsp. Or visit www.uspto.com and search "complaints."

trend since the first edition of this book. A number of firms that I am familiar with that provide these services are Evergreen IP (www.evergreenip.com), InventionHome (www.inventionhome.com), and Lambert Invent (www.lambertinvent.com). Each of these tends to have unique relationships and category strengths, so if these are a consideration, you will want to speak with each of them. For example, Evergreen provides the invention review services for Clorox and Avery and also presents to other major brands for inventors, whereas InventionHome has a presence at a number of trade shows in particular industries. If you work with one of these services, be sure you clearly understand its process and the terms of its agreement.

One thing to keep in mind is that licensing companies that operate on a royalty basis will typically reject the vast majority of products submitted to them. They are not charging the inventor large fees (usually just a couple of hundred dollars to evaluate your product); instead, they profit by sharing in the royalties of the licensing agreements they secure. Since they are assuming the cost of advancing the items they select, they must carefully focus their efforts on products that they feel confident they can place at retail.

There are some other unique new sales channels to consider when looking for ways to get your product to market.

Edison Nation (www.EdisonNation.com) is an online community that is dedicated to helping inventors license products to manufacturers. Like some of the other agents and programs mentioned earlier, Edison Nation runs product searches for manufacturers such as Fender guitars and Worldwise cat toys. It charges a modest fee, currently $25, to submit an invention and shares in the royalties earned. As always, be sure that you fully understand the obligations you are taking on and the terms of the licensing agreement before you submit. In addition to having a community model where an inventor can share insights and find like-minded supporters, Edison Nation offers additional benefits for "Insiders" who pay extra fees. And, Edison Nation is affiliated with the PBS program *Everyday Edisons* as well.

Perhaps the most innovative new website and model for inventors to consider is Quirky (www.quirky.com). Based in New York City, Quirky has taken the idea of direct consumer feedback, leveraging online "influencers," and speed to market to a new level. This is made possible through the combination of online technology and social media. Inventors can submit a product to Quirky; it then gets reviewed and voted on by Quirky's members, also known as "influencers." Products that receive a certain level of support are reviewed each Thursday with a live audience of members and staff that decides which items the organization will develop and launch. Quirky prides itself on speed to market. Once a product is launched, the organization is able to sell the item on its online store. Taking this one step further, members have an incentive to help promote or "influence" the success of the items sold on Quirky.com, as they are collectively paid 30 percent (as of this writing) of the revenue produced through the online sales as well as some percentage of the royalties earned through wholesale deals with major retailers. The inventors are also paid a percentage of each sale.

As with the other models, it is very important that you understand and feel comfortable with the terms of the Quirky model. Once it takes the item on, it retains certain rights, which you will want to understand. In addition, there could be some implications of showing your invention publicly if you have not previously filed a patent.

Finally, from time to time, companies or media outlets will run product or invention submission contests somewhat similar to those run by Edison Nation. We have done this in the past ourselves. The benefits of these include a well-organized process, with clear terms should your item be selected, and a definite response, one way or the other, fairly quickly. In addition, it is very likely that someone will get a deal.

The downside of relying on these channels is the amount of competition. We commonly received hundreds of terrific submissions during these events. This made it hard for an individual item to stand out. Staples announced one year that its Invention Quest drew more than 13,000 submissions.

What to Expect

It's doubtful that you'll retire based on licensing your first product. In fact, a 2 percent royalty with no up-front payment might actually end up being a pretty good deal. The reality is that while a great idea is an essential beginning for any product, it's just one small piece of its ultimate success. By licensing your idea, the manufacturer assumes the responsibility, costs, and risks inherent in the launch of a new product, including steps like mold and pattern development, patenting, production, insurance, regulations, safety requirements

Melanie Cruz and her whimsical product, Bebe Doos Perfect Ponies (www. bebedoos.com, pictured in Chapter 8), illustrate several of the points discussed here so far.

Her product, a headband with pigtails for baby girls, was created out of her need to create extra income, and was inspired by her sister's wish that she could give her baby daughter, who had no hair, pigtails.

Melanie initially just made her product and sold it to a local retailer. As her product flew off store shelves, she increased her distribution and eventually became a vendor selling her product to a hair goods company called Aderans Hair Goods, whose brands include Revlon. She clearly illustrated a creative way to open up an opportunity. It was through this relationship that she was able to get her product in front of key executives at Aderans. Eventually she was able to license the rights to Aderans for specific accounts while she retained rights to her existing accounts.

While the agreement had tremendous potential, internal changes at Aderans resulted in disappointing results. Fortunately, her own sales efforts have enabled her to continue to grow, and, as of this writing, she is in the process of reworking her licensing options.

and testing, sales, marketing, distribution, managing sales reps, handling returns, collections, inventory management, and so on. This is why you won't get a larger piece of the pie.

Reaping the Rewards

Generally, the further along in the development process your product is, the more lucrative the terms of your licensing agreement will be. For example, if you present just an idea to a licensee, you'll probably get less desirable terms than if you've already secured a valid utility patent, produced merchandise, and generated sales. Your deal will be unique but it will most likely contain some aspects of these three key elements:

Up-front payment. This is money that the licensee pays the licensor up front, before development or sales even begin, for the assignment of the rights. This can be an outright payment, but it most commonly takes the form of an advance against (future) royalties. The amount of up-front payments varies. However, it is not unusual for an inventor to seek an up-front payment that covers the cost of her patent filing. Another way to determine an agreeable sum is to base your payment on projected sales expectations for the first year.

Royalties. These are the payments made to the licensor based on a percentage of the licensee's product sales. So, if you make a 2 percent royalty, you'll receive 2 percent of the wholesale price of each unit sold. Royalty percentages will vary by industry and company and can run anywhere from 1 percent to 10 percent. The typical royalty range I have seen runs from 2 to 6 percent. Again, the further along or more proven the product, the less risk there is for the manufacturer and the more likely it is that you'll get an up-front payment or higher royalties. From my perspective, the royalty is the most important element of the agreement, because if the market responds to the product, the manufacturer will do well and the inventor can earn a good revenue stream.

Annual minimum. This is a contractual term that requires the licensee to pay the licensor a minimum amount of royalties, irrespective of the actual royalties due from sales. To me, the purpose of an annual minimum is to ensure that the manufacturer puts sufficient effort and resources into promoting the product. Therefore, I believe that annual minimums are most important in the initial years of the agreement—when the product is being launched—to ensure that the licensee places an adequate priority on this item when deploying sales resources. Annual minimums can be measured in terms of units, minimum payments, or some combination. They can also be crafted to increase each year. Typically a manufacturer will want 12 to 18 months lead time, as it can take that long to develop an item and place it in retail stores.

(*Note:* These negotiation points are interconnected. In other words, when an agreement has a high up-front payment, there may be a lower royalty percentage. Or if there is a large annual minimum, there may be a lower up-front payment.)

Exclusivity agreement. Usually a manufacturer will want to have exclusive rights to distribute the product globally. However, this is subject to negotiation. Depending on each party's motives, the agreement could actually divide up the markets in many ways. Some variations of an agreement could include provisions that provide exclusivity domestically but not internationally. Others might offer the license for certain types of accounts, specific named accounts, or in certain industries. The length (term) of the agreement can also vary from one year to forever.

How Patents Come In

Common licensing practice tends to assume that an inventor will secure, or at least file, a patent, copyright, and/or trademark application prior to presenting a product to a prospective licensing partner. These protections provide the inventor with a tangible asset to offer licensees. And, having a patent or patent pending status provides a much greater degree of comfort for inventors when presenting their products to prospective partners.

From the perspective of the licensee, a valid patent makes an invention more desirable because it helps the licensee prevent competitors from entering the market quickly. It also means that, in the absence of an agreement with the inventor, the licensee's own internal product development team cannot launch the product without some legal risk. In fact, many manufacturers will not even accept submissions that don't have a patent, as they do not want to deal with future accusations that they stole an inventor's idea. While some of the submission programs mentioned earlier in this chapter, such as Quirky.com, do not require patents, practically speaking, when you are seeking a licensing deal, some evidence of a patent or patent pending status (achievable with a provisional patent application) is likely to be necessary. For these reasons, the terms for the licensor tend to be more lucrative when a valid utility patent has been filed.

One exception to this is when an inventor has launched a product without bothering with a patent and has been able to achieve sales success, but has decided to license the product to another company. She may be able to use her trademarks as the consideration she assigns to the licensee. Again, keep in mind that all that manufacturers truly care about is sales. If you pass them an item that is already sold at retail, a patent may not concern them.

On the flip side, however, it's worth repeating that only 2 to 3 percent of patented inventions ever make it to market, while many nonpatented products do. Plus, as discussed in Chapter 4, high-quality patenting services are costly. So, this is not something to be taken lightly.

Note that the manufacturers that you present your items to are likely to be reluctant to sign nondisclosure or noncompete agreements or similar documents, as they need to avoid complicating their rights. Keep in mind that it is conceivable that other inventors have submitted similar ideas or that the company is already working on something similar in-house. If it signs something with you but later proceeds with a similar item that is already in development, this could create the suspicion that it copied your product idea. This is not as unusual as it might seem. During one of our product searches several years ago, we had three invention submissions from different people in different parts of the country that involved nearly the identical idea—which we had also previously discussed internally.

What Will It Cost?

The idea of licensing is often presented, for good reason, as a low-cost way for inventors to get their products to market. If you are able to avoid the substantial costs of launching a product and a business, yet get your product to market through a 2 to 5 percent licensing agreement, you have made a huge savings. However, while many of the hard costs (for example, production runs, advertising, trade shows, and the like) are avoided, the process of getting a licensing agreement can be time-consuming and can include costs such as thorough research and analysis, intellectual property filings, prototype development, and the ongoing sales process.

On the other hand, many of the most successful licensing agreements we have seen have been signed after the inventor has independently proven her product by taking it to market herself, and has invested heavily in the development and launch, but then has chosen to license it to a larger company that can assume the risk and increase sales.

Chapter Wrap-Up

Licensing can be a terrific way to profit from your idea. This is especially true if you lack sufficient financial resources or the interest to develop the product yourself. However, make sure your expectations are in line with reality. Individual licensed products will seldom produce enough licensing royalty income to allow an inventor to retire and move to a tropical island. Annual million-dollar (or even half-million-dollar) licensing contracts are rare. But $5,000, $10,000, and $20,000 contracts are not. Inventors who make their living through licensing inventions tend to have inventive minds that never rest, and they get pleasure from coming up with new product ideas. Once you go through the licensing process, you may wish to repeat the process and generate multiple sources of licensing revenue! This is another reason to view your licensees as partners. If you are a good partner, they are likely to want to see other future ideas from you.

Taking Care of Business

Watch video message: Tamara Monosoff Introduces Chapter 10

http://www.tamaramonosoff.com/tamara-monosoff-introduces
-chapter-10

Setting Up Shop

In previous chapters, we've discussed how inventing a good product is just half of the equation—you must also turn your invention into a viable business if you are to find success. Running a business requires that some business systems be put in place before you can sell your first widget. These steps may not be quite as exciting or as much fun as, say, developing your invention or testing it with friends and family. They are, nevertheless, necessary to get your business on solid ground to move ahead.

In this chapter, you'll learn about the systems, documents, and structure you will need to put in place and how taking these steps early can save you money and create business efficiencies. When I launched my business, I had absolutely no idea what I needed, and I often found myself scrambling without critical systems in place. I found myself drowning in a sea of acronyms—C-Corp, EDI, SKU, PO, UPC—that made sense to everyone, it seemed, but me. And because Mom Inventors, Inc., grew so quickly, I was under even greater pressure. I didn't know the first thing about how to ship orders, bill customers, or track inventory.

My objective here is to give you an overview of what I didn't know then to enable you to move your business forward on a solid footing. The key is knowing that you don't have to do it all on your own; there are experts and tools available in every field that you can find or use and ask for help.

Setting Up Your "Space"

It's essential that you create a defined space that's devoted to your business. Don't expect to run it from the dining room table or the kitchen counter. Not only should you set aside physical space—probably somewhere separate and defined in your home, at first—but you should also set aside mental space in which you can conduct business freely. Finding both types of space can be a challenge, especially if you have children at home.

Mom Inventors, Inc., was launched from my second daughter's bedroom! I will never forget the moment in May 2004 when NBC's *Today Show* called to consider having me as a guest for its segment on women entrepreneurs. My babysitter had called in sick that day, and I was caring for daughters Sophia (age two) and Kiara (a newborn), but because it was relatively quiet, I took the chance of answering my business phone. The moment I began speaking to the producer, Sophia decided to have a "bring down the walls" tantrum. I offered to call right back, hung up the phone, and began negotiating with my two-year-old. I promised a visit to her favorite park—and chocolate—if mommy could make just one quick phone call. When I thought the deal had been struck, I picked up the phone and dialed. The moment the call connected, Sophia reneged on our deal. I grabbed all the markers on my desk, fell to the floor with paper, and began frantically coloring with Sophia as the producer commenced her interview. Although I was invited to be a guest on the show, a smooth, businesslike interview was not the reason I was chosen.

Giving Structure, Taking Shape

Before you go further in setting up your office operations or hiring staff, you first need to establish the identity of your company. This means deciding on how your company is structured, then naming your company and giving it a "public face." This section will tell you how to begin this process.

Choosing Your Business "Identity": Sole Proprietorship, C-Corp, S-Corp, or LLC

* **A corporation.** There are two types that I will describe:

▷ Use a *C corporation* (C-Corp) structure if you think you will be raising millions of dollars and having an initial public offering (IPO). This form of corporation protects you from unlimited personal liability. While you can lose the money you invest in the corporation, your personal assets are protected as long as you follow corporate formalities. One disadvantage of a C corporation is that it is subject to double taxation. When the corporation makes a profit, that profit is taxed at the corporate rate. Then, when it pays you a salary or gives you a dividend, the salary and the dividend are taxed again at your individual income tax rate, so the money is taxed twice!

If you plan to raise capital from professional investors, a C-Corp may be necessary.

▷ An *S corporation* (S-Corp) may prove to be a better option if you don't plan to make a public offering of securities. It provides the same benefit of limiting your liability that a C corporation does, but it doesn't involve double taxation. With an S corporation, profits and losses are taxed only at the shareholder level, not at the corporate level. You must follow certain corporate formalities with an S corporation, such as avoiding the commingling of corporate funds with your personal funds. There are also some limits on the number and type of investors you may get.

◆ **A limited liability company (LLC).** This is often your best option if you don't plan to make a public offering, and it is very often the route that start-up entrepreneurs go. Its structure protects everybody, even the "managing member," from unlimited personal liability. It can be taxed either as a partnership or as a corporation; you choose. One obvious benefit is that you'll avoid double taxation if you choose to be taxed as a partnership. Also, there is no limit on the number or kind of members, and it is more flexible than an S corporation.

Note that if things change with your business over time, you can always change your structure from one type to another. There is some expense and effort involved in doing this, so you don't want to do it often, but it is not unusual. I started my company as an S-Corp but switched later to a C-Corp when we started raising capital from professional and institutional investors.

◆ **A sole proprietorship.** A sole proprietorship is the simplest type of business to start because it has few legal requirements. Basically, to form a sole proprietorship, you need only a business license to begin operating. The owner of a sole proprietorship has complete control and receives all the income. It sounds wonderful... but if anything goes wrong, you will have unlimited personal liability. This means that all your assets and future assets—business *and* personal (house, car, and furniture, for example)—can be targeted by your creditors to satisfy their claims, so it's pretty risky if you're investing money that you've borrowed and you suddenly can't pay it back. In addition, sole proprietors usually have great difficulty raising capital from investors. To save money in the beginning, you might consider starting as a sole proprietorship, then converting to another type of business entity at a later date.

◆ **A partnership.** This business entity has the same disadvantage as a sole proprietorship—unlimited personal liability. With a partnership, however, the liability is spread across the partners. *General* partners have unlimited liability, while *limited* partners are more protected. Every limited partnership must have at least one general partner, who has unlimited personal liability. Like sole proprietorships, partnerships also have difficulty raising money from outside investors.

Technically you may be able to set up your business entity yourself, but you need to make sure that you fully understand the process and your options. NOLO (www.nolo.com) is one place where you can find resources; another is your local business library. Rocket Lawyer (www.rocketlawyer.com) is another place to get some free legal advice. Most legal forms can be found at LawDepot (www.lawdepot.com).

For more information before meeting with a professional, the Small Business Administration (SBA) is a smart resource (www.sba.gov), as is the Small Business Development Center in your area. In addition, the secretary of state's office in each state has resources to support you. You can hire a local business attorney or accountant to assist with this process as well. Perhaps the easiest route, which I would probably take if I were doing this myself, is to work with a local attorney or use an online service such as www.legalzoom.com. At this site, you can set up your corporate entity for as little as $99 plus filing fees. It just doesn't get much cheaper than this.

Getting Your Ducks in a Row—Officially

After you've decided on a business entity, you'll have to make it official with your state and local governments. It may be necessary to meet the requirements of city, county, state, and federal government agencies. For instance, I had to get a city business license, file my company name with the county and with the state, file articles of incorporation with the state, and apply for my federal Employer Identification Number from the IRS. You can take most of these steps yourself, but you may also want to seek some free advice from an accountant or attorney. Often the legal bar association in your county will have free events or can provide referrals to attorneys who offer free or low-cost consultations.

To begin learning about the requirements in your region, visit the website of each relevant government entity in your area. The secretary of state's office in your state government is generally a good place to start. Another terrific resource for state and local agency information is State and Local Government on the Net (www.state localgov.net). This directory lists all the websites in a given state, from the governor's office to the smallest of counties. Click on the "Business" link on your state's official website. Most state websites will describe the business and legal requirements necessary to establish your business entity.

No matter where you reside, you'll also need to register for a federal tax ID number, also known as an Employer Identification Number (EIN), as mentioned earlier. The only exception is if you're creating a sole proprietorship, in which case your social security number will suffice. For a partnership or corporation, however, the IRS will need this number to identify your business for tax purposes. You'll soon find that large retailers will expect you to provide this number as well. (Often large retailers will expect you to complete a detailed vendor application, which establishes you as a "real" entity.) To obtain an EIN, you can apply online at the Internal Revenue Service (www.irs.gov) website.

In addition, some states require a seller's permit. Information that pertains specifically to your state can typically be found on your state government's website under the Board of Equalization. Aside from the hassle of more paperwork, the upside is that this permit, sometimes referred to as a resale permit, gives you the opportunity to purchase items wholesale and then resell them. For example, I purchased T-shirts and baby bodysuits wholesale, printed our Mom Invented logo on them, and then sold them online. I was responsible for making sure that the sales tax on these items was charged to the customer and passed through to the state.

These steps involve a lot of detail and are fraught with delays. Don't let them stop you from getting started with the other aspects of your business.

The Home Field Advantage

Having a home office offers tax advantages if your business is profitable. Discuss the possible deductions you can take with your tax accountant.

Special Start-Up Advantages

If your business is minority-owned, you may wish to be certified by the National Minority Suppliers Development Council (NMSDC) or one of its regional affiliates. If your business is woman-owned, you may wish to be certified by the Women's Business Enterprise National Council (WBENC). Such certification may provide an advantage with certain retailers; for example, some of the big-box chain stores have special departments that deal with these types of businesses. I was successful with this in our own business. After some difficulty penetrating one major retailer through the "normal" route, I decided to contact the director of the Minority/Women's Office, and I received an immediate response.

To be certified as a woman-owned or minority-owned business, a company must be at least 51 percent owned, controlled, and operated by a woman or minority group member.

For more information, contact:

National Minority Suppliers Development Council
    212-944-2430 / www.nmsdc.org
Women's Business Enterprise National Council
    202-875-5515 / www.wbenc.org

The Name Game

What's in a name? A whole lot, especially when you're building relationships and an image with buyers, vendors, and customers. That's why choosing an effective name is a vital early step in developing your business.

That said, feel free to explore and brainstorm business names! One of the most common mistakes I see is inventors giving their company the same name as their product. For example, if you invented a Day-Glo dog leash and you named your company "Day-Glo Dog Leashes, Inc." it would be tough for you to release any other pet products through the same company name. Giving your company the same name as your product can inhibit growth, defining your company in terms that are too narrow. At present, you may think that this is the only product you plan to ever develop and bring to market. However, if you truly have an inventor's mindset, you will continue to think of one product idea after another. And once you get one product placed with retailers and have a vendor number (a requirement at large retailers), the second item is much easier to place.

Another error to avoid is naming your company something that's meaningful to you but meaningless to customers. I've seen many mom inventors combine their kids' names in some way. While this is cute, it can also result in names that are difficult to remember, hard to understand, or tough to pronounce (as a test, picture yourself answering the phone all day using this name). Also, your company name needs to convey the right image for the company. Ask friends and family for their suggestions and feedback. A word of caution here—as with naming your baby, asking family members can be touchy, especially if they really dislike the name you have chosen.

Once you have decided on your company name, search the Internet and purchase the domain name that you have selected. Hopefully, no one will already own the name you've chosen. Companies that sell domain names often offer packages that include e-mail address accounts along with your domain name. These e-mail accounts can further legitimize your business and present a professional image, as opposed to using an e-mail account with a Hotmail, Yahoo!, or AOL address. Such an address is also a tip-off that you are a small (sometimes interpreted as "unstable") company. Presenting your company as a serious player from the beginning by using an e-mail address with the name of your company will allow you to prove yourself and the credibility of your company to others—retailers in particular.

Your company name and website address are important company assets. They help present a sound, professional image and help increase the value of your company to prospective customers, partners, investors, or even acquirers in the future. Once the name of your company is finalized, I recommend trademarking it. (See the discussion of trademarks in Chapter 4.)

Be Realistic About Running a Business

If you are responsible for childcare, you should harbor no illusions that your children will quietly read books and color while you conduct business. While research, planning, and writing can be carried out at night or during nap time, it is important that you arrange some workday childcare coverage, even if it is only two hours per week. If paid help isn't feasible, look to family members or community services for help. The key is to arrange the same two hours each week that you can use and depend upon to schedule important telephone calls or outside meetings. Expand your coverage when you can. You may not be able to accomplish everything on your list during these fleeting time slots, but you can begin to tackle the most critical items.

Business Planning

If you got a knot in your stomach at the two words in the heading, "Business Planning," with visions of financial spreadsheets and business jargon, *do not worry.* When I started my business, there were only a couple things that I really feared, childbirth and business planning. But, if you have read my other books, you know that I now love business planning. That is because it does not have to be done in a way that is painful, but instead can be fast, fun, and energizing. There are many good systems and styles for business planning.

I devoted an entire chapter in my last book, *Your Million Dollar Dream*, to this subject, and I have coauthored *The One Page Business Plan for Women in Business* with my friend Jim Horan, the founder, CEO, and author of the One Page Business Plan Company. It offers a fill-in-the-blanks process so that you are not starting with a blank page!

I don't intend to replicate a full book's worth of content here. Rather, I want to highlight a few key aspects of creating a useful business plan.

Your business plan is the answer to the what, why, and how you will organize and prioritize the next phase of your business life.

The One Page Business Plan for Women in Business (whether you are a woman or not) will enable you to take the dizzying array of information and options that you have, organize them, and bring a new degree of excitement to your business, all in a single page.

In this process, you are going to get clear on five key components of your business plan:

- **Vision.** What are you building?
- **Mission.** Why does this business exist?
- **Objectives.** What results will you measure?
- **Strategies.** What will make this business successful over time?
- **Action plans.** What are your business-building projects?

Each of these components has a series of exercises that enable you to create your first "One Page Business Plan" in a single sitting. In addition, Jim and I share sample plans from other women entrepreneurs to inspire you to get started creating a powerful business plan of your own.

Managing Your Business

Once you have the framework in place, you need to start attending to the nuts and bolts of building your business. These are the systems and resources that will enable your business to run smoothly, such as staff, office processes (including invoicing and inventory systems), insurance, and customer service.

It's All About the People

You don't need to hire an employee to cover every individual area of your business. Hiring "virtual employees"—those who work for your business, but on a fee-for-hire basis—is an effective alternative for small and growing businesses.

Previously, I have referred to resources that included Elance (www.elance.com), Odesk (www.odesk.com), Fiverr (www.fiverr.com), crowdSPRING (www.crowdspring.com), and 99designs (www.99designs.com) that make it easier than ever to find consultants to handle specific tasks such as website design, editing, video production, logo design, and the like. As your company grows and the workload increases, you may find it necessary to hire part-time or full-time staff. There are definitely more complexities to doing so, including payroll management, insurance issues, and more. When you do reach the point where it's necessary to employ workers yourself, consult with an accountant to know what steps you need to take from an accounting perspective.

Office Operations

To run a successful business, you'll also need certain systems and processes in place that will allow you to manage your money, carry out transactions (make and receive payments), manage your inventory, make shipments, and serve customers. Running many facets of a business can become very complicated, so these systems and processes should help simplify and streamline your business. The following is an overview of the basic systems you'll need to put into place.

Getting Paid: Merchant Accounts

If you're selling a product, you'll need an easy way for your customers to pay you. Credit cards and electronic payments are the most popular payment methods today for both end users and retailers. A *merchant account* (such as www.Authorize.net or www.cybersource.com) is a global payment-processing service that enables merchants to process secure transactions, 24 hours a day. The company that provides your merchant account will process credit cards and electronic checks and will work with many business transaction modes, including Internet, broadband, wireless, call centers, and retail. You can find merchant account companies through your industry association or bank, by searching online, or even through discount clubs such as Costco and Sam's Club. In addition to signing up with a merchant account service, you will need to open a bank account that has the capability to link to a global payment-processing service. Some banks may offer the entire package. A merchant account costs approximately $50 per month plus a per-transaction fee. Note that some banks charge initial setup fees.

Many of the website resources previously described have a payment-processing system incorporated into their offering—something that was only a dream 10 years ago! However, at times, you will need to buy things or enable people to pay you for other services outside your e-commerce store. This is where other payment options are necessary, even if you have an e-commerce tool in place.

The ability to invoice and accept payments both online and in person has changed dramatically. It seems that each day a new innovative option for accepting payment arises.

PayPal (www.PayPal.com) is perhaps the best known means of electronic payment. Anyone can set up an account, and it is convenient, as you can use it both to pay bills (this is how I often pay consultants that I hire) and to invoice others. PayPal can be used for online transactions as well as in person using the "PayPal Here" card reader. This uses a device that plugs into a smartphone so that credit cards can be swiped in person. This would be a dream at an order-writing trade show! There are additional features worth exploring, such as a debit card that provides direct access to funds in your PayPal account and "Bill Me Later" options. Now, you can even accept a check using PayPal.

WePay (www.wepay.com) is an exciting company that offers some functionality similar to PayPal at what appears to be comparable pricing (2.9 percent and $0.30 per transaction as of this writing). There seem to be some differences in the setup that are worth checking out.

Intuit GoPayment (www.intuit-gopayment.com) is another offering connected to Intuit, a company that is known mostly for its accounting and bookkeeping software. One interesting benefit is that it will automatically sync with QuickBooks if that is what you use for bookkeeping.

One of the first services to offer the ability to accept credit card payments using your smartphone is Square (www.squareup.com). Square offers both a per transaction price option and a flat monthly fee option. Its card reader is free, and you can even list your business in its community.

Note: Collecting payments from small retailers can be time-consuming and difficult. Since yours is a new company, many new wholesale clients will be reluctant to pay you upfront. We decided that it was worth it to us to offer an additional 5 percent discount for prepaid orders (usually paid by credit card). This way, we almost never fail to get paid, and our retailers appreciate the extra discount. Plus, we get the cash right away!

You Can't Fight the (Invoicing) System!

Not only will you need a conduit by which your customers can pay you (your merchant account), but you'll need a system that tells you from whom—and when—all your payments are due. Unlike a store, in which you pay for your goods before you walk out the door, you may be shipping goods and expecting payment later. So, when you send out an order, it will be accompanied by an *invoice*, which is basically a bill that details what products you've provided, how much is owed to you, and when it's due.

When I came back from my first trade show, I had about 50 new orders from retailers who wanted the TP Saver. I manually created all 50 orders as Microsoft Word documents. This was a good, low-cost way to start. However, it wasn't efficient, and it didn't allow us to scale with our business growth.

Today, you can do this in a completely different way. First, as outlined earlier, you may be able to run the transactions onsite using your smartphone or tablet. Second, this transaction will probably be integrated with your bookkeeping program.

Few things are more intimidating to some people than bookkeeping. That is certainly my feeling. When I launched my business, I had to buy a bookkeeping package for $200. In addition, I had to hire a professional bookkeeper to set it up and manage it on a weekly basis. However, the new tools available are almost enough to convert someone into a lover of the process.

FreshBooks (www.Freshbooks.com) is one such system. A single-user *free* account is available that enables a small business to handle most business bookkeeping requirements and can produce your financial reports, including the balance sheet, income statement, and profit and loss statement. Customer support is available during the week, and you can access your account any time anywhere.

Wave Apps (www.waveapps.com) is another such system that is completely *free*. Providing full accounting, including payroll, invoicing, and expense tracking, this system is designed specifically for small business with nine or fewer employees.

XERO (www.xero.com) is another system in the "cloud" that seems to cover all the bases, including directly connecting to your bank accounts so that this information automatically updates.

QuickBooks (www.quickbooksonline.com) offers similar services for a small monthly fee.

Yendo (www.yendo.com) offers an accounting system that also includes customer relationship management (CRM) capability. This allows you to associate sales with a sales representative and to facilitate better integration with client data.

Kashoo (www.kashoo.com) offers "simple cloud accounting" for about $20 per month.

Zoho (www.zoho.com) is a website that will come up again. It should be mentioned here, as this company offers an online accounting and invoicing tool.

Plenty More on Purchase Orders

You'll encounter purchase orders in two ways in your business: when you create them and when you receive them. As a manufacturer, you will hire vendors to produce things for you. Therefore, you will need to provide them with purchase orders for their work. For example, each time I order TP Savers from my factory, I provide the factory with a purchase order. This official document should state specifically what you are ordering and how much you are expecting to pay (something that you've already verbally agreed to with your vendor). Details include the date of the request, the quantity ordered, the item description, the unit price, and the payment terms.

There is also a place on your purchase order for comments. In this area, I always spell out my expectations in detail. For example, I'll note the specific materials to be used (ABS plastic and elastic), the length of the elastic in inches, and the expectations for the packaging (for example, four-color printing with a gloss finish on the front side of the packaging and the Pantone color specifications), in order to ensure that we are both on the same page. It is also important to spell out how the pieces should be packaged for shipping. For example, if I order 20,000 units, all 20,000 units cannot be thrown into a box together and shipped. One PO reads, "Of the 20,000 TP Saver packages, 12,000 pieces need to be packed individually in cartons of 6 units with 8 cartons per master box totaling 48 units per master box. Each box should then be put in sturdy bulk boxes for transport." In addition, you will want to specifically stipulate how you want both the internal and the external case packs labeled. For instance, you may want your company name, the product name and SKU number, and the quantity in each "inner" and "outer" case pack. *Note:* I figured this out through trial and error by asking our retailers (customers) how they would like to have the product delivered to them. (Go to www.TamaraMonosoff.com/Guides to get a free sample purchase order.)

Before you receive a purchase order, you will need to agree to payment terms. For example, we always ask our customers to pay net 30 (this means within 30 days of receiving our invoice). However, some of the larger stores will say that they will pay only net 45 days or net 60 days. Another term you may see is "2% net 60." This means that the retailer will deduct 2 percent from the total bill if it chooses to pay in full within 60 days.

What's a SKU?

When a retail buyer is interested in purchasing your product, it will ask, "What's the SKU (pronounced "skew") number?" SKU stands for "stock keeping unit." According to the Uniform Code Council, each product in a store "requires a separate identification number to distinguish it from other items. In inventory control and identification systems, it represents the smallest unit for which sales and stock records are maintained."

The UPC

Here's something else that may not immediately pop into your mind when you're launching your business—getting a Universal Product Code (UPC). This is the bar code symbol, that oh-so-familiar pattern that you see on just about every product you buy—a series of black bars and white spaces with numbers below. The numbers, which are encoded in the symbol, uniquely identify the product. This group of numbers, referred to as a Global Trade Item Number (GTIN), is captured by in-store scanners, which help track sales and product orders via computer. The GTIN in a UPC is always 12 digits in length.

Much the way every individual has his or her own social security number, every company is assigned a unique prefix. The prefix is the first six digits of the bar code. The subsequent five digits are the item number. The combination of the prefix and the item number represents the bar code. The final digit is called a check digit; it simply validates the prefix and item numbers.

Your UPC is obtained from the GS1 US and uniquely identifies your company within the UPC system. Once your application is accepted by the council, you'll receive the number on the UCC membership certificate that will be included in your membership kit.

Most good-sized retailers will expect you to have a bar code on your product, to adapt it to their in-store computer system. While this is not essential for small boutiques or independent retailers, it is to your advantage to purchase a bar code and incorporate it into your packaging design from the start. Then, once an opportunity from a major retailer arises, you'll be ready to go.

FIGURE 10.1

As part of the bar code, there are digits that you, as the business owner, have the freedom to change. These digits are called SKU numbers. As you add new products to your company, the bar code stays the same, but the SKU numbers change. You assign the SKU numbers yourself. For example, the SKU of one of my products is "01," and that of another is "40." This provides the ability to track different products.

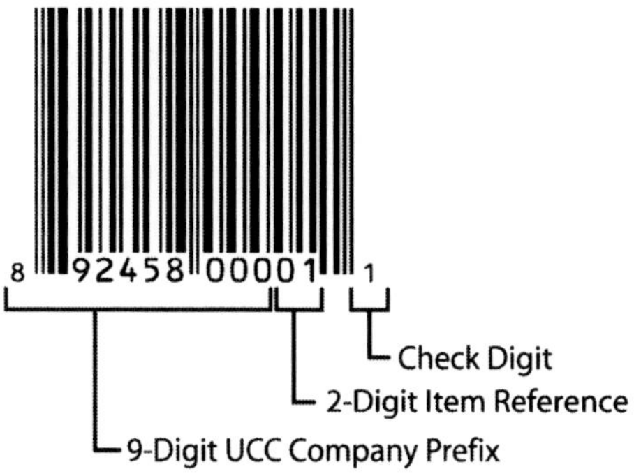

8 92458 00001 1
Check Digit
2-Digit Item Reference
9-Digit UCC Company Prefix

It sounds more complicated than it is. You can probably get set up with one call or visit to the website. To get the ball rolling, go to the Uniform Code Council, Inc. (http://www.gs1us.org).

Electronic Data Interchange

Large retailer ordering. If you land a deal with a large retailer, it will most likely require you to be set up with an EDI system. EDI stands for electronic data interchange. This enables the retailers to electronically integrate its inventory needs by store with its orders. If you have an EDI system, you can integrate with the retailer's ordering system and thereby fulfill as it requires. This is another area that has seen tremendous improvements. By simply typing "EDI" into Google, you will come up with hundreds of options. You probably will not need this until you get placement with a major retailer, so this step can wait for a bit. However, I hope that the time comes when you need it!

When selecting a system, be sure to find a solution that is geared to support a small business. Some of the solutions you will encounter are designed for very large corporate clients. In addition, look for solutions that can be integrated with your other tools, such as your bookkeeping and invoicing tool.

Shipping orders. A shipping order is a simple document that you use to request shipment of product from one location to another. If you store your products at an off-site warehouse, a shipping order provides an official request to the warehouse to ship to a given customer. This also provides a record and paper trail to follow if any problems arise.

The invoicing system you select will enable you to keep track of your accounts payable.

A new tool I am excited to share is Stitch Labs (www.stitchlabs. com). This system enables you to track your inventory as it sells through different sales channels, whether they are your shopify.com store, amazon.com, or other channels. It was built by people in the product industry, so they know the challenges that you face.

Tools, Technology, and Getting Stuff Done

Throughout this book, I have listed new tools and resources that, in many cases, simply did not exist when I wrote the first edition of this book. Once again, this section emphasizes the fact that there has *never* been a better time to be an entrepreneur. Nearly every entrepreneur who I have interviewed for this book said there is one tool he or she can't do without: the Internet. And, of course, your key to accessing it is through a computer. This section details exactly what other technology is likely to help you as you begin your business. While you may have some or all of the following resources, you may wish to upgrade them or dedicate them solely for business use. You will need:

A computer. A laptop with wireless capability that gives you the ability to work from anywhere in the house and to access the Internet for free in areas that offer Wi-Fi links, like airports, coffeehouses, and libraries, is great for moms on the move. But, you can also buy a relatively powerful desktop computer for a surprisingly low investment, so buy what your budget allows.

A dedicated telephone line. A line for business use only is essential. If you can't afford to put in an additional phone line when you first start your business, use your cell phone. Leave a professional message with your business name, and answer the phone only when you are able to speak (without the kids screaming in the background).

Become a Website Wonder

When I wrote the first edition of this book, the idea of website templates was new. The common wisdom at that time was that you should hire a talented web designer who could use a software tool to build something unique. I recall spending nearly $25,000 on a website at one point—that barely worked! Today you have an incredible array of choices for building your website. Some people will opt for a simple blog site using a platform such as www.wordpress.com or www.weebly.com. In other cases, a hosted website using a web host with e-mail and a template builder such as www.one.com or www.godaddy.com will suffice. In these platforms, a shopping cart or integration with a payment gateway such as PayPal (discussed earlier) may be necessary if the site will be used to sell products.

A cool new feature that you can add to your website is Speak Pipe (www.speakpipe.com), which enables visitors to leave a voicemail directly on your website. This makes it easy for visitors to contact you and to leave feedback or a testimonial. It's as simple as click and record. No phone calls are required!

The line indicating where the website fits is now blurred, which is why I listed several platforms that enable you to put up an all-in-one web store quickly and easily in Chapter 7.

As a small business, you need to take advantage of every opportunity you have to increase your productivity, and hence your success. The tools available to help you do this are better and more affordable than they have ever been. I see new ones every day. I cannot provide a comprehensive list, but I have listed a few that I, or others I know, have used to manage tasks and support their businesses. Just five years ago, you would have paid hundreds or thousands of dollars for these capabilities. Today, many of them are free or cost just a few dollars per month.

Hold conference calls at any time for no charge with Free Conference Call (www.Freeconferencecall.com).

Keep all your documents in one place, stored and accessible remotely and shared with others as you wish: Google Docs (www.google.com), Dropbox (www.dropbox.com), and Box (www.box.com).

Make phone calls, chat, or video calls online using your Internet connection for free with Skype (www.Skype.com), Google Hangouts (www.google.com/hangouts).

Access many affordable business tools from Zoho (www.zoho.com).

If you plan to use online presentation software for sales demonstrations, to meet vendors, or to show your engineer your latest design modification, in addition to Skype, you can use web conferencing vendors—some are *free*: Join Me (www.joinme.com), GoToMeeting (www.gotomeeting.com), and ReadyTalk (www.readytalk.com).

If you need to have customers or vendors sign contracts, the entire process can be managed securely online for free with EchoSign (www.echosign.com) and DocuSign (www.docusign.com).

If you need to send files such as large presentation decks, drawings, or videos, e-mail won't suffice. Ten years ago you had to FedEx a DVD; today you can use Hightail (www.hightail.com) or Send ThisFile (www.sendthisfile.com).

There are numerous ways to organize your thoughts and projects. Use those that work best for you but here are a few cool ones.

Trello (www.trello.com)
Evernote (www.evernote.com)
Base Camp (www.basecamp.com)

Back Up Your Data

Prepare for the unexpected! Nobody ever thinks that he will need to have a backup copy of his data—including me. Even so, I have always made a practice of backing up my office computers. Unfortunately, in 2010, I was using a relatively new laptop for a period of time when suddenly the hard drive crashed. I lost everything, including several chapters of the book I was working on! *Back up your data.* In 2006, I was paying about $250 per month to back up three office computers with a limit on data using an online system.

Today, you can back up a computer with unlimited storage for about $60 per year.

Carbonite (www.carbonite.com)
Mozy (www.mozy.com)

Similar to the importance of data backup is your virus protection. Most computers come with a program preloaded that you can easily install. I have often relied on some free tools such as Avast and AVG, as the free versions offer the features that I felt were necessary. They also offer upgraded versions. There are many other well-known providers, such as McAfee, Norton, and Trend Micro. The main thing is to make sure that you have one. *Note:* One problem I have seen is that, because so many devices are preloaded with a particular vendor solution, some people accidentally end up having two tools running on the same computer, which can cause performance issues.

Customer Relationship Management

Once you start to build relationships with prospects, customers, partners, and others, you will want a way to keep track of your ongoing communications and transactions with them. In the corporate world, the systems used to track this activity are called customer relationship management, or CRM, systems. I have listed a few of these systems. At the beginning stage, you can use anything. I don't think you will want to go overboard on this, so start with a tool that is inexpensive and easy to use, and that enables you to export your data should you decide to move on at some point.

Zoho CRM (www.zohocrm.com)
Highrise HQ (www.highrisehq.com)
SugarCRM (www.sugarcrm.com)
Free CRM (www.freecrm.com)
Salesforce (www.salesforce.com)

A Professional Answering Service

While e-mail and voicemail may be sufficient in the beginning, there may come a point in time when you need to have a live person answering your phone, yet you may not want to hire a staff person for this task. Innovation and technology have created fabulous options for even the smallest entrepreneur to have a virtual receptionist 24 hours a day. Here are two options, and there are also a host of others.

Answering Service Care (www.answeringservicecare.com)
Answer Connect (www.answerconnect.com)

Customer Service Is Key

It's critical that you take care of your customers, thereby creating loyalty and long, fruitful relationships. Depending on how your business is structured, your customers may be end users (those who buy your products and use them) or retailers (those who buy your products to sell to end users).

Order confirmation. When you receive an order, e-mail a note that says something like: "Thank you for your order. We appreciate your business. Your shipment will be sent by _____ date." Then be sure to meet or beat this date.

Tracking notice. Make sure you keep package tracking information in your customer files. Many times, a store (the large stores in particular, which have to manage a lot of inventory) will say that it never received a shipment. In these instances, tracking proof is invaluable.

Follow-up. Call after your product has been received to make sure your customer is satisfied.

Setting expectations that you meet or exceed—**underpromise and overdeliver.** For instance, if I know that my customer will be satisfied with a 72-hour shipping turnaround, I'll tell the customer that I'll meet that expectation, even though I know we can do it within 24 hours. Then, when the customer receives the shipment "early," she will believe that her expectations have been exceeded. This kind of reliability creates loyal customers.

Communicate. In business, everyone has times when she fails to meet her commitments. The key to surviving these foibles is communicating. Most customers will allow for a few mistakes if you proactively communicate and work to find a resolution. Contact and reassure customers about a problem before they have to contact you. They often have bosses too, and they don't want to look like they are not on top of things.

The Best Things in Business Are (Sometimes) Free!

Certainly, there is no one book or resource that can answer every question and challenge that arises when launching your business. Fortunately, there are some excellent free and low-cost resources that can help you get your business off the ground.

Service Corps of Retired Executives

I am dazzled by the impact of the Service Corps of Retired Executives (SCORE) (www.SCORE.org). Almost daily, inventors tell me about the great experiences they've had with their SCORE counselors, retired executives who volunteer their time to help small-business owners. Not only do they provide knowledgeable advice for entrepreneurs, but they often have contacts and resources that can be equally useful. The best part? The services they offer are free and confidential, and they can help you build your business from idea to start-up to success.

The SCORE Association, headquartered in Washington, DC, is a nonprofit group dedicated to entrepreneurial education and the formation, growth, and success of small businesses nationwide. SCORE offers advice online via e-mail as well as face-to-face small-business counseling and mentoring, with more than 11,000 volunteer mentors and low-cost workshops. For more information, visit www.score.org.

Small Business Administration

Every state has at least one Small Business Administration (SBA) district office, with multiple resource partners to support the needs of the small-business community. In addition, many districts have an office specifically dedicated to women called Women's Business Centers. Women's Business Centers (WBCs) are a national network of almost 100 educational centers designed to assist women in starting and growing small businesses. The mission of the WBCs is to level the playing field for women entrepreneurs.

According to the U.S. Small Business Administration, "Women business owners are critically important to the American economy. America's 9.1 million women-owned businesses employ 27.5 million people and contribute $3.6 trillion to the economy. However, women continue to face unique obstacles in the world of business."

There are also independent microenterprise programs offering a variety of types of training and support throughout the country. To find those in your state, visit Micro Enterprise Works (www.micro enterpriseworks.org). In addition, many community colleges offer programs to support local entrepreneurs. Also check with local chambers of commerce and community organizations to find out about special support programs.

Chapter Wrap-Up

Building your business requires structure, a plan, tools, and people to help you. There are more valuable tools and options mentioned in this chapter alone than existed when I launched my business in 2003. Some accounting software and invoicing systems that used to cost hundreds of dollars and were difficult to use are now simple and free or have low monthly fees. Conference calls, CRM tools, virus protection, project management and collaboration tools, and even e-mail are now practically *free* and are better than ever.

Now is the time to get set up, create your plan, and take off!

Conclusion

When you bought this book, you may have had a range of motivations and expectations, from, "Hey, maybe I can get my gadget developed," to, "I've decided to change my life by building a product business." Now that you have reached this point, I suspect that this is no longer a casual consideration, but instead a serious, life-changing endeavor. Recognize that you have taken the first steps on your journey. If you have digested the chapters in this book, you are as well equipped for success as any inventor/entrepreneur in America; in fact, with this information and the many new resources that are available today, you are years ahead of where I was when I started developing my first product and business in 2003.

As you forge on, carry with you the encouragement you read in the foreword from Julie Martin-Allen, a senior director and buyer from the eighth largest retailer in America. Embrace the inspiration of the more than 50 people like you who were featured in this book, who have walked the same path you are now beginning. And, carry all the knowledge and encouragement I have to share, and know that I am cheering for you from the sidelines as you now take the baton.

As with my path, and the paths of each of the people featured in this book, you will navigate curves and hills—some sharp and some steep—but as you do, never doubt that you can overcome them. In some instances, you may need to create solutions that did not previously exist. Some challenges will surely surprise you, whether it is a purely technical issue or the degree of support you receive from a partner or loved ones. Whatever shows up, never doubt that you can achieve your goals and fundamentally transform your life. Along the way, take time to celebrate your successes, large or small. I look forward to seeing your product on store shelves or selling online and adding your story to those of others who have shared their successes with me. But as you encounter obstacles, embrace them, knowing that it is these obstacles that make the experience—and your ultimate success—something that you will savor with pride. American novelist Ernest Hemingway captured this idea perfectly in his statement, "It is good to have an end to journey toward; but it is the journey that matters, in the end."

My final thought comes from a quote that was given to me by my mother many years ago and that has been with me at the precipice of every opportunity I have considered.

Leap and the net will appear.   —JOHN BURROUGHS

Index

About the Author

Dr. Tamara Monosoff is a business coach, inspirational speaker, award-winning inventor, and author of the bestselling books *The Mom Inventors Handbook*, 1st edition, *Secrets of Millionaire Moms*, and *Your Million Dollar Dream*, and coauthor of *How Hot Is Your Product?* and *The One Page Business Plan for Women in Business*. She has appeared on *Today*, *Good Morning America*, *NBC Nightly News*, *The View*, *CNN*, and the front page of the *Wall Street Journal*. (TamaraMonosoff.com.)

Invitation to Readers

For More Valuable Resources,

Tips & Tools and

Mentoring Programs

I invite you to join me at

TamaraMonosoff.com

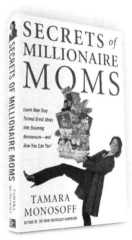

CPSIA information can be obtained at www.ICGtesting.com
Printed in the USA
BVOW02s2043140616

452062BV00008B/96/P